...ing Love

Being Love

26 Keys to Experiencing
Unconditional Love

MARK PETROFF

iUniverse, Inc.
Bloomington

BEING LOVE
26 KEYS TO EXPERIENCING UNCONDITIONAL LOVE

The following material could be considered unconventional to the reader. Mark Petroff is a Certified Coach trained and experienced in shifting clients' perceptions and strategies; he is not a licensed physician or mental health counselor. The intent of this work is to provide educational material in support of the expansion of consciousness, experiential awareness of Divinity, and relationships in general and not for diagnosis, prescription, or treatment of any physical, mental, emotional, or relationship condition without the consent of a licensed counselor or health-care practitioner. If you should exercise your right to read and/or use the information contained herein, the author and publisher assume no responsibility for your decisions, actions, feelings, or ultimate success.

Within the text, certain people's names and circumstances have been changed in order to maintain confidentiality.

iUniverse books may be ordered through booksellers or by contacting:

iUniverse
1663 Liberty Drive
Bloomington, IN 47403
www.iuniverse.com
1-800-Authors (1-800-288-4677)

ISBN: 978-1-4620-4774-1 (sc)
ISBN: 978-1-4620-4775-8 (hc)
ISBN: 978-1-4620-4776-5 (ebk)

Library of Congress Control Number: 2011914650

Printed in the United States of America

iUniverse rev. date: 09/23/2011

Contents

Foreword

Spontaneous Journey

It was a fairly dull Friday afternoon in California, and I'd just finished an exhausting week of work when the phone rang. The familiar and friendly voice coming through it told me I needed to be in Austin, Texas, for a writer's workshop that started that evening. She sensed that I would wind up meeting someone special. Because I was a single man who had painfully ended many unsuccessful relationships over the years, I assumed "someone special" meant a woman, perhaps one who could meet the lofty standards of the worn-out list I had been carrying in my wallet for several years. Graciously, I let my friend know that I appreciated her invitation but was heading to the beach to relax and take a nap. I also reminded her that as a discount shopper, I'd never purchased an airline ticket the day of travel and that there were likely none available, because it was such a busy airport. She called back ten minutes later and let me know that there was just one ticket left for a flight scheduled to depart in two and a half hours. Somehow, my steely logic was overridden by a soulful knowingness that getting on that plane would be a consciousness-expanding step, one that seemed to be needed after many trials and errors, broken hearts, and too much time alone. With curious amazement, I soon found myself in Austin.

The next day, besides being intrigued by what Julia Cameron, famous author and facilitator of the workshop, had to say, I was moved by the presence of a woman named Charlene who was assigned to the small group I was in. She too had arrived for totally illogical reasons, including the fact that she wasn't even a writer. Later that weekend, we shared some profound transformational ideas and experiences, but when the workshop ended, we said our farewells without exchanging contact information. As fate would have it, my return flight was delayed for two hours, and while sitting in the airport, I noticed Charlene walking by. After some further moving conversation, we exchanged business cards, and over the next several months we deepened our friendship. Inspiration and relationship ideas always seemed to be part of our phone calls, even though a few thousand miles separated us. One day while we shared ideas about what fulfilling relationships required and how love is a verb more than a noun, we tried to convince each other to write a book about it. Little did we know of the impact, the joy, the extreme challenges, the growth those simple words would set into motion.

During the next seven years, I listened to valuable feedback from Spirit, life, and clients who worked through their relationship issues during and after personal coaching sessions with me. Slowly I began dictating and digesting the learning into my life and growing relationship with Charlene—sometimes gracefully, other times after much resistance. The journey toward unconditional love has never stopped, especially after Charlene and I took the leap of faith to join in marriage and later have a son together. Along the way, there have been many personal tests and lessons; hours, days, and nights of prayer; moments of struggle and surrender; and breakthroughs with clients and with groups during numerous relationship workshops. *Being Love* is the outcome, which records my own deepening discovery of what works and what, if ignored and uncorrected, makes relationships difficult and painful: physically, emotionally, and spiritually.

It's been said that wisdom is the study of differences—differences that raise our awareness of what's possible and give us the power to make more resourceful and rewarding choices. It's also been said that we tend to teach best what we most need to learn. The following pages record the methods and results of my life-long yearning to experience unconditional Love. Some of the words will seem familiar to you, like a friend you haven't heard from in years and are glad to reconnect with. Others may appear curiously unusual, like food you've never tried but sense will nourish you and expand your life experience in a satisfying way. Several may challenge you in unsuspected ways.

Although the book was written through my voice, every chapter was synergized and experienced with Charlene. She has been my muse, devoted spiritual partner, compassionate listener and feedback-giver during hundreds of phone calls, meetings, dinners, late nights, emails, and full weekends together. She has also been a patient teacher of her own example of love and has contributed to the framework for many of the exercises at the end of the chapters. Without her beautiful light, devotion, and contributions to our family, this book would not have been written.

Since the chapters are alphabetized by topic, you may find yourself turning to a specific one to meet your current need, reading and applying one chapter per week as a focused way to work on yourself and your relationships, or reading the book straight through. Whatever way you are drawn to read and use *Being Love*, I want to thank you for standing for yourself and those you love. May you enjoy and be strengthened and blessed by your journey!

Introduction

Impact

What is the number one reason you don't feel loved or able to love more unconditionally at times? What if you were given some ways to overcome that? Most of us have felt blocked in relationships due to the core fear of not feeling good enough to receive or give unconditional love. In writing *Being Love*, the author asked Spirit to reveal what it takes to experience real and lasting love—love that overcomes fear, ego patterns, and changing life circumstances. Successful universal principles and practical ways to apply them were received as a result of searching, praying, studying, and experiencing relationships of all kinds over a period of many years. What will be shared is with the hope of giving simple and empowering ways to feel and radiate Love more deeply and securely.

During coaching sessions with clients, research, and my own relationship interactions, it became clear that we attract what we are; what we have become as barriers to love have been progressively removed. *Being Love* will show how to more fully connect with the Divinity within you, to identify love-blockers, and, with conscious choice and grace, to reduce or eliminate those hindrances. It will also ask you powerful questions so that your inner wisdom can reveal answers that you can integrate into your relationships. Such ideas, questions, and answers have the potential to free and enhance your relationships with yourself, others, and the Higher Power you deem sacred. Here are some of the things you can expect to find in the chapters:

- Because the capacity to love is developed by choosing moments of such qualities as unselfishness, flexibility, and appreciation, the benefits of love will be illuminated in ways to motivate you to more fully and easily become love.

- Not loving makes life hard, so the satisfaction or payoffs you derive for ignoring or refusing love (and the tremendous costs you pay for doing so) will also be laid bare.

- Lovingness and radical honesty inside you will be energized as former limiting patterns (attitudes, motives, and behaviors) lose attraction and strength.

- At the end of each chapter, guidance and exercises will be offered to apply and integrate specific aspects of love into your relationships.

- Programming, false beliefs, and fears that would weaken your expression of love will be exposed and, by your choice and through divine grace, more easily removed.

- Empowering distinctions will be shared to help you choose more harmonious connection, joy, and worthiness in your relationships. After all, it's easier to find something when you know what you're looking for.

- Finally, you'll explore how to have a more experiential and reliable relationship with the caring and infinite field of Divinity within and all around you. Your sacred journey can reveal expanding abilities and joy as you see how to progressively reflect the highest and surrender the belief in a limited self.

Principles That Free

Many of us have tried to find happiness "out there." At one time or another, we have attempted to rely on our sex appeal, intellect, money, education, career, or connections, all of which are ever changing and sometimes fail to satisfy our needs for certainty, significance, variety, love, and expansion. Strategies to "get love" are widely available, and yet our yearnings may still feel unmet. We may discover that the love we seek starts and deepens with the Presence, the godliness, within us. The need is often to expand one's capacity to perceive and express love rather than to change one's circumstance or partner. The heart of divine Love is as close to us as our own vibrating energy, as real and practical as our daily motives and life choices. Its wonderful and uplifting nature reveals itself to us through inspiration, friendship, opportunities, challenges, laughter, spiritual teaching, beauty, and healing. We feel love better as we become transparent to it—when, in degrees, we quit obstructing it.

For your ideal sense of love, you may resonate more easily with the name God-essence, Christ, Source, Higher Self, Supreme Being, Divinity, or Creator. By whatever name you use, this ever-present field of Love guides, protects, teaches, purifies, strengthens, and restores you. It continuously blesses you through light and dark times. Life has given you difficulties, some of which you may still be dealing with. All of the things that you have gone through and will go through have the potential to expand your consciousness of and capacity to love. They also have the potential to harden your heart and make you resentful or fearful. The choice is yours.

In our present awareness, we may sense and share only a limited sense of this infinite Love, and we, and our significant others, pay a tremendous cost for not feeling more connected with it at times. The quality of our relationships is largely determined by our level of spiritual consciousness—by how clearly we perceive, identify with, and express the Presence. Is it actually possible to increase our awareness of the Presence of Divinity and to more fully embody its nature with those whom we care about? The following pages offer practical and challenging facets of Love to inspire your unfolding pathway to do so.

As children of the divine One, we already have the fullness of love within, which is ready to be set free. Regardless of our pasts and human frailties, love is our design, our core, and our essential nature. We do not have to add lovingness to our true Selves; it is the way we were created to be. Yet for love to shine forth, false belief systems, distorted perceptions, and ego-based ways of being that obstruct love have to be let go. If we are clearly shown how and are motivated to do so, positive change can be ours.

Life tends to respond to our inner knowing—our demonstrated confidence in what's true. Our daily opportunity is to receive the words, examples, and experiences we presently understand about Love, and digest them into our own hearts, motives, communication, and actions. Saint John put it this way: "Our love should not be just words and talk; it must be true love, which shows itself in action" (1 John 3:18 GNT). He also wrote that God's love is made perfect in us as we love each other (see 1 John 4:12). John seemed to be saying that the only way to truly *know* anything is to *be* it—to witness, experience, and express it. Then Love becomes our reality, and the experiential nature of it can never be taken away from us. Through our learning and higher choices, we free the Love within us to naturally flow through us—to be expressed as us.

> You're here as a vehicle for Divinity to show forth Its love through your heart.

Potential for Transformation

The purpose of this book is threefold: First, to further energize your awareness of the intimate activity of how divine Love is continually operating for, through, and all around you. Second, to heal the part of your heart that may be struggling, exhausted, anxious, or pain-filled, so your revitalized wholeness inspires you to be more available to love and feel loved. Third, using new choice-giving ideas, to present opportunities for you to embrace a deeper sense of love and honesty in words and actions (where before you would not have) and to feel supported by divine resources in these expansive choices. As a result, you may shift the quality of your experience and the experiences of others whom you touch in ways that bring connection, joy, strength, healing, comfort, and peace. Is all of this possible? Because you've chosen to read this, I believe it's your destiny.

Perhaps to some degree each of us feels held captive by fear, physical limitations, emotional pain, or life conditions that keep us from fully feeling and expressing love—from having fulfilling relationships. Spirit is calling us to be set free so that we can experience divine Love as a continuously animating and progressively liberating vibrational energy in our relationships. As we become liberated in moments, we will inspire this liberation in others.

> Higher awareness reveals more resourceful choices. Resourceful actions bring positive changes.

I honor and celebrate your desire to know and experience the presence and activity of Divinity in your relationships. May this book play some role in leading you toward states of being that can heal and transform you, your intimate relationships, friends, family, and the entire consciousness of mankind! Your transformation and that of many others is to the glory of God, the All-in-All, as we come home to the fullness and radiance of infinite Love.

With profound gratitude and respect for your present expression of "being love."

Mark

Chapter 1

Feel Abundant

"And God is able to make all grace abound to you, so that
in all things at all times, having all that you need, you will
abound in every good work" (2 Cor. 9:8 NIV).

Abundant Basics

After reading this chapter, hopefully you will sense the incredible and always-available resources of infinite Love—resources designed especially and perfectly for you. You may feel a shift in what you believe is possible and how you receive blessings and take action. If you positively shift what you know and say to be true, you will then notice things to back up your uplifted mindset. In this way, you'll become more resourceful by increasing your ability to access what has always been available to you. Having been on food stamps, having seen an investment account grow from twenty-seven thousand dollars to more than a million dollars in just five months, and having to rebuild my finances after being wiped out (and recover from large debt) three times in the past two decades, this accessing lesson has come back to serve me many times.

In reality, we have all we need right now because of the great "I Am," which is within and all around us. Our job is to hold the vibration that Divinity is generously pouring out to us now from an inexhaustible supply of good. The key is to maintain this frequency with a glad and accepting heart, despite the material circumstances. Conditions change; Divinity's giving doesn't. It may take persistence and focus to actually feel that Divinity knows exactly what and how to give to us plentifully and to overcome distracting doubts, setbacks, and fears. Choosing a state of love and gratitude makes the process easier. Focusing on problems makes it more difficult.

The thoughts and feelings we entertain are like seeds that take root, grow, and bear fruit, so we should be wise about the kind of seeds we plant and how we nurture them. The harvest really begins the moment we align our consciousness with Divinity. The question is: do we persist in this way until the reward is evident?

Many areas of the world live in cultures of competition founded on the belief that there is not enough for everyone and that what is given to another takes away from oneself. The strongest and the brightest strive after seemingly limited supply and leave the leftovers for the less talented. Yet, if you look at substance spiritually, you will recognize that there is plenty for everyone. Supply tends to come from giving unexpected value to others. There are boundless ways to offer value with your presence, skill, creativity, and thoughtfulness. "Give and it shall be given unto you; good measure, pressed down, and shaken together, and running over shall men give into your bosom" (Luke 6:38). When we feel prosperous, we'll have more to share with others. If we feel restricted, we will tend not to give.

The nature of all love comes from a boundless Source. There is enough for everyone. Giving to another does not cause you to have less. In fact, giving blesses you and increases your capacity to receive more. One way for you to view prosperity spiritually is by having a plentiful supply to do what you came here to do. If Divinity gave you a soul purpose, don't you think you would also be given all that you need to fulfill that purpose?

All possibility for good exists now and always. When we resonate with divine abundance, we are sending thought waves that align with formless patterns, or spiritual blueprints, out of which unlimited manifestations can be revealed. Even physicists tell us that particles or forms come out of waves of energy, and energy is eternal and inexhaustible. When is the last time you ran out of using the number seven? You didn't, because the number seven is an idea, abundantly available to use anywhere and everywhere all the time. There is an infinite supply of 7s available for accountants, stock brokers, retail workers, and school children alike. When you share an idea with another, it multiplies instead of diminishes. When you share goodness with another, it multiplies too. True abundance never gets depleted, because its source is spiritual, not material.

If this is true for all ideas that benefit others, why are there so many people who seem to be in lack? First, it is important to understand that we do not *make* abundance; we *access* abundance. Divinity doesn't lack anything. Abundance exists right here and now, always. The real question is: what prevents us from accessing it? Lack comes from being engrossed in our problems rather than focusing on the resources and action steps available for their solutions. What we focus on or hold in mind tends to dominate our experience. Whether we feel burdened and limited or prosperous and unlimited, we'll tend to experience more of what we predominately feel.

There are other things that may be blocking you from abundance, such as forgetting to access it, believing that it's unavailable to you, refusing to ask for and/or receive help, acting deceitfully, or letting fear blind your vision. These things may make you feel cut off from available resources, and as a result, you will more likely believe you are on your own in a contracting or stagnant situation, unaware that you are part of an ever-expanding universe.

Instead of going unconscious and getting lost in the fear that you are lacking something, remember that you have a generous and divine Caregiver, that you are part of a vast network of people and supply, and that ideas and opportunities are boundless. Integrity and valuable service tend to reveal abundance. Maintaining a knowing conviction that what we have to give will serve others also helps.

Underneath almost every fear is the fear of death—the fear that if we lack something, we may not survive. You may have been tempted to submit to the fear that you will run out of whatever you need and then get sick and die. What a horrible way to live! In nearly every case, fear of death is illusory. If we run short of funds at the end of the month, we're probably not going to die, even though it may feel like it to our ego. Our job is to have compassion for and manage our egos.

Perhaps you have recently found yourself in fear and limitation, trying to get what you seem to lack but with meager results. Instead, choose to allow infinite Love to be at the center of your consciousness. Awaken more fully to the beneficial ideas and resources that are constantly being made available to you. Feel something of the essence of the twenty-third psalm: "The Lord is my shepherd; I shall not want" (i.e., "I shall not lack

> Your results and happiness largely depend on the quality of the thoughts you entertain, the feelings you regularly sit in, and the atmosphere you surround yourself with. Choose them wisely.

anything with such a capable shepherd!"). It is a good shepherd's job to make sure the sheep are protected and well provided for. It is the sheep's job to trust in the shepherd's guidance and ability to supply what the sheep needs. Divinity has an inexhaustible supply available to anyone who exercises a conscious capacity to access and accept its field of Love. Our part is to not block it by holding in mind that which limits us.

Spiritual Resources and Practical Needs

When you are feeling fear or lack, how can you shift to positive expectancy? First, realize that the fullness of divine abundance is present and available at every place in the Universe at the same time, right now and always. Regardless of your circumstances, the field of ever-present Love includes unlimited good, networking, and supply. The entire content of the Internet, with billions of pages of resources, is a small example of this. Spiritual resources and divine energy are infinitely vast and can never be depleted, so focus on Divinity's abundance instead of your seeming lack. Entertain the feeling and certainty that Divinity is working with you and others to orchestrate the fulfillment of your needs and pure desires. Then rest into the feeling that you are presently receiving what you need or asked for in order for you to be your best and to be a blessing to others. Finally, relax about the details of how it will all be worked out. If you're steadfast in your focus and feelings, you will know what to do, when to do it, and how to receive.

Spirit can communicate a single idea to you that can bring you millions of dollars. When I worked at a high school, there was a student who told me that his grandfather was once in the trucking business. He had the kind of work that gave him a limited amount of money, but he was always thinking about how he could improve highway mileage. He received the idea to put a curved wind deflector on the top of the cab of a truck. Results showed that mileage improved significantly. Later he obtained a patent on the idea and thereafter received a royalty for wind deflectors used on trucks throughout the United States and other countries. The huge amount of money he made did not take away from others. Rather, his idea helped them by increasing their mileage and profits, conserving energy, and helping the environment.

Regardless of your current or past life situations, you can decide now to be bountiful in what you believe, how you feel, and the way you take clear action. Imagine how a prosperous person would think, what he or she would focus on, and how he or she would feel, speak, and act in your situation. Accept the opportunity to walk with this same attitude and power, knowing that abundance is already present for you, because it is! By holding the conscious frequency of what is spiritually true, you will be more likely to receive what you need in the way of people, ideas, and supplies to plentifully meet your practical needs. Picture and feel the fulfillment and reality of your prayer-desire. In those feeling-filled moments, you will have experienced something of the realization and joy of your heart's intent, regardless of the physical outcome.

Abundant Qualities

The word *abundance* comes from the Latin root *abundare*, meaning to abound. The word rings of expansiveness and describes a powerful state of being. Ways of being that foster abundance include appreciation, generosity, a feeling of worthiness, expectancy, joy, and creativity. These spiritual qualities align us with the natural abundant flow of life, because during moments of expressing such qualities we are supporting life. As a result, we are naturally supported by life and the immeasurable resources of the Universe. Regardless of how our finances, jobs, or social situations look, we can actively embody and express qualities that support life and give value to others. By doing so, we will be more open to receive what best supports us. Many people let their money determine how they feel and how they treat themselves and others. Instead, we can choose to be kind, gracious, and persevering at any time, especially if our bank accounts look low. It's not so much what happens to us but how we respond that makes all the difference.

What if you were to pick one spiritual quality, such as kindness or thankfulness, and practice it unconditionally for a month? Doing this is a resourceful and challenging way to grow spiritually. It can measurably expand your experience from limitation to freedom. Other expansive qualities include open-mindedness, willingness, trust in Divinity's guidance and care, responsiveness, patience, spiritual vision, giving with joy, and purity of purpose.

In relationship with our Source, there is an attitude or posture that puts us in a better position to feel and accept abundance, such as that of a young child who is wholly dependent on his or her parents or caretakers.

An untainted, childlike posture includes having humility, trust based on a sense of deserving, willingness to ask and respond, what spiritual masters call "beginners mind," and openness to infinite possibilities of good. You may find these same attitudes critical for you to receive abundance in your approach.

We tend to receive prosperity in proportion to our belief of deserving it together with the expectancy that we will receive it. A key to abundance is to consistently practice shifting our mental state to positive expectation and feelings of deserving. Taking actions without doing this tends to limit our results. Jesus, a master of manifesting, taught that things happen to us according to our faith that they will (Matt. 9:29). He had the multitude sit down in expectancy of receiving a meal before he fed them with what appeared to be a limited supply of food (Matt. 14:15-21). Our actions tend to come from what we believe, and our beliefs are powerfully influenced by the pictures we hold in mind and the feelings we entertain about them. That's where the real work is needed!

In business, abundance tends to come from serving others, bringing them joy, and solving their problems, sometimes in surprisingly pleasurable ways. Every product or service does one or more of these, so to expand your business, feel where you are motivated to benefit others and find out what they desire and need by asking them or doing research. Then design practical and cost-effective ways to solve their problems and give them value. Use the feedback of your results to give them more of what they want and need. If the way you connect with them is done uniquely, authentically, and generously, you will have loyal clients and customers. In personal or business relationships, if you contribute to the success and well-being of others, give them more than is expected, and do so with joy and enthusiasm, you will have prosperous relationships.

> An abundant life comes from loving abundantly, and there are always rich opportunities to love.

When Abundance Happens

Will you be plenteous "someday"? Not really! Prosperity always shows up in the present and not in any other time. The reason why early stages of romance often feel so wonderful is because they have many of the rich qualities of being abundant—positive anticipation, worthiness, appreciation, limitless possibilities, fun, and unselfish motives in giving. If this describes your experience, you may remember that you were so fully engaged in the present that you didn't want to be anywhere else! Has your passion been put on pause? Are your funds in a funk? Then embody the practice of living like an abundantly present partner, fully engaged in the wonder of now, and watch how life responds to you.

Every day is like a fresh canvas, waiting for the vision of the artist. The higher Self within you is the artist of your life, spontaneously preparing you for what you most need to receive and give. For many people, the present is restricted by what happened in the past, and their future view looks like the past, only more so. As an expansive being, you don't have to anticipate that the present will have the same outcome as negative past experiences. Know that the present has new and vast possibilities. Step up to the understanding that you have the capacity to create whatever you have clear intention and commitment about. Choose to release the restrictions of the past, and come into the abundant now—the place where Divinity always resides and where whatever you need is included.

> "The same Lord is Lord over all [of us] and He generously bestows His riches upon all who call upon Him [in faith]" (Rom. 10:12 AMP).

What Hides Abundance?

Living the qualities of abundance will help you keep a clear vision of bountifulness. The converse is also true; there are ways of being that would darken your access to ever-present abundance. Here are a few signs that your abundant view may be getting clouded. Are you regularly complaining, fearful, critical, unthankful, mean, uncaring, or isolated? Are you being a taker instead of a giver in your relationships? Do you have a tendency to be angry, impatient, willful, close-minded, or arrogant? Are you feeling regretful and unworthy for some mistake you made last week, month, or decade? Do you regularly entertain feelings of foreboding or self-doubt? Do your internal and verbal languages reinforce negativity and limitations about the economy (or your own financial abilities), and why you can't do things?

These kinds of mental states haze our ability to see that there is enough right now. We may be convinced that *it*—whatever *it* is that needs to happen for us—will not happen. Guess what? If we strongly believe in lack and limitation, lack and limitation will tend to show up in our experiences. In large measure, we get what we see! Do you dwell on the problem or on the anticipation of a solution? Abundant people are certain there is a solution, so they act like a magnet to attract it. They declare what is possible and doable, take massive action, and hold feelings of impending success. Isn't it time to let go of the negativity? The payoffs for holding onto it aren't really that great anyway.

> Willfulness and fear tend to arise from an inflated sense of self. Humility and love are the way out.

Accept Help

Do you willingly turn to others for help in a time of need, or do you try to go it alone? Many times we limit ourselves when we believe we have to do things on our own. Most likely there are resources available within your circle of friends, family, and work associates and through many forms of media and technology that are right at your fingertips. Once when I was working on a community service project with seven others, we made a list of the resources available to us within each group of people we each knew. The list was amazing and included artists, marketing experts, financiers, healers, computer experts, and printers. Together we had access to everyone and everything we needed, if we were just willing to ask, which we did. Now think of the people you know who could assist you with ideas, contacts, or resources today. What will it take for you to ask for and accept help from them?

Typically, the feminine nature within us more naturally receives things without struggling. The masculine nature inside us often comes from the belief that we have to work hard for what we can accept. Perhaps this belief can be traced all the way back to the story of Adam, who was sentenced to sweat for what he needed (Gen. 3:19). Maybe this mental struggle is just a survival instinct we've inherited. The downside of believing struggle is necessary to succeed is that it can block things that are being freely given to us. After all, if the Christian Jesus had to labor for everything that came his way, he would not have been open to receiving the gold coin out of the fish's mouth to

> "I am come that they might have life, and that they might have it more abundantly" (John 10:10).

pay his tax bill (Matt. 17:27). That event shows the perfection with which divine grace cares for our needs. We only have to show up with an open heart and mind to accept available support.

Timely Action

Divinity gives us ideas through many means. When we respond to them in a timely way, they, in turn, meet our needs. You may get the idea to call a friend, read a magazine article, reorganize a file, buy a book, send an email, look at something in a new way, start a business, find a better job, or market your invention. What you do with the idea and the *timing* in which you respond to it can make all the difference as to whether you experience abundance.

One time I was trying for several weeks to sell a perfectly good car. I no longer needed that Mazda, and I couldn't figure out why it felt so difficult to find someone who did, even at a bargain price. During prayer, I was led to meditate about and feel the activity of Angels—deliverers of messages from God. Soon my despondency was replaced with confidence, and I knew that a buyer for my car would be led to me. The quiet knowingness was suddenly interrupted by a ringing phone. The caller had a thick foreign accent, which I could barely understand. She talked way too fast and was losing my attention quickly. Fortunately, I decided to help this woman instead of hanging up. To calm her down, I asked her name. She told me her name was . . . Angel. This Angel was in desperate need of a car just like the one I was selling. The next day she bought my car after her tire-kicking brother assured her that it was in excellent condition. To access abundance, I had gone from focusing on how difficult it was to sell my car to trusting in the divinely perfect way that angels communicate, to receiving the Angel who purchased my car.

> "... the earth is full of the goodness of the Lord" (Ps. 33:5).

The Infinite gives you talents, inspiration, strength, and connections in many forms. How do you use and share them? Do you treat God like a mail-order clerk when you ask for a car, a job, or a new significant other? If you are praying for new housing or a better relationship and you choose to ignore the idea you have to open the real estate ads or talk to a friend, should you complain that you still need your new home or mate? Taking timely steps when you receive the idea to do something will always lead to the next step.

Shut Out Negativity and Be Fruitful

To receive needed ideas and support, you'll need to shut out negativity, fear, and limitation. That is the essence of what Jesus taught. "When ye pray, enter into thy closet [the quiet place of the Presence], and when thou hast shut the door [on fear, negativity, and limitation], pray to thy Father which is in secret; and thy Father which seeth in secret shall reward thee openly" (Matt. 6:6, interpretations added). The Master's teaching suggests that we must go into our mental closet and shut out all the things that suggest that Divinity within us cannot do what needs to be done. In our hearts and minds, we can refuse to feed fearful and limiting beliefs, bad attitudes, smallness of trust, and stinginess. Like letting air out of a blow-up monster, such discipline diminishes the belief in lack and enables us to open our receiving hearts to the Infinite One for whom "all things are possible" (Mark 10:27).

The *real* first commandment Divinity gave to us was to be abundant! That's right; it's in the first book and chapter of the Bible: "And God blessed them and said unto them, be fruitful and multiply, and replenish the earth" (Gen. 1:28). Because most of us are no longer farmers, we don't use the word *fruitful* much anymore, but it still means to be prosperous and abundant and to bring things to success. This is our Creator's profound mandate for us: to be abundant! We wouldn't be given such a command without the complete backing to fulfill it.

Right this moment, feel Divinity's Universe giving to you. If you like affirmations, you can declare, "God's abundantly generous Universe is showering gifts on me now. I accept them, I am grateful, and I am blessed." Ideally you will not just say such an affirmation, but rather, you will believe and feel it. You may have to proclaim it regularly until you know it to be true for you. Speak it from your soul's perspective, not your human perspective. Allow it to merge with intensity into the cells of your body so the truth of it can be experienced. The more we emotionally connect with prosperity, the better our focus will be to recognize and act on it. The goal is to raise our vibrations in order to be in rhythm with Divine supply, which actually fills all space. As we progressively do this, we let God's will for us be done on earth (where our problems seem to be) as it is in heaven (where it's all abundantly worked out already).

Record Love

You may find it helpful to record on a daily basis all the ways the infinite field of divine Love gives to you and abundantly cares for you. This witnessing activity can support you to recognize and feel just how specifically and constantly you are loved, guided, and plentifully cared for. You may be amazed at how often the loving Presence of God is showing up in your heart, relationships, and life.

Life is like a huge mountain stream that we approach with thirst. We have the choice to show up to it with a teaspoon, a bucket, or a huge, ever-flowing pump piped into a limitless reservoir. If we feel and freely accept what is being given to us, we will be in an inspired position to share some refreshment with others too. After all, love is about being abundant and *sharing* abundance!

Practice Feeling Abundant

1) **Feel and Speak Abundantly:** We are the sons and daughters of the great I Am. When you say "I am," what follows those words? What you identify with and declare can make a huge difference in your experience and relationships. Honestly write down statements you have said in the past week. Did you say things such as "I am such an idiot," "I am poor," or "I am hopeless"? With heightened awareness of how the energy of words manifests, start declaring words that are true about the great I Am, which are also spiritually true about you as Divinity's creation. With this empowered feeling, you can proclaim such things as "I am multitalented," "I am resourceful," "I am prosperous," and "I am creative."

2) **Give and Receive:** To see abundance manifest in your life, you must not only give, but you must also be open to receive. Truly look at your relationship with giving and receiving. Do you accept help when it is offered, or do you insist on doing things

on your own? If it's difficult for you to accept generosity from others, stay open to saying "yes" and "thank you" when people offer to do things for you. If you're a taker, the Universe will reflect taking *from* you, but if you're a giver, you'll be more open to the Universe giving *to* you. Look for some ways you can more generously give and graciously receive this week and notice what happens.

3) **Trust in Infinite Supply:** No matter what your current situation, stay conscious this week about trusting that the infinite field of Love has already provided guidance and solutions for you in every way. When you start to get lost in thoughts of scarcity or fear, bring yourself back to the nature of God and live expansive qualities to the best of your ability. What is one thing in thought, feeling, word, or deed that you can improve in order to be more like our opulent Caregiver? For example, can you be more expectant of good or proactive in searching out resources? Practice one or more of these qualities unconditionally and then relax about how things will unfold.

Chapter 2

Appreciate

One of the strongest urges in human nature is the
desire to be appreciated.

Appreciate Yourself

Divinity is the source of your values and capabilities. Since the dawn of creation until now, there has never been anyone or anything created just like you. In a special way, you help to complete Infinity—you are that important! Your unique character and the way you express spiritual qualities are divinely precious and beautiful. Throughout your life you have shared your talents with others. Your true essence is amazing, whole, and intact, and despite all the detours and setbacks you have experienced, you are on a pathway to reveal more of your incredible essence. You may call your path spiritual growth, evolution of consciousness, or salvation. It may feel like a birthing process, a soul school, or a challenging adventure. You have faced considerable odds, and you are to be honored for your journey thus far. All you have been through and overcome has made you deeper, richer in experience, and, fortunately for you, perfectly prepared for what lies ahead. Up until now, everything has been perfect to bring you to where you are today.

If you're like most, your relationships have been challenging at times. On one or more occasions, you may have been hurt, slandered, criticized, lied to, stolen from, forsaken, rejected, let down, or disrespected. At times you've painfully sat in loneliness and fear, had to figure out difficult things, and survive through failure and loss. You've had to give when you were tired or sick, move into unchartered territory in a job or relationship, and risk the unfamiliar. After feeling unsuccessful or wounded, you somehow found it within yourself to get back up and try again. You've faced thorny challenges with family members and friends; in social circles, spirituality, politics, and health; and, of course, with the ongoing labor for money. In your own way, you are a warrior or a heroine. You have journeyed valiantly and have not given up.

Somewhere inside, you may sense there is something yet to be revealed, something deeply rich, calm, majestic, and free. Yes, you are spiritually amazing, wonderful, and beautiful, even if your nature occasionally seems to be tarnished by life's circumstances. Perhaps your life path, for all that it has delivered to you and for all you have given it, is calling you to appreciate who you are and what you have come through with total self-acceptance and love. In this way, you can more easily build on what has already worked for you and improve what has not. Appreciate who you are and what you have become, not in comparison with anyone else but in consideration of all that you've faced and surmounted, all that Divinity has gifted you, and all the opportunities you've had and will continue to have.

Like a relentless mirror, intimate relationships tend to reveal what we don't like about ourselves. They give us real-time, plentiful, and intense opportunities to love the seemingly unlovable, to embrace what has not gotten enough attention or value, and to grow beyond old and unworkable patterns. Acceptance enables us to get out of our own way so that Spirit can work through us. The love and acceptance we give ourselves opens a flowing energy field for others to love and accept us. Other's love can get in only to the degree we appreciate and accept ourselves. Also, we'll be able to expand what we give to others when we practice giving to ourselves the things we most need. What do you most need to give to yourself right now, and when will you give it? Others will feel that we're more accepting of their imperfections when we're that way with ourselves. Conversely, someone who is critical of others is usually even more critical of himself.

What could you do to connect with and nurture yourself today and daily? Appreciation invites movement and opportunities for expansion. It's easier to feel lovable and loving when we appreciate who we are, what qualities make us special, and what we stand for and contribute. Like a plant that's been starving, what is there about you that is thirsting for appreciation?

Appreciative Others

What do you believe is the number one destroyer of relationships? For many it is chronic criticism. Criticism tells people that they aren't good enough, but it also signals that the critic believes the same thing about herself. Criticism is negative energy that increases resistance and can result in a slow death to the relationship. Conversely, when we appreciate others, we align with higher vibrational energy that overcomes resistance, puts us in the flow of love, and helps us to heal feelings of inadequacy, self-loathing, and guilt. Appreciation radically increases feelings of goodness and love. Whatever gets attention tends to expand; whatever doesn't get attention tends to contract, lose energy, and die. Appreciation is a way of sharing positive attention and life-giving energy. Don't we all want to know we count, that we are valued, and that our efforts and contributions are meaningful in our home, at the office, and to our family and friends? It is a basic human need to feel significant; yet, how many of us actually do feel so on a consistent basis? And how effectively do we communicate significance to those around us?

People who appreciate us give us inspiration and motivation. They make life more enjoyable and remind us that we are worthwhile and that we make a difference to them. Our relationships with them are nurtured and strengthened by their attitudes and actions, much like a plant that receives regular water, nutrients, and sunlight. True friends have an uncanny ability to acknowledge us for who we are instead of who they think we should be.

Think of the people you know who embody appreciation as a way of being. You may find them to be:

- Joyful, inspired, and passionate

- Heart-centered, open-minded, and loving

- Contributing to the progress of their environment

- Focused on serving others and not just themselves

- Devoted to spiritual progress and to knowing Divinity

- Giving and receiving; they understand the full circle of love

- Looking for and seeing the best in all whom they encounter

- Recognizing beauty and valuing resources, opportunities, and life

- Thankful for others and the little things that make a big difference

- Expressing appreciation in writing, through verbal praise, or with gifts

All of us struggle at one time or another to feel good enough. Yet, when people express gratefulness, they inspire us to find the best within ourselves and to live from that place. They show us what appreciation looks and feels like and enable us to be more accepting of ourselves and others.

Impact on Relationships

We all want to feel that what we are contributing has importance. This is especially true in a committed relationship. A woman who wants to show love to her husband prepares a delicious and thoughtful meal with great effort. While racing to finish setting the table, she forgets to wipe up some spilled marinade on the kitchen counter. When her husband comes home and walks into the kitchen, he sets down some important papers right on top of the sauce.

Circumstances like this happen to most of us. Yet, what we do next greatly impacts our relationships. The husband may respond by quietly cleaning his papers while commenting on his wife's generosity and culinary preparations. His comments could bring her joy, because she knows that she has pleased him and her efforts were valued. Their bond is thereby deepened. An opposite reaction would be that he angrily asks how she couldn't have noticed the glob of sauce she thoughtlessly left on the counter. That one decision to ignore an opportunity to appreciate her (and instead criticize her) could lead to a night of disconnection or conflict and perhaps words they may later wish they'd never said. Choices always have consequences.

We all get impulses to show appreciation and gratitude for one another. What we do with those impulses is the crucial thing. In life we're either growing or dying, progressing or backsliding. Many relationships are starving and dying because of lack of appreciation. When a partner doesn't feel valued, they begin thinking, "What's the point?" Plants and trees cannot survive without nutrients; likewise, relationships cannot thrive without the nutrients of meaning, most often expressed by praise. Appreciation helps provide needed nourishment to a relationship that would otherwise become depleted by the stresses of life.

You may never know how incredibly you have blessed your friends, family, coworkers, and casual acquaintances. There are many people who have benefited just by your essence, not to mention your words and actions. One day while working at a high school, I was eating lunch in the cafeteria and noticed a teenage girl who looked depressed. Later I walked over to her and struck up a conversation. To my surprise, she had several cuts on her wrists. It appeared that she may have attempted suicide, perhaps even that day. For several months I befriended her, gave her encouragement, and acknowledged her strengths and talents. Years later, after she had graduated from college and was happily married, she wrote an article about the healing of her depression during that time. She called to tell me about the article's publication and to express appreciation for the support she received during that difficult time in her life.

There may be people in your life who may never tell you how much you have meant to them. Whether you have been told or not, you can be sure that you are having a positive impact on the people you are in relationship with—if you're appreciating who they really are and what they contribute. When you walk into your home or workplace today, focus on who you can appreciate and how you can do so in creative ways that mean something to them.

Very few relationships are harmonious all the time. Fortunately, thankfulness gives a lubricating quality to sticky times and helps smooth the rough patches. People who appreciate others make committee work more enjoyable and productive. As many supervisors have discovered, people don't work for organizations as much as they work for other people! Managers who inspire and appreciate employees for what they contribute are wonderful to work for. Workers will do considerably more than their normal share of work if a leader gives them sincere acknowledgment. Conversely, when a boss shows little or no gratitude, the staff often becomes drained, unmotivated, or challenging to work with.

Appreciate Source

How grateful are you to Divinity for life itself? Do you appreciate being alive and having whatever health you do, a place to live, a car to drive, a job to earn income and improve your skills, a mind to think and imagine with, freedom to believe what you want, and the opportunities to learn from all the mistakes you and others have made? What about the magnificent beauty all around you? Life truly is amazing! Even during challenging times, when some part of you seems to be struggling or failing, you can still find plenty of goodness, beauty, and blessings to be grateful for. Saint Paul's writings encourage us to "Thank [God] in everything [no matter what the circumstances may be, be thankful and give thanks], for this is the will of God for you" (1 Thess. 5:18 AMP). Appreciation awakens us to the reality that Divinity is conspiring for us and aiding our spiritual growth. In moments of clear spiritual vision, we may realize that heavenly things are happening right in front of us. Recognizing the splendor and wonder around us has the effect of shining light on it and amplifying it so that it radiates more brightly.

> One of the simplest, most deeply connecting, and far reaching prayers is "Thank you God."

In the developed parts of the world, most people have an incredible number of possessions compared with people who are impoverished. You won't be able to take your stuff with you when you die, so you don't actually own anything. Instead, you are merely a steward of your possessions during your stay on Earth. How well do you take care of and share your abundance? Cherish what Divinity has given you, not only in terms of things but also in opportunities, experiences, wisdom, and especially relationships. If you stop long enough to admit it, you may sense that you haven't gotten where you are in life on your own. By recognizing your limitations, you will see how assistance has come to you throughout your life. Guidance, encouragement, inspiration,

> If our spiritual vision was unobstructed, we would see that all people, things, and events are sacred and that all moments radiate forth Divinity.

emotional support, ideas, mentoring, and resources have flowed to you through many people, such as teachers, pastors, coaches, authors, bosses, friends, strangers, and family members. Acknowledging their positive impact—how they helped you find light, freedom, and healing—can go a long way in deepening these relationships and opening your thoughts to receive even more support.

Divinity has also given you a body. How well have you been taking care of it? It is a highly complex, versatile, rejuvenating, functional, and useful gift. Your body requires generous amounts of quality food, water, rest, and movement. Hopefully this is the kind of maintenance you have been demonstrating, and if not, today is a new day to start. Thank God we have hands to work with, eyes to see with, feet to walk with, a mouth to share our ideas with, and a heart to connect with. The deaf Beethovens, blind Bocellis, and multi-impaired Helen Kellers of the world inspire all of us to focus on what we have instead of what is missing and to value the precious opportunities our bodies are giving us to glorify our Creator and make a positive difference with others.

Benefits and Costs

One of the major benefits for gracious living is that it opens us to receive the abundance and vitality of the Universe. The winds flow in easily if we keep our doors and windows open. With respect to the flow of love in our life, thankfulness is a key way to do this. Yet, there are other benefits. One of the biggest fears of being human is that we're not good enough to receive love, which is connected to the fear of rejection. When we communicate to others that they *are* enough, we will tend to experience "enoughness" ourselves. Connection, love, intuition, inspired ideas, and supply pour more easily into and through a grateful heart. Acknowledging the good at hand will increase your ability to receive more of it. King David continually demonstrated appreciation through psalms, or songs of praise. Even through his most troubled times, he never completely lost sight of God's greatness, mercy, blessings, and power.

Appreciation has a socially energizing quality as well. The ones who call us friends are likely the ones whom we value. Honoring another is attractive; closeness and intimacy tend to result from honor. Furthermore, appreciation can help us find meaning to move past obstacles when life seems self-focused and difficult. It helps us find strength and purpose, reminding us that we are not alone but part of a much larger network of life. If we give thanks and strengthen our hearts when it's light, it will seem more familiar to summon our faith and gratitude when it's dark.

Gratitude will also support us in keeping perspective. One look at the millions of stars above us on a clear night reminds us that we are a miniscule aspect of the entire Universe. At some level, we sense that we wouldn't be able to move our finger on our own if it wasn't for the infinite field of Divinity animating and empowering us. "For in him we live, and move, and have our being" (Acts 17:28). Appreciation for any good reminds us of this, keeps us humble, and allows us to move more freely within this loving and powerful field.

If you miss opportunities and decide not to give appreciation, no one may notice. Yet, over the long term, there may be a price to pay in the quality of your life and relationships. People around you may begin to feel overworked and undervalued. They may not want to go the extra mile for you. Whether they vocalize it or not, they will sense that they "can't do it good enough" for you. Closeness and connection will fade. Some may give up, close down, disconnect, get angry, or look elsewhere for recognition. You may then wonder why your life looks so good on the outside, yet feels so empty on the inside. Your world will feel smaller and more isolated—contracting instead of expanding. You may even experience a decrease in joy, heart presence, creativity, and achievement. Remember, whatever doesn't receive attention will tend to die.

> "Therefore encourage (admonish, exhort) one another and edify (strengthen and build up) one another ... get to know those who labor among you (recognize them for what they are, acknowledge and appreciate and respect them all) ... And hold them in very high and most affectionate esteem in (intelligent and sympathetic) appreciation of their work" (1 Thess. 5:11-13 AMP).

Practice Appreciating

1) **Focus on Blessings:** When you focus on the goodness in your life, you will tend to attract more of it. Pick a time each day to reflect on all the blessings you have experienced throughout

your day. It might have been the friend who called unexpectedly to watch your children, a customer service representative who solved your problem, or a new contract you negotiated that increased your business.

2) **Appreciate Yourself:** It is difficult to give appreciation to others when you are constantly criticizing yourself. Divinity loves you specifically and without reservation. This week focus on how wonderful you are. On an index card write a list of ten of your strongest or most beautiful spiritual qualities and recognize how you express them in your own unique way. This list may include your humor, persistence, creativity, or the way you care for others. Post this card at home or work or carry it with you to remind yourself of your divine design.

3) **Appreciate Others:** This week pick two people in your life who may not be feeling your love as much as they could be. Write down some authentic and creative ways you could more actively show them appreciation and honor. You might want to acknowledge the uniqueness of their spiritual pathway, ask about and listen to what is important to them, or acknowledge their emotional needs and, if appropriate, help meet them. Then notice the positive impact your inspired words or actions have on those relationships.

Chapter 3

Attract

*When we see Divinity in ourselves and others, we
become more attractive.*

Fundamentals

Much of the current law-of-attraction literature emphasizes techniques
and strategies, some of which can yield results. This chapter will touch on
something more powerfully fundamental: the principle that we tend to
attract what we are—what we have become in character and consciousness.
It will also show how, because of limited perception, we tend to filter out
available relationships and prosperity. Finally, it will reveal what we can
do to expand our view.

By its very nature, divine Love is constantly bringing people and
resources together that support the highest good for all concerned. Our
opportunity and responsibility is to remove the blocks to this orchestration.
As our fears, ego patterns, unworkable strategies, and limiting beliefs
yield to the field of Love, we are moved toward those we need to be with
for a reason, season, or lifetime. Two people from different cultures and
backgrounds from opposite sides of the world can be brought together
unexpectedly at a conference because they have something to share with
one another. All of us have opportunities to be connected in unique and
wonderful ways, as long as we do not limit how they come about.

The most authentic and powerful attraction happens by authentically
living who we are—when our hearts are aligned with inner peace and joyous
giving rather than what we try to do or say in order to gain something. So
by truly being yourself, you will be led to do what you need to do in order

to have what your soul desires. If you set out in reverse and try to have what you desire so you can do what you want to do in order to be your best, you may be found wanting. You will be postponing true attraction.

The principles of attraction have a lot to do with trusting in the infinite field of divine supply, which is always available to us. What we consistently hold in mind and feel and declare to be true has a greater likelihood of coming to light in our experience. When we have clear intentions and let go of fear and resistance, we put ourselves in an ideal position of receiving what we need. If what we intend does not come to light, we may have to resolve inner conflict or subconscious beliefs as to why we don't deserve it or why it won't happen.

> "… things which are seen came to be from those which are not seen" (Heb. 11:3 LAM).

Being and Seeing

Are you currently experiencing what you want in your life? If not, you may want to take an honest look at the way you are being *and* how you are seeing. What you are bringing into your life and relationships often comes from your state of being (e.g., either authentic or not, positive or negative, etc.) and from how well you are seeing the best in yourself, others, and what life is offering. The way you see is filtered by your level of spiritual consciousness, which includes your attitudes, judgments, beliefs, words, revealed capacities, and actions.

We tend to attract into our experience what we include as the range of probabilities. If we are honest and kind and believe that others generally are too, we will likely experience honest and kind relationships in our lives. If we approach life with the attitude that "we had better get ours before someone else does," we shouldn't be surprised if competitive or jealous people surround us. Like a boomerang, the view of the world that we project out comes back to us.

It is much easier for a magnet to draw iron in the sand toward itself when the sand is not mucked up with mud or garbage. Similarly, it is easier for us to attract what our soul desires (what is truly best for us) when our true nature is not being covered up with behaviors, choices, attitudes, and beliefs that distort our beauty, power, and love. By cleaning up our mental environment and actions, higher-quality attraction naturally results. When we see the best in others, they will feel drawn toward us as well.

Babies are lovable, because they are so great at just being themselves—clumsy, drooling, smiling, cooing, and eagerly discovering their world. There's nothing blocking their essence, and their transparency is adorable. So is ours when we allow others to see it. The question is: how often do we let them?

We love another's authenticity, because it allows her true essence to freely shine through. Conversely, we can feel repelled by someone who is pretending. We sense fake a mile away. The important point is that others do also, and by the time we're adults, most of us have adopted some kind of act or inauthentic ways to get love and prevent hurt. We want to avoid the risk of rejection from not being liked for who we believe we are. It has been built into our genes over millennia that if we don't fit into the herd, it feels like we're going to die as an outcast. So, rejection seems like high-stakes business! Still, if we want to attract meaningful relationships into our lives, we'll have to allow others to see us authentically, including our weak aspects. This energetically invites them to connect with us and allows true relationship.

Ask yourself what blocks (the personality stuff you use to keep others at a distance) you are willing to remove so that other people can see the genuine you. Your love-blockers may include shyness, cutting wit, know-it-all smarts, seductiveness, or petty attitudes. It may require devoted spiritual seeking and healing for you to rediscover your authenticity. Yet, the rewards of soulful connection can be well worth your journey.

Attraction and Repulsion

Contrary to popular belief, most relationships don't really attract opposite spiritual qualities. Energetically, we tend to attract others who are like us in consciousness. Our thoughts and character radiate outward like a tower that transmits radio or TV signals. Others tune into what we are transmitting. The ones who are sending out similar energy waves find themselves drawn toward us. Our thoughts and actions broadcast more than we think, and they include our desires, values, beliefs, fears, intentions, and choices. When we are feeling, thinking, and acting from our hearts, it is easier to awaken and connect with the hearts of others.

Have you thought about the qualities you would most like to attract into your relationships? Courage can be attractive. So can enthusiasm and intelligence. It makes sense that expressing qualities such as integrity, goodness, and generosity more easily attract these same qualities from others.

Hold in mind the three qualities most important to you. Do you see yourself embodying these qualities at high levels? Are you committed to sending out beautiful and balanced thought-waves? What if you lived these qualities more purely and powerfully this week and this year? What if you held the intention to practice them unconditionally, no matter what? You would likely find yourself attracting relationships and experiences that more fully express these same qualities. Your way of being would align you with a field of energy that includes the potential for such relationships and experiences.

Do you want to be more attractive? If yes, are you willing to think, feel, express yourself, and live in ways that do not obstruct your unique spiritual qualities? With awareness and adjustments, you can actually make choices that will invite what your soul yearns for—that which serves the highest good. The great English playwright William Shakespeare wrote, "Kindness in women, not their beauteous looks, shall win my love." That's the great thing about qualities—they are not restricted by how we look or what circumstances we find ourselves in.

For many people, purity is engaging, and impurity is disconnecting and repulsive. Impurity is simply the clouding of a substance with something that does not belong. You may feel beclouded by a lifestyle or activity, an attitude or motive, or even a work environment or association. By removing the impurity, you actually become more authentically attractive. When you assess your life, what needs to be modified or eliminated? How could you do this? What steps could you take today?

> "It is helpful to understand that a specific level of consciousness is aligned with an 'attractor field' that, like a magnet, attracts similarities" (David R. Hawkins, M.D., Ph.D., *Discovery of the Presence of God*).

Life Filter

In consciousness, people tend to allow into their lives what they believe is available and possible to them. Think of this as a life filter that lets in only those experiences that match your focus, attitudes, feelings, language, and beliefs. This filter largely determines the content of what shows up in your life, because the filter won't let in things that do not resonate with you. In fact, much like software, the filter will work to reject, ignore, and even destroy what doesn't match its programming. As a result, you could miss out on the experiences your heart and soul are seeking. You could reject, ignore, or sabotage an idea, experience, environment, opportunity, or relationship.

Take a close look at your life filter in order to make adjustments there. Without adjusting your filter, the content of your experience will tend to be repetitive. Time won't change anything unless you change your perceptions (filter) and strategies (actions). If you believe that income has to come through a paycheck from one particular employer, then your filter will make it less likely for you to include multiple streams of income or financial gifts. As your consciousness expands, you naturally make room for more amazing things to show up in your life, and you respond to them in more productive ways. Once I had a very limited concept of what type of woman I was attracted to, and this of course ruled out many wonderful women from my dating life. Only when I realized how confining I was being did I open up to relationships that had been there all the time.

The bottom line is that there are millions of available experiences, no matter what your situation currently seems to be. But, you unconsciously screen out available options and resources that do not fit your views. For instance, if a single woman believes or repeatedly says "There are no good men left," then it is almost a guarantee that she will experience a lack of "good men" in her life. Incredible men may come across her pathway, but for one reason or another, she will either not notice them or find a host of reasons not to connect with them. Her life filter simply will not allow good men to hang around in her experience. When you awaken to how this process works, you can adjust your life filter in a way that supports you rather than keeping you stuck in lack or fear. From such an empowered place, you become a ready instrument to be used by the divine Will for that which contributes to life and your own long-term well-being.

It is important to become aware of your dominant thoughts and feelings and seek to entertain ones that support and uplift you rather than impact you negatively. Life coaches often say that "results never lie." By looking at the pattern of results in your experience, you can get a pretty good idea about the thoughts and emotions you are regularly holding in mind. From this awareness, you can choose more workable and resourceful patterns.

If what you want is not showing up for you, even though you are doing your best to attract it, then it could be for one of two reasons. It may not be what your soul really wants—what is best for your spiritual growth—or you may need to be more consistent in transmitting the thoughts, feelings, and actions needed to move you closer to your goal. Who you are *consistently* does the most powerful attracting, and often it is the only thing that blocks success. Two tennis players can be equally matched in athletic ability, court sense, and training. Yet, on any given day, the one who consistently hits his serves, ground strokes, and volleys better will likely be the victor. If what your heart and soul desires does not manifest easily and quickly, you may not be doing anything wrong. It may just be that commitment and disciplined consistency are being required of you to expand your consciousness until you reach success.

Drama or Connection

Some people don't know what it feels like to connect at the level of the heart, so they continue to connect with others through drama, conflict, pain, crisis, and negativity. Although these experiences can be huge energy drains, you may feel more alive and comfortable with such states than with boredom, dispassion, or isolation. Yet, is fighting really more engaging and meaningful than joy and harmony? The payoffs for each way of being should be deeply considered.

Instead of making life an unwinnable battle, wouldn't you rather choose concord? Even if you win an argument, your heart will still be left wrestling with guilt and aching for true connection. At some point, all of us will have to be willing to give up the secret satisfaction we are getting from conflict and negativity in order to realize better relationships. We can choose to connect through unselfishness or anger, through appreciation or criticism, through magical moments or drama. It's important that we have our needs met, but we always have the choice to do so either in low—or high-quality ways.

Feel Deserving

Do you believe you deserve what you want in your life? In every moment, you are communicating to Life what you believe you do and do not deserve. Are there experiences, relationships, environments, or behaviors that you still hold on to but that do not support what you deeply desire? There is no reason to let age, lack of credentials, what other people have told you, or anything else put limits on what you can include in your experience today. A master teacher of possibility clearly taught that ". . . all things are possible to him that believeth" (Mark 9:23). Believing is about living in a present-feeling realization of that which is not yet physically seen. You couldn't feel it if it wasn't already present in spiritual reality. Electronic instruments have shown that what one feels from the heart has significantly more energetic power than what one thinks from the head. If you hold on to the feeling in your heart of already having what seems to be missing, it will more likely show up in your life.

Understanding that we tend to attract ideas, people, and experiences that match where we are in consciousness can feel like a significant responsibility! Fortunately, it is much easier to make positive changes from a place of empowerment versus a place of victimization. Quantum physicists tell us that the observer affects the outcome. What we look for tends to change what appears to us. If we specifically look for brown cars, we'll see a lot more brown cars than if we're looking for white cars or no color in particular. Perhaps we happen to life much more than we think life happens to us. In fact, we not only selectively see what appears to us, but we selectively choose what it means to us as well. Once when I held a door open for a woman, she seemed offended, took the door from me, and with a huff said, "I can do that!" My motive was to honor her not offend her, and it appeared that her filter did not allow for that option.

Realizing that the meaning of our experiences largely come from what we predominantly hold in mind gives us the opportunity to improve our lives by making more empowering choices. As we continue to awaken to divine Love, we may sense that the Universe is abundantly on our side to bring higher experiences toward us and us toward those experiences. Our job is to more wisely focus on what thoughts, feelings, language, and character we are putting out there and confidently leave the attracting job to Spirit's perfect timing, deep wisdom, and infinitely amazing resources.

Soul Attraction

All of us have a soul-longing to feel true connection. It is only natural to want to attract people and experiences that bless and nurture us the most. Our hearts want to express who we really are. We also desire to feel understood, connected, trusted, and valued. The trouble is that there is so little in our sex-and entertainment-driven world that speaks to this yearning for true connection. Instead, a daily host of seductive, dramatic, and violent diversions are offered. The programmed effect for many is that their soul-yearning can become numbed, dormant, twisted, forgotten about, or compromised.

> If we seek to be content because of another person, then we will not be content with ourselves.

How would it be different for you if you more fully discovered and deliberately focused on exactly what your heart truly desires? What is it that you value most in relationship? Is it affection, honesty, communication, intimacy, playfulness, or spiritual growth? Perhaps you find generosity, strength, or joy more attractive. What are you willing to do and get rid of in order to have your heart's desire? By keeping clear about what's most significant, you will be less likely to compromise yourself in search of it.

Your primary job is to unblock your genuine nature, become what you are capable of, and more fully live in the feeling/being state of what you want to attract. Then be unwilling to settle for less until these attractive qualities show up in your relationships! When you stay aware of what you are transmitting, you can make adjustments to embody your true spiritual qualities. Then you will naturally attract qualities that more closely match yours. How could it be otherwise? In a loving and honest state of being, you will more easily attract and experience love and truth in relationship.

Practice True Attraction

1) **Set a Clear Intention:** Write down the top five to ten qualities that you want to attract into your relationships and carry this list in your wallet or purse. Make it a priority to more fully live these qualities yourself in all you think, feel, say, and do and make adjustments whenever you find yourself out of alignment.

2) **Identify and Remove Blocks:** List three attitudes, feelings, beliefs, choices, or behaviors that may be opposing what you desire to attract. Perhaps you believe that you are getting too old

to be attractive or that you don't have enough money to have a successful relationship. You can remove such blocks by feeling that divine Love is abundantly capable of meeting your needs and that your uniquely expressed qualities are lovable—right now, no matter what your age or bank balance is. Then ask: how am I *seeing* (e.g., critical, self-righteous, or limited)? Now notice any unworkable ways you are *being* (selfish, fearful, or angry). What could you do to uplift your ways of seeing and being in order to improve your life filter? Perhaps you will make a clear intention to look for and speak only about the best in others. Maybe you will enter a room and ask in your heart, "Who can I give to?" or "How may I serve?" Such a simple shift in motives can powerfully clear the way for more authentic ways of seeing and being.

3) **Embody Attractive Qualities:** For long-term results, we must *become* what we want to attract. Pick one action that will attract more of what you want. For example, you may want honesty in your relationships, so you will more openly communicate your feelings or boldly stand for what you believe in. To attract an honest partner, you must first speak your truth and walk your talk. If you want soulful connection, then you may want to first nurture your own soul by taking time to meditate, attend a retreat, read an inspiring book, or join a spiritually awakened group. You may discover an honest and soulful relationship along the way!

Chapter 4

Feel Balanced

Divinity understands your needs. With all your praying,
be willing to experience inner change.

Divine Adjustment

How many things in your life right now need to be adjusted, balanced, or harmonized? Do your finances, stress levels, exercise habits, or outgrown relationships need changing? Maybe it is your wardrobe, fifty-hour workweeks, the way you are living your values, or the loneliness, anxiety, or depression you feel. What if there was a Master balancer who could take care of all your needs? Imagine what a relief it would be to have everything that feels unresolved, conflicted, unhealed, or even impossible to fix completely handled by a balancing intelligent power. You might be thinking, "Back to reality, back to my problems." But before you go there, expand your possibilities for the rest of this chapter.

Balance has to do with stability and equilibrium. When something feels unbalanced in our lives, we may feel out of control or unstable to some degree. This uncertainty can affect other parts of our lives and relationships negatively. Fortunately, divine laws exist to bring us back into harmony by showing us how to adjust our perceptions, procedures, and priorities. Anything we fully love will tend to feel in balance. Anything we don't fully love may need an adjustment on our part.

If you were absolutely sure that there *is* a completely supportive field of consciousness accessible to you in every moment of your life, would you wait any longer to connect with and benefit from its phenomenal resources, timing, and wisdom? Would you hold off surrendering your problems, issues, and maladjusted list of stuff one more minute? Rest in the certainty that there *is* such a power available to you today—a power with immeasurable abilities ready to direct your heart, mind, and actions step-by-step. This masterful wisdom, this infinite field of ever-present energy, is divine Love. Today, intend to move toward balance, harmony, and beneficial adjustment in every area of your life by responding to the nature, guidance, and gifts of this perfect field.

Look around you right now and see objects—the content of your surroundings. There is also space in and around the objects. Think of this space as the field that includes the objects. Now imagine and feel that this space is filled with balancing Love so that your focus is not on your problems (the content of the field) but only on the Presence (the comforting energy) of the field Itself. Do you feel any lighter?

There have been many times when I felt like I needed the balancing activity of Divinity, especially after exhausting efforts to fix things that were stuck or broken in my life. Over and over again, I have had to rediscover that the Allness of Love is able to correct and solve each of my pressing needs with perfect resources, timing, and precision. My only job was to ask for direction and then actually do what I was being divinely led to do. Sometimes this required patience, humility, courage, or endurance. Many times I would go through unnecessary suffering until I remembered my job.

Several years ago I found myself in a very difficult situation: unemployed, in very poor health, and with more than $50,000 in credit card debt. Things felt hopeless, and I lived in an almost-constant state of foreboding and anxiety. This emotional state led to what felt like a dark downward spiral. I needed to feel Love's balancing action soon, before things got worse! I reached out to Divinity many times each day and slowly began to feel inspiration and guidance. For a while, fear seemed to obstruct divine direction. Even when I did let guidance in, the adjusting steps seemed difficult to act on, because I felt so physically weak. Nonetheless, each time I took positive action, I felt more empowered. It is amazing how well this principle works. Soon I began to eat and sleep better and even started to exercise a little. When I felt stronger and healthier, I began to look for work in the best way I could.

In six months, beyond many moments of self-doubt, I landed a sales job. Soon, I not only earned enough to meet my ongoing bills, but I also started paying off my credit card debt. My health steadily improved. After a year, I was fully recovered, and my credit card debt was completely paid off. Step by step, both my outlook and my actions had been adjusted and balanced. I am still learning lessons from having witnessed divine Love's influence and activity in my life at that time. It may be comforting for you to meditate on the understanding that there exists a divine law of harmony constantly moving you toward that which serves your highest good and the good of others. With its infinite capacities and power, there is nothing that this field of divine energy cannot help you resolve.

> Difficulty includes the opportunity for a shift in one's perceptions and/or actions in order to find a solution.

Trust the Power

You are not expected to blindly trust in divine Love, but instead to understand the nature of what you trust. When you balance your checkbook, you don't doubt the laws of mathematics, do you? You know that addition and subtraction rules work each and every time, based on principles that are unfailingly reliable and always available. You have witnessed that these rules work at home, in the grocery store, and on vacation. The reliability of Divinity's balancing love operates for you the same way. It is always available to completely realign and calm every aspect of your heart, mind, body, and life.

Nature reveals this balancing and adjusting movement all around us. Loud noises echo off into silence, winds calm down into stillness, roaring waves subside into the vastness and depth of the sea, rigid ice melts into flowing springs, the heat blasts during summer cool down into fall, and the over-zealous, playful kittens tucker into a peaceful nap. Feel the magnificence of this ever-present Power that smoothes and controls all things! How perfectly it is able to move you as well. What if you lived today and the rest of your life knowing that there is such a friendly field of energy moving in, through, and around you, guiding and balancing you the moment you become aware of it?

One key to accessing the Presence is remembering that you are not going through life on your own. Divine consciousness is within you, actively animating you every moment. You always have three choices: ignore this field, resist being moved by it, or respond to it willingly. The real question to ask yourself is: how is your life working for you right now?

If you are in need of balancing in any way, take a closer look at how it can happen for you.

Perception and Reality

Creation is perfect. Perhaps our view of creation isn't perfect at times. Nonetheless, good can appear out of that which looks less than good; beauty can appear out of ugliness; order can appear out of disorder. Problems exist on the level of perception, the way we view things and the meanings we make up. When we shift our perception, problems can evaporate. Would it be horrible if someone's income was cut by 10 percent? Your answer will be based on your perception. What if you found out that their original income was $50,000 per month? Would your opinion change? Our perceptions are often different from reality, because they are based on how we think things *should* be. Our expectations change as we expand our views of what's true—as we perceive more about spiritual reality. What you expect and know to be true today is quite different than what you expected and knew at age seven.

What if you could tap into a spiritual reality, a knowing-ness, where your current difficult situation, relationship, disease, money, or emotional problem was already resolved? What if glimpsing this reality for a few moments was enough to actually begin to alter the problems in your life? Wouldn't it be easier to simply see/feel your problems within the context of this omnipotently perfect spiritual reality rather than continuing to struggle with the unsatisfying outward details? You could be like an eagle soaring above the fog instead of getting lost in it. Just as changing the film in a projector naturally presents a different picture on a movie screen, your awakened sense of spiritual reality enables you to see your life projected, or animated, by divine control. This new way of seeing/feeling can have a dramatically positive impact on what shows up in the movie of your life.

Once I worked as a cook in a restaurant with a very difficult boss. She gave me the absolutely worst schedule and cleanup tasks and treated me with a sour and impatient attitude. Moreover, she was generally disliked by most of my coworkers. Yet, knowing that others were miserable too didn't really help me; it just re-enforced my situation. I needed the job to pay bills but couldn't go on without something changing! I decided to change me. During prayer, I asked Spirit to adjust the way I saw my boss, and I immediately glimpsed something more likable about her. The way Divinity created my boss was as a woman cherished, tenderly loved, and uniquely talented. My heart softened, and I felt some compassion for her. I sensed how things may have looked from her perspective, including the hurtful way many of the workers reacted to her. I truly felt a desire to support her and see the best in her.

The next day when I went into work, it was as if a nice body snatcher had taken over my boss. Without saying a word to her, she completely changed her attitude toward me. She walked up to me and announced that she would be giving me better hours and wanted me to do less of the dirty cleanup work. I stood there with a sense of amazement, hoping my jaw would not hit the floor. From that day forward, my whole relationship with my boss transformed for the better. It was like going to a B movie, and halfway through, somebody replaced the film with a blockbuster. By compassionately discerning something of her divinely true nature, both my eyes (what I was projecting) and the movie of my life (my work experience) were dramatically improved.

You might find your view improved through a change in your priorities, an inspired attitude, or purified motives or actions. As it is in your spiritual awareness of divine reality, so it will progressively be in your experience ". . . on earth as it is in heaven" (Matt. 6:10). Divinity fills the Universe with tender care, exquisite power, perfect intelligence, infinite resources, and awe-inspiring harmony. Understanding this, you have the potential to bring balance to all that you know. Conversely, when your consciousness is degraded through criticism, fear, or negativity, you should not be surprised if your relationships and life experience seem unstable.

Centered in Allness

When life feels complicated, it is often because we're lost in details and focused on what we don't want or lack. We're often dominated by anxiety and limitation. Such mental focus tends to go against our infinite spiritual nature. In such moments, we are not making our life about knowing and expressing Divinity. Something else has become god to us: problems, people, places, things, and situations. What we focus on has a lot to do with how we feel.

Ask yourself what is most meaningful to you, not in theory but in actuality. Does your world feel constricting? Now, expand your vision beyond what has been getting most of your attention lately. What would be most important for you to experience during the next ten years and during your entire lifetime? What would you prefer to make your life about with the time you have left? By answering such questions, your problems may be reduced in perspective. At the end of the day, unless you embody and experience ever-deeper aspects of divine Love, nothing else may satisfy you or bring you peace. The false idols that clamor for attention in your day, as engrossing as they can be sometimes, will eventually feel frustratingly unfulfilling.

Divinity's presence is at the center of all we are and all we do. Discontentment happens when we become unconscious of this great fact. We feel empty, because the Presence is missing from our awareness or focus. The easiest way to access this infinitely powerful, abundantly resourceful, perfectly balancing Love is first to acknowledge that Divinity is all there is. Scripture enlightens us: "That they may know from the rising of the sun and from the west, that there is none beside me. I am the Lord, and there is none else" (Isa. 45:6). At higher levels of awareness, all is divine; God is All-in-all. By refocusing our attentions and priorities on the infinitude of Divinity, we're moved beyond perceived material limitations. More of reality then dominates perception, and solutions become apparent. We become witnesses and instruments to progressive possibility. This feeling of certainty actually starts shifting what we experience.

When a swimmer out at sea is rescued from storm surf by a search-and-rescue team, they are lifted above the waves, not dragged through them. By centering in the totality of Allness, you have a way to lift yourself above the storm waves of your life. The intelligence of God includes your mind; the health of God includes your body, business, and bank account; the lovingness of God includes your relationships; the justice and protection of God includes your affairs; the success of God includes your capacities and activities.

> "The earth is the Lord's, and the fullness thereof; the world, and they that dwell therein" (Ps. 24:1).

Be As If

How can you connect with the Source of all balance if you are not sure what it feels like? You can start by asking for divine guidance: "Spirit, show me what perception or behavior I need to change and how to do it." Then, relax in the understanding that there exists an infinite field of harmony right here with you, capable of altering whatever needs it. In order to rule out doubt and fear, recommit to the awareness that God is powerfully and tenderly present as a field of Love in and all around you. In so doing, you become available to the wisdom and resources of this omnipotent Presence.

Enlightened ones have told us that spiritual creation is already complete and perfect. Yet, our perception of it is evolving, so the world looks far from perfect to us. Our growth is just an expanding awareness of what's real and what's not. By relying on divine principles, we can act as if what seems to be missing is already present, because, in spiritual reality, it actually is. This "act-ion" activates latent resources and potential. It puts us in a receiving stance to witness and manifest what seems to be missing. In coaching circles, this process is known as "be as if." In other words, feel and live as if the circumstances or conditions are already exactly the way you want them to be. Then take action from that feeling state. The beauty of this practice is that it awakens and activates dormant capacities and aligns us with a higher energy domain, which includes a range of possibilities we are seeking. Consciousness researchers such as David R. Hawkins, M.D., Ph.D., call these higher energy domains Attractor Fields. Aligning with such a field more easily attracts into our awareness and experience the circumstances and resources that match how we are feeling and acting. Remember, like attracts like. That's why sales people who have just made a sale are the ones most likely to make another sale—they feel like they will, because they have! It's easy to know that something will happen if it's already happened. Being as-if is a way to prelive desired experiences.

How would you act if your job, health, money situation, or relationship was ideal right now? How would you feel, think, and speak? What actions would you take or no longer take? Act like that until you experience the fruition or balancing adjustment you want. You will increase the likelihood of experiencing what your heart desires while "acting as if," embodying and expressing what you want and need.

Through his spiritual vision, the prophet Elijah was able to bring balance and safety to his frantic servant. In 2 Kings 6:15-17, we read that one day the young servant came running to Elijah in fear, because their entire city was surrounded by a strong military force with horses and chariots set out to destroy Elijah and what he stood for. Instead of becoming afraid, Elijah communicated confidence to his servant and prayed that God would ". . . open his eyes, that he may see" (i.e., that he might perceive the spiritual reality of the situation, which included their secure safety). When the servant's eyes opened, he was ruled by reality and saw the hills full of defending horses and chariots all around Elijah. Elijah never altered his state of being, and he acted from a balanced, powerful, spiritual stance. Through spiritual perception, he was able to easily defend both himself and his servant and totally adjust the outcome of the situation, which included a peaceful resolution.

Instead of acting out of fear and worry, you too can act from spiritual confidence by accessing what you know and feel of divine Love, which includes your divine capacities. This higher state of being invites divine grace, power, and success. It also develops you spiritually. Like any other strength, as you exercise spiritual confidence, it grows stronger.

There is an eastern riddle that asks, "What is the sound of one hand clapping?" Perhaps it is the sound of joy from spiritually knowing the divine hand is constantly showing up to meet our hands to produce resonating sounds of harmony and balance. We can listen for this sound with expectancy. The infinite field of divine Love has enabled us to *be* what we seem to need. If we need to overcome stress, we can feel the ease of this Presence and be relaxed. If we need friendship, we can feel the support of this field and become friendly. It is simply up to us to identify with the field and make a committed choice to act "as if"—to feel and be whatever is needed, to realize that Allness includes us. After awhile, this state of being Love will become more important to us than the result we originally sought. Like any road to mastery, the road is the destination!

Course Correcting

When the captain of a ship sails from New York to London, he or she has to make many adjustments amid the winds and currents to stay on course and reach the port of choice. Likewise, we may need to make adjustments to realign with our values and ultimate destiny. Our values and what we trust chart the course of our lives. To be on course toward success and fulfillment, we need to know what our values are. Otherwise, we may be traveling without a rudder and leaving everything up to chance. Values include the principles, standards, and qualities that are worthwhile or vital to us. In ancient times, a man's honor was commonly considered to be so important that it was worth dying for. For some, it still is today.

When you pass on, you will have given your life for something. What is it going to be? Is it your honesty, love, or loyalty? Perhaps it is your zest for life, achievements, or family. You can tell what your values have been by recapping how you have lived up to this point in your life. With that in mind, is there a gap between your life and what you say you value? Regardless of what you may discover about your personal gap, you always have the option to chart a new course for your life through new decisions and actions.

If we resist making adjustments, we may solidify the habit of being off course. Soon we can develop stubborn ways of being that are in direct opposition to our own core values. These invested-in patterns actually attract more of what we say we don't want. Entrenched negativity, willfulness, self-centeredness, and deception can hinder the progress we desire. These traits are like saying "No!" to the Presence available within us. Violating our own values will lead us to the rocky shoals of pain, suffering, and loss. The farther off course we go, the more radical the correction needed. Just as a ship captain cannot fight the winds, ocean current, and tides, we ultimately cannot fight the divine flows in our lives. We are either going to move with them gracefully or exhaust ourselves struggling against them.

Take this moment to consciously expose and write the ways of being that are contrary to your deepest values. These may include lacking discipline, compromising your mission, voicing self-limiting statements, or having some form of excess in diet, drinking, or stress. Do your weekly priorities match your values? Today is an opportunity to realign with what you know in your heart to be most important to you. By listening for needed steps and taking appropriate actions, you may find a profound effect on your peace and prosperity.

One of the best ways to experience positive change is to feel your way into it. What would it be like to already have your situation adjusted? How would that make you feel and act? What if you didn't wait for the external to change but could feel the way you want to feel, regardless of your temporary circumstances? Instead of believing that you'd be happy if you got a new job or intimate partner, you could just choose to be happy now. Feelings are actually a choice, and emotional mastery is the ability to proactively choose one's state of being. In the vastness of all-encompassing Love, problems are miniscule anyway. Nothing can resist the infinitely powerful field of all-balancing Love.

If you're ever feeling disconnected, stressed out, or out of sorts, ask yourself, "Where is Divinity in my life right now? Is feeling divine Love's nature and activity my priority?" Its nature and activity includes you! God is Love; therefore, you are nurtured and provided for this very moment. God is Life, so you are animated, energized, and unfolding wonderfully. God is Spirit; hence, you are unlimited, free, and empowered. God is Soul; you are thus rich in wisdom, beauty, and grace. God is Mind; consequently, you reflect intelligence, resourcefulness, and expansiveness. God is Truth, so you include and can inspire honesty, justice, and integrity in every detail of your experience.

Meditating this way gives us dominion, because it helps heal the belief of separation between God and us. The complex in our life can become progressively clear and simple, and clarity is power. As thoughts and feelings align with the Divine, they become effortless, comforting, and peace-giving. It's as if we receive and embody them rather than do them. When we let God be the doer, we sense that we are God's deed. Having a consciousness in which everything is included in Divinity, we are led to make decisions out of love and honesty instead of from fear or manipulation, which give us much better results in the long run. Centering in Divinity's Allness is a reward in itself; the positive changes in our life are the by-products.

With ideal timing, divine Intelligence knows what you most need and when you need it. Your alignment with divine perfection and completeness can balance your life and meet your needs in amazing ways that serve the highest good for you and all concerned.

Practice Feeling Balanced

1) **Feel Divine Presence:** Recall a few times when you've seen or felt Divinity's adjusting hand in your life. Maybe it was when you first met your significant other, when a solution to a problem at work appeared from out of nowhere, or when a stranger stopped to help you fix your car. Divine Love is continually and masterfully nudging you toward balance and harmony. Start recognizing the activity of the Presence in your day-to-day life and record these grace-driven events in a journal to increase your awareness of them. What we focus on tends to bring more of the same in our experience.

2) **Intend Harmony:** Note one or two areas of your life that currently need adjustment. Consider physical, material, mental, emotional, relationship, and spiritual aspects. It may be as simple as needing to find an important email or a piece of jewelry or as complex as healing the deep emotional hurt from a past relationship or work situation. Set a clear intention that these things will be resolved based on communing with the Presence of infinite Love's always-harmonious and perfectly balancing field of energy that totally directs you and others. Notice what occurs from this place of positive expectancy, this centering in Allness.

3) **Be "As if":** Meditate on another area of your life that needs shifting. Based upon Divinity's limitless abundance and tender care expressing itself through you, feel and spiritually act as if the problem or situation is already resolved. Then, let Divinity move you and others to take care of the details.

4) **Take Aligned Action:** Pick an area in your life that is out of alignment with your values. Write in a journal about the behaviors, thoughts, words, or feelings that are blocking you from feeling peace and power. Now develop a simple action plan to bring the way you live into alignment with your core values. For example, if respect is one of your top values, you could be on time for others out of respect for them. If inner strength is important to you, stretch yourself by courageously doing what looks hard, even when you don't feel like it. Stay open to whatever solutions are revealed to you and commit to following through when you receive inner direction. Then listen for and act on the next step.

Chapter 5

Beautify

Along with your seeking and desires, include the aim to have
new eyes to see what has always been here.

Beauty Shines Forth

Color, movement, contrast, dimension, texture, sound, contour, and light—these are just some of the ways beauty is communicated to us. Nature and artists bring us beauty through mastery of light, perfection in rhythm and balance, and engaging variety. The inner or spiritual sense of beauty is transmitted intuitively, energetically, intelligently, and often with feelings of soulful awakening. We *know* beauty when we feel it, and such experiences can be transforming. Beauty can lift us above a heavy mindset and take us on a shortcut to experience the timeless and divine. In reality, all that exists belongs to Divinity and is its magnificent expression. Our role is to perceive and experience this underlying essence and, in so doing, access Divinity and benefit our relationships.

Each of us expresses and reflects divine beauty in our own unique ways. Beauty that we see in another is also present within us or else we would not be able to recognize it. If we see that our beauty is an expression of the Infinite rather than as a personal possession, we can more easily feel its nature radiating within us. By recognizing the true source of beauty, we allow it to freely shine through us instead of having it obstructed by pride or self-criticism, which are two sides of the same coin: a belief in personal authorship. We don't originate beauty, but it is up to us to recognize and appreciate it. With humility we can see splendor in the twinkle of our own eyes, the perfection behind nature's design, and miraculous light that dances off of everything around us, and the music of the sounds of life around us.

In the presence of people who love us, we seem to feel even more wonderful. Why is this? They see our uniqueness and our very best. This has the effect of magnifying what is radiant within us. Whatever is undesirable gets outshined by what is lovely. Professional photographers know how to use and capture light in order to bring out the splendor of seemingly insignificant objects. Witnessing to the beauty within ourselves and others enables the divine Light to shine more brightly within our own consciousness and through form. Beauty is a gift, and so is the capacity to recognize it.

Connecting deeply with beauty can bring immediate healing, joy, and love. It can take our focus off of the past and future and unveil the wonder of the present. Beauty can uplift consciousness, enrich life, provide hope, expand our awareness, and bring peace. It is that powerful. It enables us to see the good and wonderful, the soulful and real—the lasting qualities of whatever the light of Love is animating in people and surroundings.

More than Skin Deep

Most of us want to know that at least some people find us attractive. But, unless we appreciate our own spiritual beauty, all of the cosmetic adjustments and adulation in the world will not satisfy us. Glossy magazines with airbrushed photos promote one type of allure. Glamour is surface only, often unrealistic and never permanent. Changing trends, gravity, and time guarantee the latter. Conversely, one's character can deepen and shine brighter as years go by, and it is unaffected by gravity.

The infinite nature of divine Love reveals itself in desert flowers, parting storm clouds, laughing children, peaceful winter shorelines, and our own motives and hearts. Spirit declares its wondrous spiritual creation to be "very good" (Gen. 1:31)—beautiful! Is this the way you are witnessing this same creation, of which you and everyone you know are manifestations?

Children are classic examples of how clearly beauty can shine through, especially when they are provided nurturing role models. One nineteenth-century definition of the word *beauty* was "truth." Children typically live genuinely, speak honestly, and have an innate sense of innocence. Their authenticity lets their beauty fully radiate without obstruction. How important it is for all of us to express our essence, to let the childlike within us glow.

By honoring beauty, we magnify it and participate in revealing it for others. Conversely, there is a tremendous cost for ignoring, rejecting, or disfiguring that beauty. Emotional wounds, low self-esteem, restricted self-expression, and disconnected relationships are just some of the consequences.

What can you do if you feel unable to perceive beauty in yourself, your partner, your friend, or your coworker? What if the landscape was unable to feel the sun? The adjustment need not take place in the sunrays, but only in what is blocking them. When clouds disappear, the light and warmth of the sun shine through and nurture the beauty of the land. The same principle applies to uncovering the truly exquisite within yourself and those around you. Simply remove what is blocking beauty in your perception. Let's take a closer look at how to do it.

> "Let the beauty of the Lord our God be upon us ..." (Ps. 90:17).

Unblocking Perception

How do blocks originate? Often they come from holding on to beliefs, attitudes, judgments, or perceptions that do not serve us. They becloud us from witnessing what is divinely stunning within ourselves and others. Perhaps you've held to concepts or associations that have existed for years. You may be thinking that your beauty does not match the perfectionism promoted by TV and fashion magazines. Perhaps you have emotional scars or critical judgments that distort how you view yourself. Maybe you hold the belief that only a certain body shape or hair color is attractive to the opposite sex. These types of attitudes could obscure what is radiating from within you. Up until now, your investment in and attachment to such associations may be stronger than your desire to perceive and bring forth the truly wonderful and lasting in character. So, are you willing to change your perception and beliefs if it means more freedom for you?

Each and every moment, you have the opportunity to shift your focus and uplift what you are holding in consciousness in order to entertain feelings that are supportive to you. The rewards for doing so can be life enriching. For a few moments feel that you are releasing hurts, resentments, negative thoughts, anger, fear, and pride. Imagine those feelings floating away from you and disappearing. This letting go is what breaks up the dark clouds and lets in the ever-present light of Divinity, beautifully and uniquely expressing itself as you. Forgiveness, compassion, gentleness, humility, and courage can bring clarity to your sight and empowerment to your feelings.

One year at holiday time I found myself struggling with several members of my family. One was going through addictions and criminality, another was miscommunicating and causing strife, a third was having health issues and not facing them, and on and on it went with several other siblings and relatives, each having difficult concerns that were weighing me down. Because I felt frustrated and overwhelmed, I called someone for help and told her about the magnitude of "my problems."

The woman listened quietly and then explained that problems are like balloons: it doesn't matter how big they are; they're still just full of air. This challenged my perspective, but after yielding resistance, I went for a long run on a beach at sunset. Because it was wintertime, the beach was deserted. I then prayed to purify my thoughts about the family member going through addictions until I felt at peace. To my surprise, a balloon washed up on the beach. Feeling a little freedom, I picked it up and decided to run with it. About a half mile later, after I cleared my thoughts about a second family member and found peace, another balloon washed up on the shore. The same thing repeated for the next five miles; each time I prayed and purified my thoughts about another person in the family, and when I did, another balloon became visible on the shore. When I neared my exit from the beach, I felt a powerful sense of joy and peace, because no negativity remained in my thoughts about the family. Just then I noticed one more balloon, which had Spanish writing on it. When I got home, I secured all the balloons to the balcony overlooking a beautiful sunset on the water. Then I hurried inside to find a Spanish dictionary. The words on the last balloon translated: Happy Baptism! Indeed, there had been a baptism in consciousness that carried through to happy holiday celebrations. Since then, whenever I feel upset with someone, I ask myself: If the way God sees this person is different than the way I do, who needs to clean up his view?

"Deck thyself now with majesty and excellency; and array thyself with glory and beauty" (Job 40:10).

Infinite and Always

Recently, I asked my wife Charlene what she has learned about inner beauty from treating hundreds of clients in her healing practice. This is what she had to say: "There is that part of us that is connected to something much bigger than our body and our past. Some people call it their true Self, Spirit, Soul, essence, or Christ nature. My clients have used adjectives such as loving, joyful, peaceful, bright, inspiring, calm, happy, all knowing, wise, and the Infinite to describe this Presence." She went on to share a story of a three-year-old girl named Emily who was confined to a wheelchair.

"Her head and eyes were deformed, and she was blind. She was able to express herself only by making sounds—no words—and was unable to walk or even sit up on her own. She appeared 'uncomfortable in her own skin,' and I was told she spent hours in her crib moaning, restless, and crying inconsolably. Within just a few minutes of putting my hands on her, I could feel the energy of her inner essence expanding in her body. Softly, I asked Emily to feel herself in the middle of her chest and to recognize her true Self, the beautiful Self created by God. As she began to connect deeply inside herself, she became calm, relaxed, and quiet. Her connection deepened and intensified, and then she began to express sounds of joy and laughter. She started to reach out and explore the shape of my face with her hands, smiling and cooing with delight. Her whole face lit up like a sunbeam."

Why the drastic change? Charlene believed that Emily recognized that she was unified with a Presence that was much greater than her body. Within each of us there exists a deep and constant connection to the field of divine Love. It's here that we vibrantly live without an ego and beyond a body and life circumstances—where we exist as an expression of Divinity in beauty, joy, peace, and creativity. In this place, we sense that everything is already perfect—nothing needs to be added to us; nothing substantial or real could ever be violated or taken away from us. "I know that whatsoever the Lord does, it shall be for ever; nothing can be added to it and nothing taken from it; and the Lord has so made it that men should reverence him" (Eccles. 3:14 LAM).

This awareness of the God-presence within allows us to transcend the physical and emotional circumstances of our lives, which really do not define who we are. During her treatment, Emily seemed to discover the beauty of her true godlike nature radiating deep in the middle of her chest.

Her recognition of this Presence enabled her to realize that even though her body had many physical challenges and limitations, her essence could shine forth beautifully and bring comfort and joy.

Emily's beauty was always waiting to be recognized and set free. So is ours. When we let go of beliefs, attitudes, judgments, hurt, anger, resentments, and pain by connecting with our totally intact, wonderfully beautiful essence within us, we clear the way for our inner beauty and greatness to shine forth from its infinitely divine Source. We have this enduring promise: "He hath made every thing beautiful in his time . . ." (Eccles. 3:11). The mundane parts of our lives will become extraordinary as we perceive Divinity and the beautiful within the seemingly ordinary.

Practice Beautifying

1) **Take Notice:** See it, smell it, taste it, hear it, touch it, feel it, and be it—beauty is everywhere. Choose to more fully connect with the beauty that is always present within you and all around you. Be willing to use your spiritual insight as well as your eyesight. Let your awareness and experience of beauty soulfully enrich the quality of your life and of those you touch. Each day, set an intention to notice or, better yet, record what is lovely in your life—in nature, relationships, architecture, music, food, and art.

2) **Let Your Beauty Shine:** Identify and write down three of your beautiful qualities. Embrace them and feel these to be your true essence, the way the Divine is expressing as you. You have a body, but you are not your body. Your spiritual essence is so much more amazing. There is a light in your eyes that comes from and goes to the Infinite. Your individual expressions of kindness, compassion, patience, courage, creativity, joy, and humility share enriching light with the world. You may have experienced the inner critic that tells you that you are not good enough, smart enough, pretty enough, or successful enough. During these times, it is especially important to reconnect with spiritual qualities. The divine Presence is animating within you. Recognize your own uniqueness as a child of God and realize that in spiritual reality you are already enough, very good, and beautiful!

Chapter 6

Celebrate

Life is given to us not only for spiritual growth but for our enjoyment. It's also about knowing where you are going and why and not forsaking meaning and depth for speed and activity.

Celebrate Divinity

Do you take time to celebrate what you've experienced, learned, created, contributed, and accomplished in your life? The first story in the book of Genesis illustrates that our Creator took an opportunity to celebrate and reflect on what had been created and accomplished. Many of us are familiar with the account of the seventh day of creation, when God rested from all that He had made. Yet, it was on the sixth day that the acknowledgement and celebration began. After heaven and earth were finished, we are told that, "God saw every thing that He had made, and behold, it was very good" (Gen. 1:31). This story says so much about the spiritual way to live. First, let the spiritual light of the ideas unfold; next, bring those ideas into manifestation; then acknowledge and celebrate what Divinity has accomplished; and finally, rest in the joy of it. Imagine how such a practice could help you and your relationships.

With Divinity as your designer, you have uniquely wonderful qualities and talents to appreciate and share with others. David's psalms recognize the tender specialness with which all of us are made: "For [God] created my inmost being; you knit me together in my mother's womb. I praise you because I am fearfully and wonderfully made" (Ps. 139:14). You may have formed a belief that says you do not measure up to others, are not rich or successful enough, or don't have something worthwhile to share. From the vantage point of your spiritual identity, these limiting beliefs are simply not true. You will never be enough as a personal ego. Yet, the authentic you is enough because Divinity is enough and has created you to be enough. With this understanding, actively celebrate your own spiritual qualities and talents, and those of others.

It's the nature of divine Love to celebrate all that is positive and good in us and to encourage us to live and share our highest attributes with others. Celebration is a way to allow these qualities to unfold and become more brightly expressed. One of the great ways to demonstrate love and devotion to the Supreme is to praise Its nature and activity in and all around us, especially when we're having a hard time seeing it. Devotion really has to do with being dedicated to removing what's in the way of, and thereby magnifying, divine Presence.

Reenergize Yourself

In ancient Greece the definition of happiness meant using one's powers in the direction of excellence. To achieve success, many alpha personality types focus on driving hard and achieving at whatever cost, often to the point of exhaustion. When one achievement is completed, they are off to the next task, with little time to enjoy anything. They're always on the move while never really arriving at a place of fulfillment. Yet success includes achievement and fulfillment.

Sometimes we get so busy with details and problems that we lose the sense of what is truly meaningful. Achievement without a sense of fulfillment will likely feel empty. Besides being an opportunity for spiritual growth and contribution, life is meant to be celebrated! The Source of life is also to be celebrated, along with the work that Divinity enables us to do. If we celebrated our completed work more often, giving gratitude to the divine Creator who gives us the hands to do the work, we would be better motivated and energized to begin the next project. It's been wisely said that we should enjoy our achievements and not just our plans.

Several years ago I knew a married couple who owned a business. They had agreed that whenever they met a business or financial goal, they would reward themselves. They did this by going to their favorite Hawaiian island, taking a relaxing cruise, or staying in a luxurious five-star hotel for the weekend. They made a point of physically, emotionally, and financially celebrating their wins.

I used to wonder how much time and money this must have cost them. Now I realize that their victory parties were major energizing times that supported and motivated them to continue to succeed. Eventually they became happy millionaires. It seems my friends knew the importance of acknowledging and appreciating all that God had given them and what they had achieved in order to fully restore themselves before beginning something new. The kindness and generosity they gave to themselves allowed them to be their best to expand their business and enjoy the journey. Your own happiness will be proportionally related to doing what gives you lasting joy and fulfillment, and not doing (or undoing) what doesn't.

Celebrate Others

As a boy, I played football, basketball, and baseball. Through the years, I participated in many team successes and won many trophies. But, to this day, I've saved only one—the one that was awarded to me in the sixth grade. At that time I was not tall or exceptionally athletic, and I was never picked for basketball teams at recess. One day while feeling discouraged, I walked over to a newly built obstacle course on the far side of the playground. The course had monkey bars to swing on, a wall to scale, tractor tires to run through, uneven parallel bars to get across, and a pole to climb. I decided to challenge myself, so for several weeks I went there alone and worked out during recess. Later I learned that the contractor who had donated and built the course announced a timed competition that was to be held soon. When the day of the competition arrived, all of the best athletes showed up, along with most of the other students, teachers, and administrators. I was an athletic nobody, so it seemed miraculous to many of them that I won the obstacle course contest by defeating some of the same boys who had refused to pick me for the basketball games.

To my surprise, the contractor handed me a two-foot-tall trophy. I will always remember the way my mom celebrated my victory with me when I got home. She was so proud of me and was amazed that I had received such a big trophy. The celebration, accomplishment, and recognition I felt have stayed with me. Those few moments of celebration helped to anchor my developing identity as one who is able to overcome obstacles in life. My mom taught me what it feels like to be lovingly cheered for one's accomplishments. Her acknowledgment made all the difference to me, my athletic career, and, more importantly, my life.

Remember how it felt for you to be recognized for who you are and what you contributed. This may help you be more conscious to see what's important to another. Is there somebody in your life who would feel inspired by your celebration with them? You could be the one who impacts his or her life for years to come. Praising another has the power to shift focus off of your own limitations and problems and to expand your horizons.

Raising children may feel so demanding to you and the details so constant that there seems to be little time left to celebrate meaningful things and magical moments. Yet, celebrating can actually give you more energy and motivation to meet all of those demands. Everybody has a need to know that she's special and valuable. When you applaud the good that somebody does, you will contribute to both your own and her happiness. You will also support her self-esteem and ability to grow and be a giver.

Support Life

About twenty years ago, I heard the story of a tiny village in the mountains of the Far East. The people there reportedly lived very long lives. It was not unusual to find several people in that village who were older than one hundred. Scientists studied them to find out what was unique to these people. Was it the good mountain water or air? Their conclusion was probably not, because there are other places in the world that have pure mountain water and clean air but don't have people who regularly live that long. Was it their food? No, there are many people on the planet who have more nutritional diets.

> To feel more joy, move where you are celebrated instead of devalued; toward those who support your priorities instead of undermine them.

After many other factors were eliminated, the scientists concluded that what was unique about these people was they had no greed. When one of their members accomplished something, they all celebrated together. When someone suffered loss of any kind, everyone compassionately grieved as a unit. There seemed to be no competition and no sense of lack. Everyone celebrated each other's wins and achievements without rivalry or a sense of scarcity. They apparently operated with the understanding, based on true caring, selflessness, and celebration, that there was enough for everyone. Celebrating may or may not give us a longer life, but there is no doubt that it can improve the quality of the precious days and years we have been granted.

You have something special to contribute through the expression of your spirit and inner beauty, the way you communicate, and your unique talents. When you celebrate yourself and others, you are supporting the very nature of infinite Love's creation. One of the most spiritual things you can do on Earth is to live in joy—to love life. Think about how much more fulfilling your life and self-esteem would be if you rejoiced in a way that truly recognized and encouraged yourself and others. Feel what it would be like to see more of the Divine—to be more connected with the flow of life within and all around you. Today and every day you have the opportunity to acknowledge the qualities and successes of your intimate partner, business associates, friends, and children. For some people, nothing is a miracle; for those who are inspired, many things are; for the enlightened, everything is. Which approach do you intend to live by?

Practice Celebrating

1) **Celebrate Source:** Take time each day to acknowledge and give gratitude to Divinity as the Source of all of Life. Be thankful for the ways that you are guided and for the multitudinous ways your needs are met. Keep a daily gratitude journal to specifically acknowledge the nature and activity of infinite Love expressed through and around you. Fill your mind and heart with praise and delight when you exercise, pray, work, talk, or sing.

2) **Recognize Your Uniqueness:** Actively focus on all of your God-given attributes and skills. Write them down on an index card, carry it with you, and refer to it often, especially if you ever feel insignificant. Let go of self-criticism and the false belief that you are not good enough and claim that you are enough because the completeness and Presence of Divinity is expressing itself as you in a beautiful way. Show forth your amazing uniqueness in what you think, do, and say.

3) **Reward and Restore Yourself:** Remember that life is about fulfillment, not just achievement. Take yourself out for a nice dinner, schedule a massage, enjoy a good nap, or plan a luxurious trip. Reward yourself for the discipline, perseverance, and commitment you have demonstrated to grow and get things done. Pick a tangible way to celebrate your qualities and accomplishments and notice if you feel more motivated and energized before you begin the next project.

4) **Celebrate Others:** Start to notice the unique qualities and accomplishments of your spouse, children, friends, and coworkers. Actively celebrate what you see. Acknowledge the unselfish long hours your husband or wife puts in at work, the determined effort your child puts forth to learn something new, or the way your friend actively stays in touch with you. The act of celebrating can be as simple as a phone call or a kind note or email. Let the impulse of love move you to act in a timely way and notice how much more meaningful life becomes.

Chapter 7

Communicate

Only what comes from the heart can reach the hearts of others.
Only a deeply caring heart can finely tune to the
hearts of others.

Communicate Love

The future of your relationships will largely be determined by the conversations you have with yourself and others. Your words are like seeds that will take root and come to harvest with feelings, meanings, actions, and consequences. The quality of your love comes from who you are and the way you communicate. Every communication you have creates either connection or separation. It brings you closer together or takes you farther apart from the heart of another. The word *communication* has a root which means "to commune," to be at one with another. Is this most often the result of your communication?

Words have an energetic pattern. Harmony and connection tend to result from words that vibrate with love and truth. Discord and separation tend to come from uncaring and dishonest expressions. In many respects, your feelings and experiences are defined by the language you use to describe them. Was your day good or fabulous? Did you feel a little frustrated or uncontrollable rage? Each phrase creates a different emotion and experience. We can actually alter our experiences and feelings by choosing words wisely. A world of richness and fullness is available to you if your communication includes discovery, laughter, emotional connection, compassion, creativity, intimacy, intelligence, or fun. Your relationships are built on the way you communicate, so isn't it worth a closer look to see just how you do it?

Thoughts Communicate

Some obvious ways that you communicate are through your speech and actions. Just as importantly, your thoughts and feelings communicate very powerfully. Think of someone you are not getting along with as much as you would like. Perhaps they made a remark you reacted to, didn't show consideration for your feelings or needs, or forgot to include you in a social gathering. If you truly want to improve your connection, honestly examine your thoughts of that person. This is where the change begins. Do you think well of him, value and respect him, or even like him? What you think about someone energetically alters the quality, tone, and depth of your conversation and actions with him. Your thoughts and feelings about him can considerably impact your emotional, mental, physical, and sense of spiritual relationship.

Often we can trace the source of relationship breakdown back to when our thoughts or feelings of that person began changing for the worse. This is not as bad as it may seem, because with awareness, we can do something about it.

For several years as a young adult, I had a difficult relationship with my dad. With a thousand critical reasons rolling around in my head, I felt justified to have negative feelings toward him. Only when I started to let go of defending my position and began to choose supportive thoughts about him did my heart soften. With renewed compassion and the desire to bless him, his wonderful qualities became easy to focus on. He was a wonderful cook, had artistic sensitivity, possessed keen intelligence, and had overcome many difficult trials in his life. The things I didn't like faded into the background. Guess what happened? My father started changing right before my eyes into a better dad who reached out to me and was appreciative and generous toward me. Ever since I uplifted my thoughts of him, our communication and relationship have improved.

Ultimately, our relationship with another exists in our consciousness of them. The way we hold and position people in our minds *is* our relationship with them. Whether or not we currently communicate with them, we can seek to find resolution in what we perceive and hold to be true about them. If we hold the best of them in mind, even if they're no longer here, watch what unfolds.

Energy Communicates

As the poet Ralph Waldo Emerson surmised, who we are speaks more loudly than our words. Most often the messenger is the message! What and who we are communicates more than we realize. Words either verify our character and actions or nakedly expose a gap between them. Many studies have set out to determine the number one form of communication. Things such as body language, choice of words, intonation, pitch, inflection, and eye contact have been considered. Guess what many believe is the most powerful form of communication. Energy! Have you ever met people and instantly liked them? How about people you couldn't stand since day one? Energy was probably the dominant reason. We can actually feel other people's energy as soon as they walk into the room!

There is a clear and identifiable high energy to integrity and love. Conversely, deceit and fear emanate an energy that vibrates at much lower and heavier frequencies. If you are paying attention, you can feel the difference and not be fooled by either charisma or homely looks. The vast majority of your communication is energetic and nonverbal. Who you are in character and the energy behind the words you use and actions you take, broadcast directly to other people. If you want your communication to improve, start with being clear about what you are broadcasting. People who resonate with your energy will be attracted to you, and those who do not may want to keep some distance.

> "If you would be loved, love, and be lovable" (Benjamin Franklin).

Motives Communicate

Our motives are not as hidden as we may think. We can say the right words, but if our motives are not aligned with the highest good for all concerned, this will not go unnoticed by one who is consciously listening. At a dinner party one evening, I found myself sitting next to a long-time minister of a nearby church. I asked her what she felt was the thing most needed within her congregation. She looked at me and started singing the Billy Joel song, "Hon-es-ty . . ." She went on to explain that dishonesty in communication is perhaps one of the most common reasons for strife in families and the world. From her comments I sensed that a widespread shift to integrity would have considerable impact in helping to stabilize our close relationships, workplaces, communities, and planet.

Motives are *why* we say what we do. Using identical words, one person may communicate with healing motives and another for antagonistic reasons. For example, we could ask a coworker how her project is coming along. One motive might be to see if she wants some help to succeed. Another motive might be to see if we can look better to our boss because our work might be finished before hers. Although the words are the same, they have two entirely different motives. We perceive what is behind another's words, and others do the same with ours. Poor motives convolute communication. Higher motives bring clarity and expansion to communication.

If you assume your motives are not communicating, then you could be in for a surprise, or even suffering. Relationships tend to decline when less-than-positive motives enter into the communication. Moreover, relationships are reenergized and nurtured when pure motives serve to rebuild the communication. Truthful and loving motives create conversation that is natural, spontaneous, and connecting.

Consider the most positive *and* negative relationships in your life right now. How would you rate the motives of your communication in each category on a scale of one to ten? Is it any mystery why those relationships have evolved the way they have?

We cannot be responsible for another person's motives. We only have to own our motives. Uplifting your motives may or may not positively influence other people to do the same. Their responses are not your concern anyway. When two people are genuinely looking out for each other, they have a natural sense of partnership and team play. They do not have to worry about defending their positions or questioning the other person's intentions. Communication and life are easy and unselfish between them. The relationship is not about a power struggle where one must be a loser, but about alignment, support, and discovery. Is that how your closest relationships are? If you find yourself constantly defending your positions or being critical of others, check your motives and make the adjustments there.

Keep Agreements

When someone keeps her word with you, don't you feel valued? When your actions match your agreements (i.e., when you walk your talk), other people feel respected and cared for. If you fail to "show up" for a friend in the way you have promised, she may feel disrespected and devalued. If you want to notice an immediate improvement in your relationships, start keeping your agreements and commitments—all of them, even in the little things—especially when no one else may notice. Your integrity-filled actions will communicate loudly and clearly, so watch how life starts shifting around you.

As a caveat, if a situation arises where you will not be able to do what you said, then ask to renegotiate your agreement. If the other person accepts your new agreement, then you are not bound by the former one, so be easy with yourself.

Gifts Communicate

For some people, to receive a gift is the most significant way to feel loved. To find the right gift takes time, thoughtfulness, and life energy. A person who likes to receive gifts will appreciate these efforts. This type of person can tell when a gift has care, creativity, and consideration behind it and when it is just a "get it checked off the list" kind of effort. If your gift shows an understanding of another's needs and desires, it can be the catalyst for deeper connection between both of you.

For many, the precious gift of time is most important. Someone you know may feel loved or unloved based on the quantity and quality of the time you share with him or her. Do you show an interest in and an understanding of that person's life and circumstances, or are you half interested and distracted? A few powerful questions you can ask to enter in the heart of another's world are:

1. What's great in your life right now?

2. What's most challenging to you?

3. What's most meaningful to you?

4. What would make things better for you?

5. How can I be most supportive of you right now?

Sometimes the gift of communication is not about efficiency or problem solving but simply being with another person, fully present and unrushed. Some people use material gifts to make up for their lack of giving quality time or sharing from the heart. Ultimately, loving presence with another person is irreplaceable. If you go beyond knowing what another thinks and get to the place where you feel what she feels, you will have communicated with excellence. If the other person does this for you, communication will be expansive.

Quality Matters

What qualities do you demonstrate while speaking and listening? Are you respectful, considerate, and compassionate? Does your communication come from a place of giving rather than from pride, fear, or defensiveness? When you speak, are you open, clear, and unpretentious? Do you listen with great eye connection when the other person is talking? It has been said that one's eyes are windows to the soul. Are you heart-connected with your words in a way that feels sincere? Moreover, are you interesting to listen to because of the dynamic way you speak, the passion you broadcast, and the substance of what you have to say? Or are you as boring as fog or like a narcissistic, nattering nabob, drowning others with nonstop trivialities and self-centered drama?

None of us communicates perfectly all the time, but thoughtfulness can help us include both words and their essential meaning. It's important to ask yourself, "Does the way I'm communicating create a quality, connecting experience?" With feedback, humble awareness, and intention, you will be guided to make any needed alteration.

Creating a space of vulnerability is also essential in quality communication. When others feel they don't have to be so perfect to share with you, you become more approachable. Your humanness allows them to easily connect with you and show you their more vulnerable sides. You may find that the people closest to you are the ones you have opened up to the most and vice versa.

Compassion is another significant quality. It not only helps communication and connection, but it can also bring healing. When someone in your life is hurting or troubled, show her you understand in a way that makes her feel comforted and no longer alone. Just as compassion can heal, poor communication can cause sickness or disease. Many of us have suffered, sometimes for years, because of the few choice words of another. Knowing this, choose your own words more carefully and hold the intention to bless others. You will have less burdensome guilt to deal with and be freer to express your highest Self.

Lastly, life can become way too serious, so help lighten it up with your wit and humor. It is a great way to interrupt heaviness and awaken spontaneity and enthusiasm in others.

Speak Your Truth

It seems reasonable that if we want the benefits of truth, we need to be willing to stand up for truth. If somebody wants to be called your friend, he shouldn't hinder your highest expression nor impede your growth. If he does, perhaps your friendship should take a different form. For a relationship to grow, we must be willing to speak our truth when wisdom calls us to do so. In life, there is always our truth, another's truth, and the Truth. Ultimately, all of us are on a pathway of experientially knowing, versus just knowing about, the Truth. Part of our journey is to honestly state where we are, what is important to us, and how the world looks to us. Giving our relative truth a voice invites feedback. Receiving feedback (another person's truth) is one of the main ways we experience learning and shift the ways we perceive, say, and do things.

Without information from air traffic controllers and airplane instruments, a commercial pilot would not be able to fly successfully. In fact, there would be great danger for many if the pilot refused to receive and respond to guiding messages and signals. The same holds true for us on our journeys in life. To navigate more successfully, we not only need to let others know where we are by speaking our truths; we also need to openly receive their perspectives. We could try traveling through life alone, but we would probably miss some grand opportunities and rewards that the feedback of relationships has to offer along the way.

Potentially, there could be great costs for not voicing what's in your heart. If your truth gets repressed or emotionally stuffed inside you, it may show up in some ailment in your business, body, or bank account. We have all heard the question, "What's eating you?" It might be wise to honestly consider this question and then do something about it before it manifests physically. Emotions are most often a clear call to change our perceptions and/or actions. You or someone you know may be holding fear, anger, grief, guilt, and resentment inside, which may be showing up in bodily form. People suffer through cancer, back and neck pain, migraines, arthritis, anxiety, and deep emotional hurts, yet they still do not speak their truth. Emotions of apathy, passive-aggressive feelings, jealousy, hurt, depression, and fear can fester for years because of a lack of expression and healing. Time doesn't give freedom; honesty and loving action do.

Stored up emotions can be released by honestly sharing what is on your mind with your Creator, friend, partner, personal coach, therapist, counselor, or other advocate. Writing in a journal can also be a great place to process, even before you speak what is on your mind verbally. This can allow you to sort through some things prior to impacting someone who may be unprepared to deal with your unsorted confusion.

Deeper truths often arise in layers, similar to finding the pearl of the onion under several layers of onion skin. Your pearl of truth may need a voice in order to be located. As you give it expression, more information, beliefs, and feelings will likely be uncovered. Find a safe avenue of expression—be it with a coworker, mentor, or twelve-step group—and watch how your self-esteem and confidence grow in the process. Share your needs, priorities, and vision. "Now" is just a snapshot in time anyway, so let others know that this is just something you are going through right now. By communicating what is difficult for you *and* what you truly want, you open yourself up to receive what will be supportive to you.

> "What we learn to do we learn by doing" (Aristotle).

True conversation happens when there is a change of heart through compassion, inspiration, joy, or learning. Without one of these, the dialogue may lack depth and real connection. Honor the best in another by communicating what is true and best for you. As you speak more genuinely, you will enlarge the capacity to discover your own heart and influence the hearts of others.

Your relationships will be greatly influenced by your flourishing ability to communicate. You have the potential to express love and truthfulness—to connect, heal, expand, inspire, free, energize, comfort, support, create, and be honest. How do you intend to communicate today?

Practice Communicating

1) **Identify Separators:** Our thoughts and feelings are most often the source of our words and actions. Loving thoughts tend to create connection, while critical and negative thoughts create separation. Think about a relationship in your life that needs repair. Honestly write down the thoughts and feelings you are having about this person. Has your expression of love toward them become obstructed by what you are holding in mind about them? Write down three qualities of thought that would change and support this relationship.

2) **Transform Energy and Motives:** Most of our communication is nonverbal and energetic. When speaking, become conscious of the energy behind your words. Are you frustrated when you ask your partner if he remembered to take the garbage out or pick up certain groceries? Do you say "I love you" and really feel the words coming from deep within your heart? Next, become aware of your motives. How often do you need to be right or make others wrong? Is your motive to gain something or to give to, see the best in, and bless others? Actively choose motives from a place in your heart that communicates honesty and love. Your choices will strongly influence the direction of your relationships.

3) **Communicate Quality:** The people closest to us are usually the ones with whom we freely open up. Vulnerability with others allows for quality connection. Write down what other qualities in communication create connection for you. Which qualities could you more fully embody to create ease with others—flexibility, understanding, humor, or consideration? The quality with which you communicate creates both a space and an energy attraction for others to be authentic with you.

4) **Give Truth a Voice:** What suppressed thoughts or feelings have you been harboring? Perhaps you don't feel understood or listened to. Maybe you are angry over what someone did or did not do, or you have been ignoring your passion. What are these emotions calling you to change? What can you do to give these parts of yourself a voice? Honor what is in your heart! Try journaling, speaking to a friend or mentor, voicing a prayer out loud, or courageously declaring to your significant other what you want or need. You may find your voice getting stronger as you exercise it with wisdom!

Chapter 8

Complete

Only a childish dreamer stares at the distant future without recognizing what needs to be done at hand and doing something about it.

Completion Brings Freedom

When we resolve what is nagging us, we become more powerfully available for Divinity and relationship. Incompletion is a distraction and energy drain that makes us weak and unavailable to some degree. Imagine how free your life would feel right now if everything on your mental and physical to-do lists was completed! Imagine the peace of mind and liberation you would feel to have finished your kitchen remodeling, incomplete conversation with your friend, art project, letter you have been meaning to write or respond to, or apology you have wanted to give or ask for. For a moment, feel the purpose, power, and self-esteem you would have upon signing up for the class you've always wanted to take, succeeding with your diet or exercise program, proposing to or breaking up with your significant other, or leaving your unfulfilling job and getting the one that you truly want! Consider the fun and excitement you would feel to have saved for, booked, and paid for the vacation of your dreams or to have paid off your entire credit card debt. In relationship, something magnificent happens when we complete what we set out to do, keep our promises with ourselves and others, and get rid of that annoying sense of unfinished business. Completion is also directly related to love.

What can be done any time or someday will likely not be done at any time. Let's face it: there will always be more to do in your life. Yet a greater measure of freedom and fulfillment is available to you right now by doing what is yours to do. "Completing" is a loving and honest way to treat both yourself and others. By letting things go undone, there may be a part of you that feels like you're not living up to your full potential or cheating what you came here to do. Your self-esteem may feel challenged, and your sense of burden may gain weight and pressure over time. This can lead to a sense of confusion, overwhelm, and malaise. Just by taking care of business, you may actually feel more clear-minded and empowered to live your purpose and enjoy relationships.

If something is irritating us, we are either enabling it or encouraging it instead of changing either ourselves or the situation. We are also getting some benefit and paying some cost for letting it continue. For example, by having big problems, we may be getting significance from them, but at the same time we are paying the cost of not showing up with joy and ease in relationship. Lastly, we may be

> Great achievements are the result of those who are driven to complete what they start.

avoiding some information (i.e., truth) or action that could allow us to have what we really want in relationship and life. Until we identify these, we shouldn't expect things to change. Finishing things is what stretches us, makes us feel in integrity, and increases our self-esteem and others' trust in us.

The nature of Divinity is complete and is unfolding through our perceptions and expansion of consciousness. By aligning with this loving field, we feel guided to do what is necessary and important to finish our work. Think for a few moments how many things you have going on in your life right now that are unfinished, unresolved, or even stuck and going nowhere. Go ahead and make a quick list of your tolerations and irritations. If you are like many people, you may have easily put together a list of twenty or thirty things. Wow! No wonder you have so much on your mind! There is a more powerful, satisfying, and freeing way to live than to let such a list multiply. Let's take a deeper look.

Eliminate the Drainers

On a physical and emotional level, all of us have a limited amount of time and energy during each day. Unfinished things may take your focus multiple times, causing you to waste energy and feel like you have less time than you actually do. Step one is to identify the things that are draining your energy and distracting you most from enjoying a phenomenal quality of life. The next step includes a yin and/or a yang style of taking care of business. The yin method is to look at your energy drainers daily and take some action on one or more of them whenever you feel led. After thirty days, notice what has been reduced, eliminated, or completed. Some people work best with this method. Others prefer the yang style, which can be done by prioritizing the list, connecting with why each one is vital, aggressively blocking out time to complete the drainers by specific dates, and measuring performance regularly along the way. You may find that a combination of the styles works best for you. Either way, watch how the Universe supports your clear intentions and commitments synergistically with resources, ideas, and people. Be grateful for incremental steps of progress and not just the ultimate goal.

With each item of your unfinished business, you might consider doing one or more of the following: do it, schedule it, delegate it, delete it, or organize it. Most things can be put into one of these simple action categories. Knowing this removes some of the stress and confusion.

Order also supports clarity and power. It tends to increase productivity, add beauty, and give higher feelings of safety. Disorder can detract from what is essential and lead to instability and inefficiency. Disorder often shows the lack of a strategy or system to make decisions and maximize priorities. One practice that has been helpful to me is to block out thirty minutes per weekend to organize my home and office. The compounded effect of this has been amazing.

> "How soon 'not now' becomes 'never'" (Martin Luther).

Focused action in finishing what is most important doesn't have to add pressure to you; it can actually alleviate it, because your action will allow you to see things with a greater sense of order and ease once the mental burdens are removed. You will then feel freer and more energized to enjoy life. The impact and blessings of even the simplest completions can be profound for both you and others. The ripple effects may reach well beyond what you ever hear about.

There was a woman I knew who, for more than a year, had an estranged relationship with her mother. Their communication was difficult, feelings were hurt, and neither was willing to talk about the source of the discomfort between them. The woman suffered anxiety, stress, and loss of energy and spent months feeling unloved. One day she decided to live the love that completes. She spoke to her mother, shared her experience of how she had felt for the past year, and expressed her desire to understand her mother and have a meaningful relationship with her again. To her surprise, her mother explained that she had interpreted a past conversation (i.e., incompletion) to mean that her daughter did not want to have a relationship with her. The woman quickly cleared up that misunderstanding, assured her mother that she loved her, and explained that she desired more than anything to have a relationship with her built on love and respect. The result was a reopening of their communication and a renewed potential for a rich and rewarding relationship for years ahead. The added blessing was that both of them stopped wasting time and energy over an incompletion!

A wishbone approach to life will never accomplish what backbone will, as the American pioneer Will Henry reminded us. Ask yourself what you're currently unwilling to complete and why. Instead of just wishing, ask yourself what you're willing to do and stop doing in order to actually have what you want. Then decide to take some action each and every day toward completion and watch how your efforts compound during the next few weeks and months. Do you want to have more energy, productivity, and peace? Then complete just a few of the important things that have been sucking your energy. How long have they been ignored? Has it been for weeks, months, or years? Also, by emotionally sensing how exhausting habits of procrastination have felt, you may become highly motivated to reverse those behaviors. After you take positive action, notice how much lighter you feel and how motivated you become to resolve other areas you've been tolerating. Really anchor in the momentum of these positive feelings, so you can use them to tackle other items. Remember that whenever you face a difficulty, you always have two choices: change the condition or change yourself.

> You will change when you can no longer tolerate a condition.

Now Is the Accepted Time

The practice of completion will build your self-confidence, self-trust, and trustworthiness. It is also a great way to nurture yourself and expand your creativity by removing burdens that may be blocking your potential. You cannot expect to find peace without the courage to actually do what is yours to do. To the degree that you have incompletion in your personal business and relationships, you may not have been totally courageous or demonstrated complete integrity. Integrity includes giving priority in thought, time, and action to what you value.

The nature of completing love reveals that we need to stand up and speak up and not let things go unfinished and unsaid. Saint Paul referred to the essence of such honest love and our Christlike nature: "speaking the truth in love, we will in all things grow up into Him who is the Head, that is, Christ. From Him the whole body, joined and held together by every supporting ligament, grows and builds itself up in love, as each part does its work" (Eph. 4:15-16 NIV). We all have our parts to do—to speak what is in our hearts truthfully and lovingly and to faithfully complete things in our relationships, homes, and workplaces.

> Nearly every significant thing that has ever been attempted was done while fears, obstacles, or objections remained.

If you knew that today would be your last day on earth, what would you not want to leave unfinished? What are you waiting for? Tomorrow is not promised to anyone. Today is a precious day; now is the accepted time. Some people believe that aging is from the compounded burdens of unfinished business, uncorrected conversations, and lack of action—the baggage and regrets of incompletion! Rather than collecting burdens, unload them by doing what you are called to do, using the divine potential you have within you.

Practice Completing

1) **Get Honest:** Make a full list of all the things in your life that are incomplete, drain your energy, or cause you anxiety or disharmony. This may include home projects, auto maintenance, conversations that need to be corrected or finished, belongings that need to be recovered or returned, finances that need to be put in order, or relationships that need cleaning up. As you dedicate some time and thought to this list, you may think of new things days later. Add these items to the list as well. Clarity is power. You must honestly know where you are to get to where you want to go.

2) **Feel the Impact and Ease:** Review your list and notice how it feels to have all of this incompletion in your life. Write down what each item is costing you in terms of emotional or physical health, peace of mind, quality of relationships, and other ways. Are there one or two items in particular that really feel like a huge burden and drain to your energy? Meditate on how wonderful it would feel to have them completed. As you do this, does your body feel easier, more relaxed, less tense, and energized? You may want to ask Spirit to show you what steps you can take today or this week to bring resolution to the items on your list.

3) **Take Meaningful Action:** Select three things from your full list and set a clear intention to complete them this month with the yin and/or yang styles. For each item, write down the following: 1) the measurable steps you will take to complete it, 2) the date when it will be completed, and 3) the benefits you will feel and the costs you will avoid when it is finished. This last step is crucial to empower you to overcome obstacles along the way. When you get emotionally connected with why you want to do something, you will have more motivation to see it through. Remember, you are declaring an intention and making an agreement with yourself to bring your life into integrity. Don't you want to be more available to life and relationships? Afterward, witness if you feel more free, energized, motivated, at peace, and available to Love!

Chapter 9

Be Courageous

*Wishing and hoping cannot produce the results of
moving with inspired action.*

Vulnerability and Risk

Several years ago I moved from Missouri to California. After six months
of settling down in my new location, I had not made any significant
new friendships. I worked at home alone, and one day I realized that
new friendships were probably not going to come knocking on my door.
Without reaching out, talking with strangers, and trying some new
activities, my quality of social life would remain scant. Within the next six
months, I'd joined a running group, found a wonderful place of worship,
become a close friend with someone down the street, started singing in a
community choir, and begun actively dating. We tend to change when
what we want becomes a must. When burning desire becomes greater
than our trepidation, we will no longer settle for the status quo. My desire
for connection, fun, and purposeful activity became greater than my fear
of rejection and the familiarity of isolation. When our love of what we
want is greater than our fear of what we don't want, fear won't stop our
courage.

Openness and vulnerability draw us closer to the heart of another.
Finding this closeness often requires courage, which could mean being
exposed to hurt, loss, rejection, or embarrassment. Yet, nearly all positive
change that has occurred in history has happened because someone was
willing to walk toward the unknown and take risks—risks that could
have potentially made them look bad (and often did in the short term).

Historical giants such as Isaac Newton, Thomas Jefferson, and Louis Pasteur had a passion for progress that was greater than their fear of failure or rejection. For this reason and others, they changed the course of their own lives as well as the course of history.

The same principle applies to progress in relationships. For them to grow, we must be willing to step into the unknown, go deeper than we have gone before, ask questions that could make us look bad, and share things about ourselves that require us to trust the other person and vice versa. Reaching out and opening up gives the other person an invitation to connect with us in new ways. We also give that person the opportunity to let down his guard and show what's on his mind and in his heart. If both of us do that, many benefits and rewards can result, including soulfulness, learning, fun, laughter, spontaneity, adventure, and spiritual growth. If we don't, nothing progressive may happen.

Sometimes risk is imaginary. If we are without a job or close relationship and we make inspired efforts to obtain one but don't succeed, what have we really lost anyway? Even though our efforts may not yield our desired outcomes, we gain experience. So, we can actually come out ahead.

Doing Nothing

Many years ago I saw an advertisement that showed astronaut Neil Armstrong standing on the moon. It appeared that an eraser had removed part of him and his space suit, as if to imply: What if it never happened? What if Armstrong, NASA, and America did not take on the daring venture of flying to the moon? What if they took the greater risk of doing *nothing*? It's been said that when President John F. Kennedy boldly stated in his 1961 State of the Union address that the United States would put a man on the moon before the end of the decade, some of his scientifically minded aides were in shock. Afterward, they informed him that the United States had not successfully tested technology for landing astronauts on the moon and then returning them to Earth. Scientists had not yet solved issues with such things as rocketry, payload design, and communication systems for such a journey. Unshaken, Kennedy simply told them that they now knew what to get to work on. Fortunately, scientists and engineers developed an uncompromising determination to land an astronaut on the moon and return him home safely, and this they did with Apollo 11 in 1969. Their love and commitment for the idea involved many risks and tests of character and ultimately yielded incredible rewards for the United States and all of mankind.

For a relationship to travel to new heights, you also might be required to take expansive risks. Are you willing to search for your truth, to speak it as you are discovering it, and to deeply listen to others? If you have hesitation to step into the unknown, remember what connection feels like as a motivating factor. Some of the benefits of true connection include joy, synergy, aliveness, and comfort. Let the desire for the feelings you want drive you to go for exploration, true passion, and adventure. When your desire to be connected becomes stronger than your doubts or familiarity with the status quo, then your relationship can soar.

When things are not going well, it may be tempting to shut down communication, pull away, get angry, or discontinue affection. Yet, openness and realness can be the very things that lead you to healing a rift. It only takes one person who is willing to reestablish connection by asking what seems to be missing, what she could do better, or to share what she's been feeling and experiencing. This kind of vulnerability is often the beginning of something wonderful showing up, such as deeper closeness, understanding, and meaningful affection. Every choice you make involves risk, including the default choice of doing nothing. The real question is this: which choice will lead you toward your desired destiny?

Some of the greatest achievers are those who have made the most mistakes and who have received great learning from doing so. Their lives serve as a statement that doing nothing in life in order to avoid a mistake could be the greatest mistake of all. All of us will have windows of opportunity to take needed action. What we actually do during those openings will make all the difference in our success and fulfillment.

Courage and Meaning

What is the main reason we do not take the risks necessary to deepen a relationship? It may be the fear of looking bad, losing what we have, being rejected by another, failing to make it happen, or even actually succeeding and arriving in unfamiliar territory. It may appear that it is safer not to be courageous, do the hard thing, or step into the unfamiliar. We are designed to move toward perceived pleasure and gain and avoid perceived pain or loss. Sometimes we need to update our perceptions.

The great philosophers such a Socrates have told us that at any given moment, we tend to do what we think is best for us, even if we actually don't know what that is. Perhaps you believe that the pain you could suffer from speaking your mind, making that call, sending that email, or giving that invitation is greater than that of being stuck in your current situation. Only by stretching yourself beyond your sense of normal can you discover deeper meaning and capacities, including the capacity to confront your fears. Only by courageously doing it anyway will you know if your imagined fear of pain or hurt plays out or not. Perhaps the discovery of meaning and freedom is directly unleashed in proportion to your demonstrated ability to go for it in life and relationships.

Relationships end when there is no compelling reason to keep them alive. Relationships thrive on meaning and fade when the meaning starts dying. Individuals walk away from careers when they no longer find reasons to be there. People check out, figuratively and literally, because life loses significance and purpose. To move beyond our fears, we must walk through them and have strong motivation to do so—motivation that comes from finding empowering reasons.

The way to find passion is to live wholeheartedly in whatever we do. In doing so, we know a greater measure of what our lives are for, what we are capable of, what we have to give, what we are no longer afraid of, and who we truly are. To the degree that we refuse to face our fears, follow what is in our hearts, take action on what is most important to us, and passionately honor our divine calling, our lives may feel unfinished and not as meaningful as they could be. Playing it too safe, it seems, may not always be that safe after all. There is a compelling purpose and host of gifts within each of us, and we will feel growing anxiety if we continue meandering toward our graves while leaving our purposes and talents caged within us or sheepishly sedated.

Power and Ease vs. Fear

Along with pride and willfulness, fear is probably the most common thing that would try to stifle our courage and hold us back in life. One key to developing courage is to shift your focus from fear to love; focus on what you want to create or be and not on what you're afraid of. For a few moments, choose what you prefer in your relationship. Do you want to experience confidence, joy, and connection? Then focus on the feeling of what it would be like to already have these qualities being expressed between you and your significant other. Align with the state of being and beliefs you'd experience during such ideal conditions. Through the power of intention, the moments of embodying these feelings and beliefs can actually increase the likelihood of them showing up in your experience.

What about telling the truth about ourselves? It can be risky business, right? In personal transformational courses, twelve-step groups, and group therapy, participants often share their weaknesses and secrets. People reveal painfully difficult personal experiences such as rape, addictive behaviors, or past mental breakdowns. Amazingly, rather than being rejected, the other participants are often drawn closer to the people most willing to share. The energy field that is felt when one person is willing to be real is one of openness and acceptance. It gives other people in the room permission and freedom to also be genuine and trusting. We're all human, fallible, and mistake-ridden. When we openly reveal our mistakes, weaknesses, fears, limiting beliefs, and secret dreams, it allows others to better understand us and share what's in their hearts. What we will discover in the process is that our humanness makes us more approachable and lovable. It engages the feeling that we're all in this together; we're all riding this blue, green, and brown sphere at the same time; and we have much to share to make the journey more meaningful and satisfying.

The fear of being vulnerable quickly disappears in the presence of realness, because love and acceptance are energetically many times more powerful than fear. If you are feeling held back by fear and self-doubt, just choosing to be giving can lift you to a place of confidence. The act of giving increases the strength to open up, share more, and receive what the other person is giving back to you. From this open space, you can experience freedom of expression, aliveness, and soulfulness. The walls, anxiety, and labels that would try to isolate you don't have to obstruct who you really are. When realness dominates, there is heart-connection and ease in communication.

One of the greatest fears for many people is the thought of having to give a speech. Many top speakers have found a key to overcoming nervousness: removing the focus from themselves and instead putting it on how the message is benefiting their audiences. This sense of giving takes away fear and helps them establish feelings of inspired purpose and connection. In the same way, your conversations that have a giving focus will feel easier, because they will be in alignment with the field of infinite

Love. The divine-consciousness, expressed as you, recognizes and connects with the Divine expressed as another. You don't have to make it or force it; just allow it to be. It is what is left when inauthentic ways are eliminated. The love energy we feel frees us to be who we naturally are, and this true Self is lovable by all who recognize it. Ultimately, we all want to feel at home. At some level, we want the feeling of unity, which love helps us feel. Experiencing authenticity and vulnerability in a relationship is a form of feeling divinely connected. Check in with yourself to see if the rewards of this experience are worth the risks of going for them and what you might miss out on if you don't.

> "The Lord says, 'I will make my people strong with power from me! They will go wherever they wish, and wherever they go, they will be under my personal care'" (Zech. 10:12 LB).

Risk and Reward

Why should one navigate the perils of risk and the chance of being wrong, judged by others, confronted with opposition, or looking bad? No risk should be undertaken without the promise of at least a proportional or greater reward. Professional stock-market traders typically have a rule of entering a trade only if the potential profit is at least three times greater than the potential loss. Traders without such standards rarely survive more than a year in the business. In life, we too should know our risk/reward ratios, not just in a mathematical sense but in essence and quality of life. Is the risk of keeping the unmotivating but decent-paying job greater than doing what would better allow you to share your gifts and passion? Is the risk of expanding beyond the familiar pattern of self-concern safer than not realizing the satisfaction of service to others? Is it more profitable to fit in socially and avoid the risk of rejection or to sleep soundly at night, knowing that you are living in alignment with your values, actually following your priorities?

There are two perspectives with risk/reward—that of ego and that of Spirit. The ego is about playing it safe, avoiding change and the unknown in order to maintain control, and going for short-term gain. It has a need for certainty, usually at any cost. The ego has no way to defend itself against the unseen or unknown. When we are deluded into believing that the ego is in charge of our survival, going for change in whatever degree will feel like going against ourselves and against our own well-being and safety. No wonder we resist it! From this perspective, the ego will only allow us to step into the deep end if we are assured that we will be rewarded with temporary gain and pleasure.

The Spirit's vantage point is different. Its design includes stability, but it is also about expansion, spontaneity, newness, and variety. Have you ever found two identical sunsets, landscapes, or fingerprints? Spirit is always original and isn't based on the past. Spiritual rewards for apparent risk usually aren't about anything temporary, and your comfort along the pathway is not a primary concern. But, if you jump faithfully with Spirit's leading, what you gain is a truer sense of the Self that will last. Of course, you may lose other things to win such a prize. For most people, the rediscovery of authenticity comes at quite a cost. It may mean going through a physical, mental, business, or marital breakdown prior to a breakthrough. It may involve going through the proverbial wilderness or desert, each with its own elements and privations. Your higher Self (the Self that is the true you, unobstructed by ego) isn't concerned with how long you struggle against the path of the Soul, but it is designed for you to give up ego-based motives and concepts of self-success for the ultimate success of being directed by Divinity.

As William Shakespeare wrote in *King Lear*, "Nothing will come of nothing." It takes spiritual courage to risk losing what the ego fears and to go for something big—what the Self wants—so that we don't live a painful life of compromise, selling out, unfulfilled potential, or as Henry David Thoreau's *Walden* put it, "quiet desperation." The main trouble with compromise of one's ultimate calling is that it will make one show up in relationship as a half man or three-quarters woman, depending on just how much compromising there is. It doesn't take an expert to determine what this does to the polarity and passion in a relationship. A man who is certain about his life's mission and his contribution to others will typically show up in relationship with powerful masculine energy. A woman who is clear about her soulful identity, radiance, and lovingness toward others will be a beautiful and attractive feminine energy to engage with.

If passion is missing from your relationship, or if you don't have a relationship but want one, don't look to glossy magazines for a quick fix. The issue could have more to do with finding and courageously obeying your calling or more fully owning your sacred masculine or feminine energy than some cheap strategy to lure and snare the opposite sex like an animal trap or fly zapper.

> "What right do we have to claim the spoils of truth if we have not the love, the courageous love, of truth?"
> (Anonymous)

Ultimately, risk and reward have to do with meaning, and before you make your risk decisions, be clear about what life means to you and what is most important. Then you'll have a decision-making standard. Just what is worth living your life for?

All or Nothing?

There will be times in our lives when we have to jump across the ravine to experience the other side. We see the opening, feel the nudge, and have some evidence and faith that what we are going for will pay off and that what we are leaving behind is tiresome. Then we leap. But just like when we were kids, not every leap works out. Sometimes we skin a knee or two; sometimes we cry or grieve. As an adult, the thought of actually getting a raw knee can make us cringe. Back then, it was just another summer day, and we got through it just fine. Scabs healed and tears dried. We received feedback from our environment, got new shoes, and learned how to prepare better and jump more wisely. Taking risk was natural. So what has changed?

For one thing, there is so much unease projected by the media that many people live the vast majority of their lives in fear—fear to express themselves, travel, accept opportunities and responsibility, commit to a partner, start a business, or even take a twilight walk in the neighborhood. Staying home to watch TV isn't too risky, or is it? The result of supposedly playing it safe is that the other side of fear, which contains love, dominion, freedom, personal growth, and wisdom, never gets to be fully experienced. Success cannot be achieved if we let the fear of failure, or fear of making the wrong choice, stop us from using our potential. We tend to think that decisions have permanent consequences, when, in fact, most decisions (and their results) can be modified. Without reframing our false programming, we won't take as many risks to improve our lives.

Progress doesn't always have to come with leaps. Most of the time it comes from incremental steps forward, and there are times when a leap would be far too risky anyway. Vincent van Gogh, who painstakingly worked the brush strokes on his landscape paintings like a farmer works his fields, stated that great things result by bringing together a "series of small things." Getting more information and experience, building some savings, and getting to know the partner before doing the deal or becoming exclusive are small, natural steps that replace the unknown with progressive wisdom and certainty.

It has been said that there is no failure in life, only results. Results give us information about what worked and what didn't and how to make adjustments. In light of this, failure is just a contrived meaning we make up that probably doesn't serve us that well. The key factor in meaning is often time anyway. Whatever time frame we choose to focus on strongly influences the opinion we derive from the event. How we frame things is totally arbitrary.

An event is really a *perceived* event, because each of our views of it is unique. An ancient story goes something like this: The old farmer had a son. "That's great!" said his neighbor, but the farmer responded, "It is what it is." When the son became a young man, he broke his leg while plowing one day. "That's terrible," said the neighbor, and again the farmer proclaimed, "It is what it is." Shortly thereafter, there was a military draft, and because of his injury, the young man did not have to go to war. "That's terrific!" spouted the neighbor, but the farmer restated his equanimity, "It is what it is." To replace his son's plowing time, the farmer bought a horse, which, of course, the neighbor was sure was a progressive step. But then one day the mare ran off, and the neighbor thought it appropriate to console the farmer for such awful bad luck. To his surprise, the farmer just smiled and said, "It is what it is." A week later, the mare returned with a stallion, and the neighbor couldn't believe the farmer's double good fortune! And so on.

This may be how we interpret our own lives. What is a setback in one time frame is linked to huge progress over a more expansive one. What looks like a failure in one relationship gives us the understanding and character we need in the next. Is it failure or feedback? Is it the end or the beginning? Pick a difficult, challenging, or negative period in your

> Character, like muscle, isn't developed in the lazy armchair of comfortable surroundings. It's developed in the demanding gymnasium of life, through exercise of fortitude during challenges, the unknown, and many forms of pain and loss.

life. Was it darkness or the coming dawn? Were you in wasteland or being redirected back to your soul path? What you decide and the meaning you give to events in your life have a lot to do with the joy and quality of your life. How much you resist what is and how well you courageously step up to receive what's next will come from the time frames and meanings you choose.

Divine Model

From what the great spiritual teachers of all time have taught, the divine Self within us openly shows us how to understand its nature, feel its love within and around us, and more fully express its qualities of Truth, Life, and Love. Power is unleashed within us as we feel the divine impulse directing us and as we use available resources to move in the direction given by this impulse. Divinity is making its mighty and exquisite field of leading Love ever available to us. With it we can feel blessings, guidance, and strength. Perhaps we could become more conscious to just how intimate and knowable Divinity's unconditional Love is.

In Scripture, God called David a man after his own heart. David is a model for how to get real with Divinity. His psalms show just how very vulnerable he was throughout his life. He openly expressed when he was depressed, tired, feeling alone, wanting guidance and safety, or filled with dancing joy and appreciation. David did his part to have a true relationship with God. He was willing to overcome his fear of being rejected. He loved God that much. Even during and after his greatest moments of weakness and mistakes, David approached God with humility and sincerity. After he committed adultery with Bathsheba, David prayed this prayer: "Create in me a clean heart, O God; and renew a right spirit within me. Cast me not away from thy presence; and take not thy Holy Spirit from me. Restore to me the joy of thy salvation; and uphold me with thy free spirit" (Ps. 51:10-12). Because the nature of Divinity is Life, Truth, and Love, whatever in us aligns with aliveness, honesty, and devotion resonates with its Presence. If misaligned, we can always find our way back with David-like realness.

> Have courage: if you listen with undistracted expectancy, you'll hear the heart of Divinity vibrating with ineffable tenderness, exquisite care, and confident power within you.

By giving us free will, Divinity allows for the possibility that we may reject Its nature. No matter how many times we have forgotten or rejected divine Love, Divinity still loves us unconditionally. Love cannot help being what it is. If you connect with the amazing essence of this unconditional field, you can be inspired to bring a growing expression of it to those who need you to be authentic, truthful, and unconditionally caring. One small step in this direction is enough to give your relationships a wonderful impulse of new life. When a portal is opened up within your hearts, divine Love easily floods in. You may be the one required to take the first step to create the opening through humble and courageous willingness to be real.

Practice Being Courageous

1) **Expose the Fear:** Take a close look at a part of your life that is calling you to courageously take a risk or to be more vulnerable. Write down why you have been unwilling to do so up to this point, such as, "I might look bad," "I might fail or be rejected," or "They might not listen." Exposing fear to the light of honesty often makes it easier to face and overcome.

2) **Assess the Costs and Benefits:** Considering this area of your life where you are hesitating, list what it is costing you in terms of anxiety, dissatisfaction, and undiscovered potential. Now write what the benefits will be if you take a forward step. These benefits may include healing a relationship, gaining a deeper intimacy, or receiving a potential pay raise, as well as more joy, connection, opportunity, and growth. Exposing the costs and focusing on the benefits can give you the leverage to courageously overcome fear. Remember that sometimes the greatest risk in life is doing nothing.

3) **Overcome Self-Doubt:** Fear may be the only thing keeping you from what you really want. Remember that your love comes from a divine Source and is able to eliminate all self-doubt, as we are promised: "perfect love drives out fear" (1 John 4:18 NIV). During prayer or meditation, focus on what you would

love to experience instead of the fear. Imagine yourself living your dream, speaking what you're passionate about, or taking the next step because you deeply want what's on the other side. Feel the light-giving power of your devotion actively dissolving self-doubt.

4) **Connect through Vulnerability:** It takes risk to be vulnerable, and yet this is what invites others to open up with you. When guided by wisdom, be vulnerable. You might be led by Spirit to tell a close friend a secret, reveal a fear to a significant other, or tell your boss what kind of experience you really want to create in your work and why you deserve it! Witness how these types of wisdom-led actions create positive movement and connection in your life.

Chapter 10

Feel Empowered

"Finally, my brethren, be strong in the Lord, and in the power of His might" (Eph. 6:10).

Weakness Made Strong

Raised by Egyptian royalty, the patriarch Moses was directly connected to a human sense of power. But he felt torn from his true Jewish heritage and had yet to discover power based on a relationship with the Divine. When he witnessed a Jewish slave being abused, Moses murdered the Egyptian aggressor and then fled in fear to the land of Midian where he hid out for the next forty years. In addition to being gripped by fear, Moses was also a man who was "slow of speech," hardly motivating characteristics for a revolutionary leader-to-be. Still, in Moses's pathway to becoming spiritually empowered, he heard God's voice, saw a bush burn without being consumed, witnessed a stick change into a moving serpent, and experienced the instantaneous healing of his own leprous condition.

All these demonstrations taught Moses to feel the nature of Infinite Power and Presence that had always been with him. They also prepared him for receiving even greater demonstrations of dominion. Through these experiences, Moses grew confident in Divinity's ultimate care for him and his people. Moving with spiritual authority, he realized that Divinity was directing his every action. Ultimately, he gained the trust and courage that he needed to face down the Pharaoh of Egypt, the apparent pinnacle of human power at the time. How do we act when we need to face the most powerful person in our workplace, family, or social circle? Perhaps all of us can learn to be more empowered from Moses's example.

With a show of force, Pharaoh sent his army and hundreds of chariots to destroy Moses and the Israelites as they fled toward the banks of the Red Sea. It appeared that the Israelites were trapped and doomed, yet Moses relied on what he already knew and had seen of the divine Power. He rallied his fear-filled people with this declaration: "Fear ye not, stand still, and see the salvation of the Lord, which he will shew to you today" (Exod. 14:13). Do you find your spiritual center and powerful stillness when the outward circumstances of your life appear fearful—when you feel trapped by some situation? While Moses faced potential death at the Red Sea, verbal tradition as recorded by Flavius Josephus in *The Antiquities of the Jews* has it that Moses declared out loud, "We are in a helpless place, but it is still a place that thou possessest . . . the sea also, if Thou commandest it, will become dry land. Nay, we might escape by a flight through the air, if thou should'st determine that we should have that way of salvation."

Amazingly, Moses didn't plea for God to help or tell Divinity *how* to do it. He just stood confidently on the spiritual fact that the powerful nature of Divinity would bring salvation for the Israelites, no matter how it came. It was not so much that Moses was *trying* to have faith as it was that he was standing firm on references he had previously experienced.

How can we more fully embrace our references—what we already know of Divinity's power and protection for us? How can we act as if we *know* that the power of Infinite Truth and Love is fully on our side, ready to show us what to say and do, and able to provide us with strength, resources, and opportunities so we can accomplish what we need to? The point is that we are weak on our own, but we are mighty based on the Supreme Presence within us. It has been said that one with spiritual reality is a majority. Saint Paul seemed to be in touch with this powerful Presence within him when he declared, "I can do all things through Christ which strengtheneth me" (Phil. 4:13).

You too have the innate design to radiate divine Power by embodying what is honest, kind, just, safe, wise, and trusting. You have been given spiritual ability to exercise such qualities in everyday circumstances of your life. Every time you act from your highest essence, you will learn to feel even more empowered.

Powerful Source

> Things will seem more difficult when we refuse to face up to them with the courage and resources we already possess. We'll feel a surge of strength and certainty by connecting with the divine Presence within and by taking direct action.

Imagine what it would be like to truly know that there is an Almighty Power on your side in every situation, such as when you enter your business meeting, speak to your significant other about something you have been afraid to discuss, travel to a foreign country for the first time, learn a difficult computer skill, or stand up for what's progressive or in the face of large opposition. Over time the ancient Israelites discovered that they had divine Power on their side. That is what gave them the ability to defeat armies that vastly outnumbered them, find abundant supply when there was widespread famine, overcome fear, conceive children beyond normal childbearing years, break out of bondage, receive healings of every nature, and even overcome the clutches of death. How mighty was their God? All powerful and ever present! How powerful do you believe your Source is, and is this divine Being the reason you claim power and take action?

If you consciously stood on having a connected and power-based relationship with your Source, what would be possible for you? Through a growing awareness of how the supreme nature of Divinity expresses itself in and around you with a field of Love, a whole new world can open up to you.

Empowered vs. Victim

Empowered individuals take responsibility for creating their own experiences. Granted, we can't control every detail of what happens to us, but we do choose our responses. To think otherwise is to forfeit our power and play the victim of circumstance. The disempowered believe that their experiences are in someone else's hands, so instead of responding with choice, they blame the government, their parents, siblings, bosses, teachers, racial prejudice, weather, and just about everything else rather than looking

> Know that the power of God is moving through you, producing the highest good for everyone, including you.

within themselves and seeing how they have chosen to respond to their circumstances. There is no doubt that difficult conditions, faulty governments, less-than-perfect parents, and racial prejudice do exist. Yet, empowered people use these difficulties to grow and make a difference to others, while the disempowered feel defeated or stuck in hurt or resentment. Do you want to live from a place of choice or from reaction? The destiny of each is entirely different.

An amazing example of one who overcame extreme difficulties by choice and without resentment is Nelson Mandela. Before victoriously becoming the first democratically elected black president of South Africa, he endured the extreme challenges of Apartheid and twenty-seven years of imprisonment. Instead of being defeated, he chose to use his prison time to learn the language of people he would later lead.

The disempowered live lives of limited or no possibilities, because they believe that something external is responsible for their experiences. Their imprisoning perspectives make them feel disadvantaged, since they believe they must wait for their circumstances to change before they can. Sometimes their circumstances never do change. Disempowered people focus on the past to find reasons why their futures will not change. Empowered people live their lives with a sense of fresh possibility and refuse to limit their experiences based on what happened in the past. They focus on maximizing the present in order to build a brighter future. They realize that when they change for the better, so must their lives.

Empowered people realize that they alone are in charge of how they experience life. They decide their own focus, attitudes, meanings, actions, language, and happiness. In a sense, they realize that they largely create their own heaven or hell by their responses to people and circumstances and by how they use their time, gifts, and feedback from life. You have a new moment right now. How will you respond to it? Will you add to your heaven or to your hell?

Purpose, Power, and Energy

Living with purpose comes from having a clear sense of identity and from totally owning one's choices. Identity is rooted in core values and includes a directed intention to live those values. Identity is also about decisively asking for what you want from life and committing to what you want to give to life. What you consistently affirm to be true for yourself and others is enough to change your direction positively. Language such as, "My purpose is clear to me, and I am drawing to me everything I need to fulfill it," can sharpen your focus and empower your sense of activity.

> Your experience will not be defined by what happens to you but by how you respond to life—by how you derive meaning and use it to progress or retreat.

Empowered people have the priority of clearly standing for what they believe in versus just trying to look good and be socially acceptable. Many people are afraid of rejection, so they don't really show up with an influential sense of character. Instead they have an energy that seems muted or dispassionate. Empowered people are spontaneous, motivated, and vibrantly animated. They do not obstruct the flow of Life energy; instead, they move with enthusiasm, passion, and internal freedom.

Even if you feel empowered, you'll still have challenges like anyone else, but you'll know that there's a solution. You'll learn to trust the unlimited and caring Universe to supply your needs. You'll also trust your own process of learning to receive divine care. By considering your life events in the context of the greater benefit for all concerned, you may sense that all things ultimately work together for good. This will allow you to more easily live in abundance through ups and downs, move in divine rhythm, and be in harmony with divine Will. Self-empowerment based on the ever-present omnipotence of divine Power will enable you to receive resources, opportunities, and synergistic ways to take action. You'll also be in a position to share support and encouragement with others who are in need of discovering their own growing expressions of divine energy.

In contrast, those who play the victim tend to live in confusion, resentment, criticism, and lack. They stay stuck because of fear, social conditioning, false beliefs, or hurt. They give off an energy that is repetitive, flat, disconnected, angry, or full of resistance. Disempowered people are inclined to have problems instead of challenges. They often try to convince themselves and others just how impossibly huge their problems are, perhaps to meet a need for significance. The difficulties of their stories are usually more important than their possibilities, positive visions, and progressive actions. They frequently struggle with the process of change and ignore the assistance that Spirit is constantly offering them. Their lives seem filled with inadequacy. They are focused on short-term limitations and drama instead of on the unlimited potential that lies dormant within them.

Which kind of person are you? Perhaps in specific moments or certain areas of our lives, we have all felt disempowered or like a victim. To be compassionate, when we're in fear, we typically want a way out but haven't found it yet. It's common nature to play the victim role until we tire of it and find a better way of being. With awareness of how we are negatively acting, we can always choose again to embody divine Power and live lives of purpose and self-expression. The unrestricted Self expresses itself as love, truth, and life. This

> We haven't come here to buy into what the world says we should think, say, or do but to keep the Light in our souls radiating, boldly moving us toward the calling in our hearts.

is the power that resides within each of us. It's the grace that motivates deeper levels of honesty, strength, and creative possibilities. By holding love and truth as your intention and by following through with inspired and unselfish actions, you have the ability to dispel fear and experience inner power right now.

Make the Shift

If you are feeling weak kneed, how can you change? What if I suggested that most fear, anxiety, and worry are self-focused? They are like a hypnotic spell that has gotten out of hand. What about a solution? The first step is to align your heart with the Infinite Presence that is right where you are, filling all space. Many people sense this as an energetic fullness radiating deep from within their chests. Place your hand on your chest and feel this energy. Divinity is centered within you, animating your potential. Feel that you're powerful because Divinity is all powerful and is expressing Itself as you. Its infinite field of energy includes you, regardless of what you have or haven't done! You really can't stop this energy. You can only become unconscious of it or with awareness magnify the effect of it.

Leverage can make a difference too, because most people tend to change in order to avoid pain rather than to gain pleasure. Realize how much the feeling of disempowerment has cost you in terms of health, mental unease, quality of relationships, productivity, and achievement. Once you become aware of the price you've been paying, you may be driven to regain your power and take positive action. Seek the change from within, instead of waiting for circumstances to change outside of you.

Humility is always a heart-opening key as well. It includes first taking complete responsibility for our own experiences and asking for help in order to feel divine supply. There is no separation between you and divine capacities (Divinity expressing Itself as you). It is easier to take clear, bold, and timely action from this heightened state of awareness.

If you ever feel that you are struggling, be kind, gentle, and patient with yourself. Self-acceptance will help you make the shift from weakness to strength more gracefully. Every day you are given moments to decide how to design your path and destiny. How will you choose?

Intention and Devotion

Without a compelling vision, we tend to flounder, lose energy and motivation, and feel weaker in facing obstacles. An inviting sense of future makes us feel expansive and capable. Forward steps to your more empowered experience will come from intention and devotion, just like they do in every other area of life. When you declare an unselfish desire and commit to having it, Divinity will provide the way to fulfill that desire, as we are promised by Christ Jesus: "Whatsoever ye ask in my name, I will do it for you" (John 14:13 LAM). Clearly state what you will unselfishly be, do, or experience and then take each step that Spirit reveals to you. Next, feel as if you've already received what you need or desire and witness how power thereby awakens within you.

There will be times when you can empower yourself by asking for help: "I will find someone to help me, to heal me, and to show me how to be unafraid." There was a time in my twenties when I felt a strong desire to find a spiritual teacher. Although I was living in St. Louis, the same week that I set an intention to find such a teacher, I suddenly felt impelled to book a trip to tour Boston. While standing in a cafeteria line in a Boston high-rise,

> Until you choose a definite direction, and thereby cut off lesser options, you will not invite divine supply to move with you. You will be tempted to retreat when faced with opposition, and you will be partially blinded to resources made available to you for your development and success.

I met a spiritual mentor who generously taught me for the next twelve years. What pure desire do you have? Are you committed to having it, no matter what? Then let Spirit open the way for you to connect with it.

Vocal Power

Human justice requires action. There is a time to speak up and be heard. With wisdom and power, you will know when that time is. Divinity gives you both a voice and the timing to use it. It is up to you to speak what is honest, just, and good for all concerned. Is there vocal action you should be taking now? What will it take for you to stop putting up with things you have been tolerating? How much more pain, suffering, confusion, or loss will you endure until you've finally had enough? In what way do you currently need to speak up and demonstrate more responsibility for your experience, environment, and quality of relationships?

Earlier in life I worked in a warehouse. During my first day on the job, I noticed many pornographic pictures that workers had posted on the wall above the shipping station. At first I was cautious; then I felt impelled to take action. Over time I methodically began taking the images down. After several days, a three-hundred-fifty-pound coworker challenged me about the missing Donna, Michelle, and Victoria posters. I found myself boldly voicing what happens to many women in the porn industry, including the abuse and drug addiction they go through, and how women should be appreciated and respected, not thought of and used as sex objects. A fight nearly broke out, and several days of tension followed. Word spread throughout the corporation about what had happened, and eventually upper management got involved. They brought me in and questioned me about the events, but I felt no motivation to back down. The workers had a right to view pornography on their own time in private, and I and others had a right not to.

Within a very short time, a Nonsexual Harassment Policy was defined and put into place by the company, including the edict that no pornographic images were to be displayed anywhere on company premises. Soon after, a female chief financial officer was hired. She was the first woman ever to be hired in upper management in that company's history. The real point was not whether my viewpoints on porn were right or wrong (my methods were definitely more puritanical than the way I approach things now) but that a personal sense of integrity was followed in the best way I knew how at the time. Using my voice felt empowering and ultimately freeing. Your voice will strengthen as you use it with wisdom, graceful directness, and love. If you don't stand for your truth, don't expect your surroundings to change.

Empowered Steps

We have the innate ability to claim dominion over our thoughts, speech, and actions. We move toward power any time we feel, think, communicate, and act with honesty, clarity, courage, excellence, and love.

What steps will you take and what are you willing to let go of or stop doing in order to become the empowered person you were born to be? Think of what you could become and experience with true power and what it will cost you not to step up to your calling. Your individual expression of divine Power is always available to you to be identified with, yielded to, and embodied. Are you ready to take the next step?

Practice Feeling Empowered

1) **Embody Divine Power:** Meditate on qualities that you believe are empowering, such as self-honesty, courage, unselfishness, or willingness. As you meditate, focus on what it would feel like to more fully embody these qualities in your daily life. Just as Divinity initiated Moses, It is constantly guiding you to live an empowered life. From the things you have been shown intuitively, what action steps could you take today? The next step will unfold as you take the ones that are already clear to you.

2) **Develop Awareness:** Identify two areas of your life where you are thinking, speaking, feeling, or acting like a victim. Write down the focus, feelings, or belief systems that may be blocking you from your potential. Also, expose weakening inner language such as, "Nobody will listen to me" or "I don't think I'm smart enough to do that." Use this honest awareness to make decisive changes in what you focus on, believe, and say.

3) **Fuel Desire:** Now write down and declare three ways in which you will choose to live as an empowered expression of Divinity. For example, "I will speak my truth," "I choose to live my values," "I will set clear boundaries with my parents," or "I will find work that nurtures my soul." .

4) **Take Empowered Action:** Decide and declare which circumstances and behaviors don't work for you and what you will stop tolerating. With power that comes from the Presence in your heart, give a voice to what you will do. "I will demonstrate the discipline to stop procrastinating," or "I claim the courage to ask for forgiveness so that I can let go of guilt." Take responsibility for your own experience so you can be the change that you desire. Step by step, it will become your natural way of expanding.

Chapter 11

Forgive

*Forgiving brings strength and buoyancy, because it includes
giving up that which weighs us down.*

Context and Compassion

Perhaps all of us have had family members or others who have said or done things to us that seem unforgivable. Can you remember a circumstance when you spoke hurtful or hateful words and later recognized that you did not really mean them? The context of your life affected the content of what you said. Perhaps you were feeling tired, afraid, angry, stressed, or hurt. In that moment, you just had to defend yourself, get some space, work through anxiety, or vent some frustration. If people had fully understood how you were feeling emotionally, mentally, and/or physically at the time, they could have more easily forgiven you, right? Likewise, if you understood more about the people who offended you, you could more easily forgive them. Picture someone specific before you right now and ask him to tell you what the context of his life was like at the time he offended you. Listen to what he says. What you hear may radically alter your desire and ability to forgive him.

When we go to the theater and watch a feature-length period film, we may make some judgments about it. The leading actor did a decent job, but the cinematography and screen writing didn't make sense, and the movie was a letdown. We believe our perceptions are well informed and accurate. We always seem to be right about how things look to us—at least more right than anyone else! We think our truth is the Truth, and that's where the problem lies.

If we watched only two minutes of the film instead of the whole feature, we'd be substantially less informed. In judging others, we often base our perceptions and reactions on a very short piece of their "life movie"—the limited and interpreted part that affects us. So, our judgments may not be as wise as we believe they are. We don't know every desire and fear they've entertained or every decision they've made. We don't know what they needed most for spiritual development or how much they were influenced by various people and environments. How can we possibly know everything about another's past and all that determined the context of their life? Perhaps that is why the great beings throughout history, such as Jesus, taught that true judgment belongs only to God, because our judgment simply does not see or experience the full picture. It's not as much that we shouldn't judge others as we're simply not equipped to do so. There is so much that we really don't know about the movie of another's life or, as some believe, another's *lives*. If we saw the private journals of our foes, we might read about their inner struggles and suffering and walk away with a more compassionate sense of who they are and why they are that way.

What if you understood that based on a person's spiritual level of consciousness, human limitations, genetics, beliefs, and past choices, he probably could not have done things any differently at that moment? Is it possible that if you'd lived that person's entire existence for him, you may have done exactly as he did?

If we not only watched an entire movie, but also learned about the making of the film; the screenwriter's, director's, and actor's backgrounds and intents; and the entire history of the era in which the movie takes place, our perceptions would shift, and our understanding of the movie's context would expand. We would naturally have more insight and compassion. That is what understanding filmmaking brings. The same principle applies to understanding another person and her life movie. Being compassionate with others based on expanded understanding is the key to opening the door of our hearts to forgiveness.

Most people are simply unaware of just how unloving they seem at times or how their negative actions impact us. Maybe it is easier to find forgiveness when we connect with the climatic words Jesus spoke while his body was being tortured and crucified: "forgive them, for they do not know what they are doing" (Luke 23:34 LAM). For someone who has been killing your spirit, your words might be, "The man had no clue," or

"I see now that she did not have the awareness or capacity to do it another way at the time."

When you closely examine some of your own repeated poor choices, mistakes, and verbal offenses, you can be just as gentle with yourself by understanding your own context. You did the best you could at that moment until you progressively learned to do it better. Awareness and compassion lead to acceptance of what was and what is without resentment. It is like your heart says, "Of course it happened that way; now I understand." With this higher wisdom, you no longer have to fight the past as if it shouldn't have been. Coming to such a realization may not be a painless process; it may be challenging and require radical humility, a deeper search for the truth, and emotional healing. Nonetheless, if you check in with the results, you may find that this pathway is easier than continuing to lug around the heavy weights of hurt, anger, and resistance that keep you stuck and deplete your life energy.

> "... to whom little is forgiven, the same loveth little"
> (Christ Jesus, Luke 7:47).

Forgive Yourself

True forgiveness will free your own life energy and support your expansion of consciousness. Yet, until you see your own life with compassion and acceptance, you will find it difficult to be gentle and compassionate with others. You may feel tempted to reject yourself for many mistakes and shortcomings. You may not like the way you look, how smart you are, how much money you earn or save, or what kind of parent you are. You may not like what you have made of your life so far. Perhaps you are unhappy about your morals or laziness, how muffled you are in speaking the truth, or several less-than-perfect choices you have made. If you are like most people, you have had feelings of guilt, shame, remorse, or self-judgment that followed your unproductive behaviors or errors. Nonetheless, if you focus on your shortcomings, life may feel self-defeating. So how can you find a more supportive view of yourself?

Everything you did, said, put up with, or failed to say and do happened within a context of how well equipped you were at that time spiritually, mentally, emotionally, and physically. You were born human and fallible, not completely animallike or angelic. Perhaps you are on a journey, moving from a survival-based mentality and toward one that knows Divinity at a deeper, experiential level—as the true and only reliable life support. When you consider your capacities, environment, genes, and background, you probably did the best you could with what you had. Forgive and accept yourself for what you have become so far. If you do, you will be in a much better place to move forward. If you don't, life will seem more difficult, because you'll be dragging around past regrets. You are love expressing itself in the best way you know how at this time. In some, the light of love shines through more brightly, but this light and potential comes from the same Source and is fully available in everyone.

Does something about you still seem unforgivable? You shouldn't have done something or said something or allowed something. Right? Is that really true? Perhaps the fact that it happened is proof that it *should* have happened. In fact, you should have done everything you did to bring you to this point in your experience. It couldn't have happened any other way to get you where you are right now. Understand that you did it the way you thought would benefit you at the time.

We all tend to do what we think is best for us in the moment in order to gain pleasure or avoid pain. This is as true for the heroin addict as it is for the brain surgeon. In order to live more fully and freely, we need to accept ourselves where we are. If we don't, we will continue to have the same life we now have, only with more accumulated lead weights of self-rejection and criticism in the future. How does your future look so far? Do you think being easier on yourself would make your life look more dazzling?

There is spiritual wisdom in the Lord's answer when he was asked by a disciple how we should pray: ". . . forgive us our offenses, as we have forgiven our offenders" (Matt. 6:12 LAM). This wisdom also applies when we have trespassed against our own integrity and values. All of us feel some level of guilt when we violate what is most important to us, but being stuck in self-rejection is no pathway to freedom. It is just another trap that will hold us in a pattern of self-destructive bondage. The way to greater freedom is through simple, honest regret, and a recommitment to actually live our values in our daily lives, followed by demonstrated action.

If you went to buy a couch for a thousand dollars, and it was the last one of its kind available, how would you feel if the salesperson wanted to charge you another thousand dollars before allowing you to leave the store? And what if you decided to go ahead and pay double the originally expected amount to secure your purchase, only to find out that you still wouldn't be allowed to drive away with your couch without paying another thousand dollars? Sound bizarre? Most of us have done something similar. We've kept ourselves locked up in an ongoing storehouse of negativity over past mistakes, errors of judgment or omission, and indiscretions of character. Part of us wants to move forward, and another part won't let us out, because it demands that we pay not just three times but hundreds of times for our mistakes. No wonder change feels difficult. Awareness of this pattern provides a saner choice.

To forgive yourself allows the opportunity to experience a fresh start, so you can walk ahead freely. Stop spending your energy in regurgitating the past like some old pasture cow chewing its cud. Instead, use that energy to take meaningful action toward what you truly want. At any moment, you have the choice to focus on what you want to create or on what you don't want (which, many times, is more of the past). Which choice would best serve you right now?

Imagine waking up tomorrow feeling forgiven for all of your past mistakes and disappointments, no matter how big or small. For a few moments, let yourself know that you deeply and completely love and accept yourself. If there is a mirror nearby, look deep into your eyes while doing so. Meditate and live from this place of freedom, and you will more likely bring resolution into your experience. Whatever dominates your thoughts will tend to manifest, so why not focus on what you most want to experience and take action toward that? Before healing someone crippled by self-guilt, Jesus would often say, "Your sins are forgiven." Once you have a humble, heartfelt regret, you can also be treated this way by the Christ within you. The question is this: are you are willing to treat yourself with such love?

> "He has showed you, O man, what is good and what the Lord requires of you, that you shall do justice and love mercy and be ready to walk after the Lord your God" (Mic. 6:8 LAM).

Hidden Gifts

Mistakes have consequences. How much agony and frustration have we felt resisting this fact? If we would just accept, learn from, and deal with the consequences, then we could live a higher quality life. This doesn't have to be a big process, either, unless we resist it. Mistakes are an inherent and major part of human existence, and we've all messed up hugely at times. That is how we learn to do things better.

Christ said that he came to call "sinners to repentance" (Mark 2:17). Perhaps sin isn't as mysterious or complicated as many people and institutions have made it out to be. From its historical root, sin simply means "to miss the mark"—like an archer whose shot does not hit the bull's-eye. In ancient times, the ring just outside the center of the archer's target was called the area of sin. The target in our lives might be something of a higher purpose, such as to live a life of honesty and love, raise healthy and happy children, achieve excellence in a field of endeavor, or make a positive difference with everyone we know. The goal seems simple enough, but then life happens, and for something that seemed like a good reason at the time, we forget about our life mission or intention; we sin, miss the mark, forsake the high prize, take a detour, or screw up. What we make that to mean and what we do next are the important things.

A man once called me to say that he felt like he'd ruined his life. His feeling was based on a high school test that he'd shown up late for decades earlier, which later affected his inability to follow a family-chosen career path. Together we were able to redefine the meaning of that missed exam, which included his ability to follow an artistic career path, the one that his heart preferred. He forgave himself based on a revised perspective, and he is now a successful filmmaker.

There will be many times when your thoughts and actions will feel off target from your ultimate purpose and values, or less than truthful and loving. So what will it take for you to get back on target? Simply adjust your stance (what you're standing for), aim (what you're going for in life), and follow-through (with purposeful action), like a developing archer.

What about this repentance stuff? True repentance isn't just feeling bad about a goof-up; it includes changing our ways. Entrenched patterns of missing the mark tend to lead us to painful and fearful places. Repentance is recognition that our aim is off plus the willingness to correct it. The movie *Groundhog Day* (Sony Pictures, 1993) masterfully illustrates how actor Bill Murray as TV weatherman Phil Connors had a new day to do things differently, which he didn't do for many repetitive days, until he finally began to actually change. First he made surface changes in order to manipulate people in his environment, but he hadn't really changed his narcissistic motives. Ultimately, he had a real change of heart and wanted to be of true service to others. You too have a new day today, but if you don't remind yourself of your real target, correct your aim, and follow through with action, you could leave something undone and have to repeat life lessons in one or more of your own Groundhog Day-style experiences.

Part of the required learning is for us to make amends whenever possible. This may impel seemingly impossible action, such as finding some long-lost person we have offended or resolving an issue with a family member who has passed on. Nonetheless, in humble prayer with God, anything is possible if we are deeply willing and committed.

Once I heard the story of a man who had a severe conflict with his father who died shortly thereafter. The man felt there was no way to reconcile things with his father, and he couldn't forgive himself for leaving the relationship where he had. As father and son, they had played a lot of baseball together when he was growing up, but times changed, and the man later ached for the closeness that he'd once felt. After the funeral, he was led to write his dad a letter in which he poured out his heart, asked for forgiveness, and told him how much he loved him. He had repented, changed his ways, and felt a huge release from the guilt that had been burdening him. The next morning when he opened his front door, he looked down, and to his awestruck surprise, he saw an old baseball sitting there for him.

Life gives us constant feedback. Missing the mark is one of the main ways we learn to hit the bull's-eye. You have been granted a new day today, so what will you do differently? Mistakes can be your best teachers and greatest hidden gifts, *if* you receive the learning they hold for you. The patterns of your repeated choices can reveal a lot about you. Those patterns often expose core issues that need the real attention, such as issues about how you've linked up pain or pleasure with an experience or interpreted the meaning of it (which may not ultimately be true) and what beliefs and behaviors are truly serving you and others. They also show what vehicles you use to get love, avoid rejection, and navigate fear. If you have enough courage to expose the patterns and their results, you may uncover what truly needs to be forgiven, healed, or changed. Then your life no longer needs to be defined by your mistakes but by who you are becoming through learning from and overcoming them.

Forgive Others

You may think you are hurt by what someone said or did, but if you look more closely, you may find that what really hurts is how someone did not become what you think they should have or by what they didn't do. "They should have been more considerate, unselfish, kind, or honest! They should have understood my needs and been there for me. Dammit, they should have been more evolved, right?" Well, maybe not, if we understand that people actually can't be at a different place in development right now than they are. We get hurt (and then often angry) by the other person's underdeveloped lovingness or wisdom or integrity, at least according to our perception and expectation at that time. And, without knowing it, we assume we know everything in the universe all at once, so we're experts on where that person should be. Sure we are!

The story you've told yourself ever since that momentous event (whatever *it* was) is built on your perception and the meaning you chose from that experience. "She didn't call or email when she said she would, so that means she doesn't love me." Is that really true? Is there a rare possibility that there was another valid reason (or ten other reasons) why she didn't contact you? Is it possible that her electricity or cable service went down, or someone came to visit her unexpectedly? Our interpretation, no matter how justified or evidence-filled it seems, has to be hugely limited and skewed. Often just asking the person for a reason is enough to rewrite our story.

Do you know why there is that piece of dust on your coffee table today? Of course! It's because you left the window open last night or because your roommate forgot to clean the living room last Saturday. Amazingly, scientists have calculated that there are well over 100 million reasons why that dust particle is there, including the entire evolution of the universe up to now, give or take a few millennia. Not so sure about your story any longer?

Your story and the meaning you assigned to it, together with the unrealistic expectation that someone should have been different than they were then, could be the very source of the energy you waste and the hurt you feel. Are you absolutely sure you know why they did or didn't do what they should or shouldn't have done? Could they have been more loving or truthful or smart than they were at that moment? Remember that piece of dust before answering.

When we see with new eyes, the world around us becomes new too. The observer affects the outcome. Our view of another affects the way he or she interacts with us. When we see the formerly unforgiveable person within an expansive and compassionate context, we don't have to *try* to forgive him; there is simply nothing left to forgive. If we ask, Holy Spirit can shift our perceptions and recontextualize what happened so that we don't need to change what happened in order to find peace.

How would it feel for you to be denied forgiveness for one of your misdeeds with no hope for resolution or opportunity to make things right ever again? Do you think that someone who offended you may feel the same way? All of us have wanted and needed a second chance, a new beginning. What will it take for you to give that other person one? Granted, it may take courage, persistence, and compassion to work through your emotions in order to forgive someone who has caused you pain. It may even take professional support. There are hundreds of pathways and many qualified healers of emotions ready to help if you're willing and committed to find who and what works for you. You have the gift within you to remove your own self-guilt for not giving another person the opportunity to make things right with you. You can give them an opportunity to be different if they choose.

In the act of forgiveness, you are not implying that the action against you does not matter. Actions have consequences. You're not discounting divine Justice either. But, you can say, "I choose to forgive so that *I* can heal. I want my freedom to be my best. I'm tired of feeling dead inside, guilty, weighed down, and imprisoned by the past. I want to live life fully with new possibilities." Your soul urges you toward forgiveness, because it is ultimately in your own and the other's best interest to go there. It is a powerful way to find peace and renew the life and love within you. Shakespeare poetically put it this way in *The Merchant of Venice*: "The quality of mercy is not strained; it droppeth as the gentle rain from heaven upon the place beneath. It is twice blessed—it blesseth him that gives and him that takes."

Why are certain people in your life? Who you are and the spiritual trajectory you've chosen tends to attract people into your experience who will best help you grow, both spiritually and emotionally. Some people and experiences may seem extremely difficult to deal with. They may stay with you for months, years, or even decades. All of them are there for your learning and ultimate freedom. In personal transformation work, it is not uncommon for a facilitator to say to a struggling participant, "The only thing keeping you from having what you want is the story you keep telling yourself about why you can't have it." What's your story—the reason your life can't be better than it is—and is there a better version waiting to be written by you?

Whether an experience was difficult or not, what if you accepted what happened, knowing that it was the perfect thing to help you grow? Would such a meaning feel more empowering to you than your original version of the story? It has been said by enlightened beings throughout the ages that there are no accidents in this perfect Universe. What if you are going through things with people for perfect reasons (even if you do not currently understand all of them)? Could this perspective make the rest of your life a whole new story, one that gives you a greater sense of love, freedom, and peace?

These are big questions. You still have the choice to become resentful, bitter, or defeated from difficult people and experiences. Millions do, but those who seek truth, compassion, forgiveness, and wisdom will persevere until they find the answers and growth they need. They will benefit spiritually, no matter what they have gone through. Saint Paul recognized this when he wrote to encourage the struggling Corinthians, "For our light and momentary troubles are achieving for us an eternal glory that far outweighs them all" (2 Cor. 4:17). Paul's momentary troubles included being unjustly beaten, being put in prison, being dishonored and called an impostor, getting mobbed in a riot, going without food, and having sleepless nights (2 Cor. 6:4-8). He must have had a powerful meaning to help him endure those things without getting bitter or giving up.

Resistance makes life seem like hard work; acceptance makes it easier. If you truly understand that offenders come into your life to bring you a gift of teaching, you will be able to receive them with less resistance. Jesus taught his followers to "Love your enemies, bless them that curse you, do good to them that hate you, and pray for them who despitefully use you, and persecute you" (Matt. 5:44). Have you ever wondered why he challenged us to such lofty ideals? Could it be that these types of people, these enemies, bring us perfect teaching for our own spiritual growth? Recognize how persistent your persecutors are until you get the lessons. It may take many layers of courageous self-honesty, courageous action, humility, and emotional healing before you do.

Once you receive the teaching that your offender brings to you, you'll be in a better position to offer inspiration, healing, and support to others going through such trials. Imagine coming to the point where you willingly accept your enemies and actively bless their appearance in your life. Think about how difficult it would have been for you to evolve thus far without such individuals. See how much they have caused you to dig deep within yourself to find fortitude, resourcefulness, and trust in your inner Self-knowing. Recognize how they stretched and pushed you like a relentless coach. Is there now a glimmer of hope that you can actually love them for all they have given you?

You may have the opportunity to bless them back. Forgiveness is a gift that allows oppressors to change too. Your freedom becomes an invitation for theirs. It is not up to us whether they actually do change. That is between them and their God. Your job is you. To win a game, you first have to know what game you are playing. The spiritual growth game seems to be all about forgiveness, truth, and love. Christ Jesus gave us a master example for understanding this big picture. He lived the limitless Love that forgives unconditionally, because he had an enlightened understanding of his purpose, identity, and relationship with Divinity. Because of his supreme goodness, nobody else overcame the amount of injustice that he did while maintaining an egoless, forgiving heart. The blocks to our own pure Christlike heart can be progressively removed through this same understanding and through divine Grace, as we're willing. If you are feeling pain, anger, remorse, or guilt, time is ticking. How much longer will you suffer and make those around you suffer?

> "Great Spirit, help me never to judge another until I have walked in his moccasins" (Sioux Indian Prayer).

Come Back to the Present

For our learning and joy, the most important moment is always now. If this moment doesn't feel like infinite possibility, something or someone may still need our forgiveness.

All of us are learning and evolving, and our pathways are rarely linear. They are more like ascending circles. We learn and relearn some of the same lessons over and over, and one day we really get it. Then, to our surprise, we learn the lessons again at yet a higher or more refined level.

Some people learn faster than others. Does that really matter in the eternal scheme of things? If we don't feel compassion, we can pray to Divinity to enable us to feel it. Holy Spirit can help us to learn what we need to learn from the past and reframe it, instead of being imprisoned by it. We could pray, "Show me what I need to learn from what happened. I am willing to own my part in it, make amends, and receive the lessons that I need. Free me from the burden of my mistakes and soften my heart in view of others' mistakes." After such a prayer, receive what you need as answered prayer before doing anything. Then your action will more likely be timely and wise.

There is always a way to let go of the pain, resentment, and self-judgment of the past in order to live in the present, where life is unfolding before your eyes in beauty, splendor, and wonder. With an uplifted vision, you can see that people in your life are expressing love in the best way they know how right now. If you stay open for divine Grace to soften your heart and heal your emotions, burdens can be removed from the other person and you. Forgiveness always has multiple blessings. Isn't it time to set your love free?

Practice Forgiving

1) **Feel the Cost:** Focus on a person or circumstance that has been calling for your forgiveness. It might be the misbehavior of a partner or spouse, an unsupportive parent, a friend who let you down, an ungrateful coworker or child, the driver who cut you off in traffic, or your own shortcomings. No matter how big or small the incident, recognize how your body feels when you focus on it. Do you feel tight, anxious, or emotionally drained? Perhaps you feel sadness, anger, or hurt. If left unhealed, all of these reactions will cost you energy and affect the quality of your life. Write in a journal the emotional ways you have been paying for this lack of forgiveness. Next, write about the payoffs (i.e., the false sense of protection, benefits, or satisfaction) you've been getting by remaining unforgiving. Look over your list and ask yourself if these payoffs are good investments in the quality of your life.

2 **Divine Forgiveness:** Recall some of the life lessons you've had to learn over and over. Imagine how patient and forgiving Divinity has been with you during those times when you just didn't get it. How would you describe the nature of divine Love, which has readily forgiven you? Whenever you are struggling to forgive another, meditate on and feel this loving nature that has continued to love you unconditionally. Notice if you feel a change of heart.

3) **Forgive Yourself:** List two or three of the biggest mistakes you've ever made in your life. What judgments about yourself or negative emotions are you still holding onto around these? Ask Holy Spirit to show you what you need to learn from these mistakes, what you need to do to make amends, or how you can see these events in a more empowering way. Find deeper acceptance of yourself by resting in the thought that everything you did was perfect to bring you to this point in your spiritual consciousness. Recognize that you did the best you could until you learned to do it better. If judgments about the past come to mind, be gentle with yourself by understanding the total context of your life movie, including things you may be unconscious of.

4) **Forgive Others:** When someone behaved in an offensive way, that person actually believed that it was the best decision at that time. That person's actions may have been due to stress, fatigue, fear, cultural programming, past choices, or selfish desires. His capacity for love was filtered by the context of his life at the time. Remember, if you would have walked in the offender's shoes for his entire existence, you may not have acted any differently than he did. Understanding this can build a bridge that leads to forgiveness. Write a letter *from your offender to you* describing what it was like to be him—what fears, desires, pain, and needs he was focusing on then; why he did what he did; or why he didn't do what he should have done. Read it in that person's voice. You may receive revelations and changed perceptions from what you read.

Chapter 12

Receive Guidance

"Trust in the Lord with all thine heart, and lean not unto thine own understanding. In all thy ways acknowledge him, and he shall direct thy paths" (Prov. 3:5-6).

Willing to Be Guided?

Recently I received a call from a woman whose life had been a mess several years ago but now sounded incredible. Back then, she had been slowly drinking herself to death and destroying her mind, body, and relationships. One day, at pit bottom, she admitted that she couldn't control her life. She yearned deep within herself to feel guided by Divinity. On that day she voiced these words to God: "Let me know the joy of being used by you." As I spoke with her this time, I realized that she had indeed found that joy and *was* being used for higher purposes in her work and relationships. Her willingness to be guided—to surrender her life to divine direction—had a profound impact on her. As a result, she had recovered from addiction, obtained gainful and satisfying employment, found a wonderful place to live, and established caring friendships.

Feeling guided is perhaps one of the most awe-inspiring feelings on earth. Divine Love is continuously guiding our thoughts, motives, speech, and actions. Our responses to this guidance have the potential to bring the highest good to us and others. If guidance is so readily and perfectly available, why don't we seek and feel it all the time? One reason is that we may not be willing to be guided; we get used to doing life on our own. Despite all the mistakes, loss, pain and suffering we've experienced, we haven't yet reached the proverbial bottom described above. We choose to go about living life our way, as if we really know what is best for us. The sad reality is that willfulness and a false sense of independence can hinder our ability to be led by Divinity, and we may miss out on true joy and connection.

Often we don't ask Divinity for help because we are preoccupied with our own agenda and concerns. We forget that we are part of a much larger concern for all humanity. We fill up our time with entertainment and all the things we have to get done instead of leaving space for inspired direction. There is little room for the Holy Spirit to operate in a consciousness filled with distractions and focus on problems of everyday life. It is up to us to clear the way in our hearts and minds.

Other times we don't feel guided because we forget or ignore the help that is already available to us in the form of teachers, teachings, and resources, such as a dusty book on a shelf that was once inspiring; however, we didn't actually follow its suggestions.

Imagine how your life will change if you ask for and receive guidance in everything you do—what to wear, how to invest your money, who to enter into romance with, what books to read, how to spend your time off, and the best way for you to help others. To request and receive guidance in the everyday things will tend to build your confidence to accept spiritual guidance in the bigger issues of life.

Control vs. Surrender

Several years ago I met a man whom I will call Michael for anonymity. He was a highly paid advertising executive. Even though Michael had phenomenal material success, he struggled with cocaine addiction and severe grief following the tragic death of two of his children. Michael's brokenness had also brought him to the point of surrender. He too wanted nothing more than to be guided by God. His addiction was healed, and his burdens were lifted. Now he wakes up every morning, and the first thing he says is "Good morning, God. What do you want me to do for you today?" He gave up trying to control his life alone and is now one of the most joyful men I've ever met. Daily, he actively serves others in ways that are healing and inspiring.

One key to Michael's new way of being is his understanding of the power of gratitude. He has been giving gratitude daily for several years, and it has become as automatic as his breathing. He is thankful for everything

God does for him throughout the day, no matter how incidental. How much would greater gratitude increase your awareness of all the ways you are being directed? How might it open your eyes and heart to receive further guidance? Other qualities that can increase the divine support you perceive are clarity, openness, spontaneity, heart-centeredness, resourcefulness, and certainty that you are being led by a caring field of intelligent energy. Such ways of being have a resonant frequency that will make it easier for you to listen and feel directed.

Humility is another quality of character that allows us to feel more consistently guided. At some level, we don't like to admit that we actually don't know what is best for us—in spite of the unproductive roads we have traveled in the past. There have been times that we didn't know who we should be with, where we should go, or what we should do or say. Yet, we continued to act like we did! Our culture promotes individualism and independence. We are *supposed* to know what is best for us. It could be embarrassing not to, and sadly, some people have taken their own lives rather than face social embarrassment. If we make social pressure the most important thing, then feeling led spiritually will take a back seat. There are times when our job titles, college degrees, or years of experience can't get us through the challenges we are facing. When life becomes unmanageable, nothing else will work for us except to surrender to the care of divine Grace: a power infinitely greater than our human mind and efforts.

Perhaps the times when we have the most pride of "going it alone" are when things are going great and we are highly successful! But pride attracts attack and makes us subject to having our bubbles popped. If we weren't unconsciously fearful of the future, why would we need to act prideful? How many times have we had to relearn that old proverb by experience: "Pride goes before destruction" (Prov. 16:18)? Suffering, loss, and regret have an enduring way of returning us to the place of humility. Many people will not ask for directions when they get lost on a trip. What about feeling lost in a marriage, a career, or raising a child?

Ask, Receive, Respond, Give Thanks

There is no better way to remember to seek guidance than to start by asking now with a sincere heart. Each time you catch yourself doing something without divine direction, stop for a moment and then simply ask. With this positive conditioning, you will become more and more conscious of remembering to ask again. You probably don't forget to leave the house without your keys, wallet, or cell phone, because you can't stand to be without them. When you can't stand living without divine guidance, then you'll be more likely to ask for it. Progressively notice when you don't choose to have Divinity lead you, just as you notice when your keys are missing. Someone said that guidance is like a beautiful, graceful dance. G-U-I-Dance—God, You, and I Dance. Spirit will lead; your job is to follow.

Much like what a newspaper reporter looks and listens for, you can be guided in several specific ways: 1) *what* you think, do, or say, 2) *how* you do it, 3) *when* you do it, 4) *who* you do it with, and 5) *where* you do it. Get specific in asking which ways you most need to be guided. For example, "God, show me the best time to call Michelle" or "I want to know who needs my encouragement right now."

The ability to hear your inner guidance is strengthened by practice. The steps are simple: ask, receive, respond, and give thanks. The practice becomes more natural when we do these steps in the little things instead of waiting for a major challenge. If and when a crisis does come, we'll be better prepared to work through it, because our trust in divine direction has been proven. We'll have references to back our trust and faith. Before David faced Goliath, he'd already learned that he could trust Divinity's guidance in defeating a bear and a lion while defending his sheep. This gave him confidence to face another giant in order to defend his people. David's life was filled with asking, receiving, responding, and giving praise. He didn't always do these perfectly, yet even after major screwups, he always returned to these steps.

Timing and Options

Sometimes there is a waiting period between asking for and receiving guidance. Depending on divine timing, this could be a few seconds, a day, a week, a month, or even several years. Michael, from the story earlier, once said, "We tend to go to God like an overnight delivery man. We bang on God's door and yell for His help, and before we hear a response, we're tearing off halfway down the street assuming nobody was home." The way divine communication really works is in the way the prophet Isaiah related: "before they call, I will answer; while they are yet speaking, I will hear" (Isa. 65:24). Divinity knows our needs long before we try to make It aware of them, but we'll receive the answers we need in Divinity's timing, not our egos'. Sometimes the answer we receive won't be what we want to hear, and sometimes it won't be *when* we want to hear it.

Just because you experience a delay in getting an answer, it doesn't mean that you have been denied the answer. There could be one or more reasons for the delay in receiving an answer from Spirit. It may not be best for you or others related to your situation to receive the answer right away. You or someone else involved may still have something to learn or do. Perhaps what will be given to you may still need to be coordinated for the good of all concerned, just as a violinist must wait for the conductor's wand to cue her first note in order for the symphony to be played most beautifully.

You won't feel spiritually guided if you are told to do something now but wait four weeks to take action. By then it may no longer timely for you or another. Your efforts won't have the same result if you fail to respond in ideal timing. Every time you wisely listen and respond with appropriate action, you will likely feel a boost to your energy and power, and to a degree, you will overcome that which would try to inhibit your spirit. Every time you don't listen, you may feel more alone, confused, and weak.

Specific opportunities arrive, but they don't hang around. It has been said that the right thing done at the wrong time is no longer the right thing. If you are like most people, you fail to respond because your ego overanalyzes, questions, and doubts. Recognize the tremendous cost to yourself and others by refusing to respond in a timely way to inklings you have received. Again, with awareness you can choose to act more resourcefully.

Another typical block to receiving guidance is going to Divinity with options. You ask for help in choosing option A or option B. Maybe Divinity wants you to do something completely different, like option C or D. You may ask, "Should I go out with Denny or Mike?" Spirit's answer may be, "Don't go out with anyone right now. You need to develop in character first." You won't hear option C if you are only listening for option A or B. True surrender to divine care comes from putting your own agenda aside and being open, without preconceptions or positional requirements. Nonattachment to methods or outcomes will support you to receive the ideal result at the ideal time.

Believe to Receive

Receiving the answer you need may require your humility, patience, and acceptance. You also have to *believe* that you will receive an answer. Isn't that what the master of manifestation, Jesus, said? "If you believe, you will receive whatever you ask for in prayer" (Matt. 21:22 NIV). He was very clear about the necessity of having the inner certainty that you will receive an answer before it can get through to you successfully. Believe that you have received it, and it is yours.

The way you receive guidance may be outside the box, so have the willingness to receive direction unconventionally. For instance, you may think that the guidance you seek needs to come from a pulpit or your mother, and instead it appears on a billboard or in a dream. Breaking the mold on how the guidance has to come to you will help free you to receive it. There is no limitation to the form in which divine Love's communication can appear. Societal beliefs may tell us that such things as love, children, and careers have to come to us in a particular way or by a certain age. Choose to be bigger than your culture or family stereotypes. Humility, patience, and confident belief, based on understanding of the continuity and completeness of divine guidance, will support you to receive what you most need.

> "I am always with you; you hold me by my right hand. You guide me with your counsel" (Ps. 73:23-24 NIV).

You Need What You Get

If we ask for bread, will we be given a stone (see Matthew 7:9)? This isn't the way divine Love works, *if* we really need the bread. Grace comes in a form that is both ideal and compassionate. If the real need is for us to expand spiritually, we may not receive our preconceived concept of an answer. For example, you may need to learn perseverance, so it might appear that God doesn't understand your material need or isn't listening. But, in fact you *are* receiving guidance, just not in the form you wanted. Receiving what you need will help you in the long run. Receiving what you temporarily want or think you need may not.

From a perspective of soul development, the timing and form of the response that you receive may affect many other people. Spirit orchestrates its guidance to have the best possible impact for all concerned, not just you! What you receive is what you need in relation to others too. There could be millions of positive consequences to your willingness to give up what you want and instead accept what you need. Isaiah left us a legacy of what Divinity promised us: "I am the Lord thy God which teacheth thee to profit, which leadeth thee by the way that thou shouldest go" (Is. 48:17); "And the Lord shall guide thee continually, and satisfy thy soul" (Isa. 58:11). The Supreme One knows what you need to satisfy your soul more than you do and will deliver what is best for you in the perfect way and time. Your job is to focus on what Divinity is doing for and through you, not on what your limited self can't do. Divinity's job, by its very nature, is to focus on you. Keeping these two roles straight makes life easier. All of life is conspiring to give you what you need, no matter how it looks temporarily. Because the ego resists change, some things may not look positive to you, but can be significant for your growth and destiny.

Love, Honesty, and Guidance

Divinity is both merciful (compassionately loving) and just (reliably truthful) at the same time. How does this impact us? If our motives and actions are moving in accord with the nature of divine Love and Truth, then the guidance we receive will support our motives and actions. If they're opposing Divinity's will for us, then the response we receive may serve to adjust and correct our motives and actions. Ultimately, all of us will be guided back to standards of love and honesty, no matter how much we veer from these standards temporarily (for days or years). Seem simple enough? As we know, simple does not always feel easy, and the process of being realigned isn't always without challenges, pain, loss, or regret.

> "Live by the principles of love and justice, and always be expecting much from him, your God" (Hosea 12:6 TLB).

If we were able to perceive the full picture of divine Love's precision and constant care for us, think of how wonderfully listened to and cherished we would feel. If you feel that you have messed up your life by choices and mistakes, you can still receive direction and answers today in order to get back on track. Do your problems seem too big to resolve? Your most difficult and convoluted questions or circumstances can be easily untangled with the divine hand's brilliant touch.

Once we catch even a whisper or glimpse of spiritual guidance, it is up to us to take action—to change our perspective, attitudes, beliefs, self-centered motives, and habits back to the freeing sense of love and honesty. Unselfishness and honesty are simple. Our resistance to them makes our life situations feel complex and painful. We may have been getting the same answers for the past ten years. Do we expect Divinity's answer to change even though we haven't changed? Like constant gravity, the infinite field of Love will wait us out.

Divine Mind vs. Ego/Mind

How do we know when it's Divine Mind or ego/mind that is influencing us? Here are some distinctions:

1. Divine Mind gives us the ideal answer. Just one answer is given at a time, one that is based in truth and love. The ego/mind often presents a sea of confusing and distracting options that are based in fear, greed, or pride.

2. Divine Mind's guidance has an unselfish quality about it, which includes the understanding that abundance is available to all. The answer given is for the greatest benefit for all concerned. When we're focused on serving, it's easier to hear this guidance. The ego/ mind is only concerned with self and survival due to its core fears of scarcity, rejection, and loss.

3. Divine Mind gives inspiration and motivation that enable us to yield to Divinity. The ego/mind resists surrender to God. Because of fear, ego/mind would rather be in control and play god itself, no matter how difficult things get.

If you truly surrender to Spirit's guidance, you won't be willfully attached to an outcome. Instead you'll simply want what is best for everyone involved, whatever it looks like. The ego/mind has to have things turn out in a predetermined way and feels anxiously out of control when things don't match its concepts. Think of this the next time you feel anxious and realize you can relax back into being guided, without attachment to the form of the outcome.

How do you get better at knowing what feels divinely impelled? Start where you are. Begin by asking, receiving, responding, and giving thanks in the ways you already know. "Which way should I travel to work? Who should I call or email this afternoon? How should I best resolve the situation with my boss?" Like any other area of growth, we start learning and then make refining adjustments. Check in regularly and see how you have been doing with asking, receiving, responding, and giving gratitude. Then adjust your course of action, just like an airplane does in flight. Planes actually don't fly in a straight line. The plane has to zigzag the whole way because of the curvature of the earth. The pilots, or their autopilot computers, are constantly making adjustments so everyone gets to their correct destination. Without making corrections, they would veer off in the wrong direction and miss their landing target. The same applies to you in your approach to life.

Relationship Guidance

Divinity shows us which people we should nurture relationship with and which ones we should distance ourselves from. People are brought into our lives for a reason, and we often hold onto a relationship far beyond its designed purpose. Sometimes, due to our choices, the opportunity or purpose passes by, and the relationship is no longer supportive or necessary. Bring your current relationships to mind. Are any of them no longer serving their purposes for you and/or the other person involved?

We're not actually stuck with relationships as much as we think we are, even with so-called blood ties. We become invested and believe that we can't change our role in a relationship, or we may believe that it's unloving to end a certain relationship. These are just belief systems that can restrict us into making decisions based on what is no longer a blessing to either person.

Likewise, we need to stay open to include relationships that are a blessing, no matter how unconventional they may look. Can a grandmother learn something from a teenager down the street? Can a fast-food clerk be a blessing to the corporate mogul? The movie *Crash* (Lions Gate Films, 2004) powerfully showed just how interconnected seemingly unrelated people can be and how each impacted the other.

Clearly, spiritual commitment in relationships is vital, and if we look at Jesus, we'll see that he was committed to Truth and Divinity, not to personalities. The ones who could handle this stood by him; those who found his teaching too demanding quickly scattered: "From this time many of his disciples went back, and walked no more with him" (John 6:66). Commitment is beneficial as long as it contributes to our own or another's spiritual growth and the highest good of all concerned. Holy Spirit moves all things for its purpose, which includes us.

We have the freedom and opportunity to choose to be part of this movement. Today is another precious day to choose to ask, receive, respond, and give thanks. Will you? If so, will you believe that you will be guided?

Practice Receiving Guidance

1) **Ask:** Bring to mind a situation in which you need divine guidance. It is important to be as specific as possible so you don't miss Divinity's guiding response. Write down or proclaim what it is that you want or need. For example, "I want to know what to say in my letter to my friend to heal our rift," "Guide me in the best way to help my husband with his business dilemma," or "Show me how to be less anxious about my child entering kindergarten."

2) **Receive:** An important step to receiving answers is taking time to get quiet, so you can hear and feel how you are being guided. Find a quiet and comfortable place to sit or lie down. Recall your question from above and set an intention to receive guidance. Next, surrender to divine Will no matter how it looks. Then, *believe and feel* that you will receive what you need. Quiet your mind by bringing your awareness into your body. Feel how it is being supported by what you are sitting or lying on. From this quiet and grounded place, what do you know the answer to be from deep within your heart? Remember, divine Mind's guidance is clear, decisive, and based in truth and love. Learn to trust what you hear from this quiet, grounded place.

3) **Respond:** Recognize the guidance you receive from your prayer or meditation and implement it in a timely way. For example, if

you feel divinely led to call a friend, sign up for a dance class, or join a book club, then act on it! Taking action in a timely way will increase your confidence in divine Love's direction. It will also tend to bring results that best support you and others.

4) **Give Thanks:** Offer gratitude for the guidance you received during meditation or prayer, for the action you were able to take, and for the support you received from others. Bring to mind other ways in which you were guided this week and express gratitude for each of them. God is continually leading you. To expand you awareness of this, simply set an intention to notice this and give thanks throughout your day. Remember that giving thanks actually increases your capacity to receive.

Chapter 13

Heal

"I am the Lord who heals you" (Ex 15:26 TLB).

Return to Wholeness

Healing may include freedom from pain and suffering. Yet, true healing is a return to wholeness, not just in the body but also in every other aspect—spiritual, emotional, and mental. The Latin root of the verb "to heal" means to "make whole." Our bodies, emotions, and lives are largely an expression of our conscious and unconscious beliefs. Our health is directly influenced by what we hold in thought to be true for us and by the emotional feelings we entertain. When our consciousness is aligned with hope, love, joy, honesty, and peace, we're strengthened, and the body's natural healing processes do what they are designed to do.

This chapter will focus primarily on bodily healing, but the principles can apply to healing a relationship, business, or bank account as well. Form comes forth out of consciousness. Therefore, an uplifted consciousness doesn't just impact the healing process, it *is* the healing! Thought is the capacity we have that can mediate between discord and divine awareness. Thoughts that align with Divinity, such as life, truth, and love, support all aspects of healing. Fear-based thoughts can detract from healing.

Relief vs. Transformation

Relief from pain is different from true healing. One's symptoms can be chemically altered without affecting any change in one's consciousness, motives, beliefs, attitudes, character, or actions. When dealing with a physical challenge, do you ever consider the images and feelings you have been holding in consciousness? Do your dominant motives, beliefs, and way of living invite progressively worse physical conditions or support healing ones?

Divinity is the foundation and structural designer of consciousness. Consciousness precedes and dominates what is held in mind. What is held in mind is then projected onto the body. If something is blocking clear consciousness, it will affect what is held in mind and thus how the body functions. By starting with what is primary (i.e., consciousness), you have the opportunity to access a spiritual principle that underlies health and vitality and then feel this principle purifying what you are holding in mind and projecting forth in your body. It is then possible to go beyond temporary relief to complete transformation and a return to wholeness.

What is this principle based upon? It is a Supreme reality in which divine Love creates and spiritually maintains perfect health in us. This Infinite field provides exactly what we need to unblock our perception of innate wholeness. Within us exists a wise and caring Presence that can support our transformation by removing false beliefs, fears, and unsupportive actions. We are always focusing on something in consciousness. The question is this: is it leading us toward health and vitality? The thought waves we send out to our bodies either bring balance or discord. Balanced and light-filled thoughts foster healing in the body. When consciousness is filled with harmony and Divinity's Allness, the supposed presence and activity of discord and lack have no space to occupy. Perhaps the Mind of Christ is a mind that's so filled with divine consciousness and Power that anything unlike it is overruled.

During the process of healing a disease or illness, we may have life lessons to learn, inherited beliefs or programming to let go of, character to refine, or fear or pride to eliminate. We may be led to realize higher consciousness or find resources and people who can further our healing. There may be times when we seek temporary or alternative methods of healthcare to quiet pain or fear so that we can more easily fill our thoughts with hope and healing.

Ultimately, true healing leads to changes within us that reveal something of our higher Self—the essence within that is always certain, at peace, whole, and unafraid. What we call healing is really the return to perceiving the dominion and peace of Divinity expressing Itself in us. All of us can experience moments of the nature of divine Love guiding and comforting us—transforming our state of being to be more like the fearless Self instead of the fearful ego.

Transformation, or the unblocking of the Self, can bring results that show up in many ways. A man stops working in an emotionally toxic environment, and his migraine headaches disappear. A woman lets go of the fear and guilt from her teenage pregnancy, and her fertility issues clear up. A child stops feeling responsible for his parents failed marriage, and his chronic depression suddenly lifts. The stressed-out, selfish executive with a heart condition discovers the joy of unselfish giving, and he finds his heart gaining strength and natural rhythm.

The ever-present field of love is constantly operating on your behalf to heal your heart, body, and mind. As your growing freedom influences your consciousness, mentality, and actions, life tends to flow more easily. This may result in positive changes to your body, relationships, business, and/ or finances. Or it may result in your being less attached to life conditions and more concerned with your spiritual progress. Because you live in a participatory universe, when you change for the better, the nature of your world must also change. Divinity's nature includes concord, wisdom, kindness, fruition, vitality, harmony, and joy. With blocks removed, the transformed, authentic, and powerfully loving essence within you radiates forth. Also, when Love's presence is operating in your heart, awareness of it serves to inspire and heal others in your life as well.

Allness Heals

A day after hiking in the woods, an itchy silver-dollar-sized patch of poison ivy appeared on my arm. Knowing that what appears on the body is dominated by what is held in mind, that mentality is dominated by consciousness, and that consciousness is designed by Divinity, I decided to go straight to Divinity. The all-presence of Divinity filled my awareness and included the inflamed spot on my arm. As the Sunday school saying goes, there is no spot where God is not! For the next ten minutes, divine Love's control of all things dominated my mindset. Purity, wholeness, and perfection felt most real to me, and I could feel the body being healed right then and there. The itching stopped immediately, and the dollar-sized spot decreased to light pink spot the size of a dime. Within the hour, my skin was completely normal. The real healing had already taken place in an uplifted consciousness, and the body had to yield to express a purified form.

Spiritual mindedness is simply dwelling in the consciousness of all-powerful and ever—present infinite Love. The field is so mighty that even a moment of its Allness held in mind can heal. Instead of just thinking that Divinity is in you, you can also acknowledge that you are completely in Divinity. All are presently included in this total field of wholeness and Love. Ultimately, there is nowhere else to go and nothing else to do or be. Of course, such an ideal must be realized experientially, not just intellectually. Nonetheless, it helps to know what is possible. When Aramaic, the language of Jesus, was commonly spoken, the word *darkness* simply meant ignorance or lack of understanding. *Light* meant enlightenment and understanding. Spiritual healing takes place when the light of Truth and Love replaces a darkened, fearful, or misinformed consciousness. If it's in your highest good, a reformed consciousness will enable you to experience a regenerated body.

By being filled with a sense of the Allness of Infinite Perfection, there is no room for an opposite (or block) to remain. Healing starts and continues with Divinity's total power, presence, knowingness, and infinite Love. Infinity contains everything and everyone; it includes nothing unlike itself. Because the real you is included in this wholeness, claim and feel a return to wholeness. Accept your spiritual status as God's expression, and know that you are subject to sickness, disease, and injury only to the degree you believe you are, consciously or unconsciously. Take a stand for the health that's yours by spiritual nature, subject only to perfection. Exercise your spiritual immunity.

Regardless of what your body seems to be going through temporarily, let your consciousness be filled with Supreme reality, which knows only wholeness. Anything opposing divine Allness in belief will have no room to exist or function anymore. Either Divinity is totally helping you or incapable of it. Which is true? Enlightened understanding corrects a distorted or dim sense of things. The two cannot exist together at the same time. Clarity always rules over lack of clarity. A light switched on in a room always rules over the prior darkness. Darkness cannot dispel light. After all, darkness is not substantial or real; it is just the absence of light. If you light just one candle in a dark gymnasium, much of the darkness immediately disappears. If you flip on the floodlights overhead, no darkness remains. Because of the Allness of the Presence, be not afraid.

Feel what's true about God's Presence that negates the difficult appearance of your mind or body or other aspect of life needing change. An uplifted consciousness must always, in degrees, cast out darkness, discontent, disease, and other imbalances.

Not Healed Yet? Don't Fret!

If healing seems to have eluded you, there are some essential questions to ask yourself: Are you willing to recover? Do you believe and feel that your condition is being healed right now? Do you see your body and mind becoming healthy and whole again? If not, the following may help.

Fear is often the main thing that stands between us and healing. Spiritual development includes learning to courageously face up to and/ or surrender fear. Where do the courage and wisdom to do so come from? They can start from an understanding of and trust in the infinite power and love of Divinity, for whom all things are possible. No matter where you are spiritually, it is possible to feel something of Divinity's healing hand in your life. Do you believe that this loving Presence is designed to completely heal whatever needs to be in your heart, body, home, workplace, and mind? There is no disease, emotional pain, broken relationship, or financial condition that is so complex or far gone that Divinity's wisdom and love cannot transform it into wholeness and ease. The question is not whether divine Love is receptive to your needs, but rather, are you willing enough to let go of fear in order to be receptive to Divinity's unconditional, exquisite care for you? If not, ask Holy Spirit to show you how.

You can also ask yourself why you believe healing has not yet come to you. The answer to this may lead to your transformation. Is it because you believe you are not worthy of healing or that healing is not possible for you? Do you have some guilt or unforgiveness to resolve? Have you been investing in the difficulty or images of the condition, convincing yourself that it is too tough to resolve? Do you fear that God is powerless to change your diagnosis or the effects of your past decisions? Do you focus significantly more on the problem than on the solution? Be honest about what habits and beliefs are running you and decide if they're actually true or supportive for you. Then shift them toward the results you would rather have.

Concepts, unless uplifted, can also present an obstruction to healing. You may be holding a concept of what healing must look like. Thus, you may become frustrated, fearful, or depressed when your concept of healing does not take place. The real healing may be a more tender heart, lighter approach to life, compassionate concern for others, surrender of pride or fear, or more truthful conversations in your relationships. When the preciousness of such changes is your primary focus, then your attachment to what *should* be going on in your body, business, or bank account is lessened. Your life circumstances will become subservient to your spiritual growth and character. Receptive alignment with divine Will puts you in a vibration where physical adjustments can most naturally take place to serve the highest unfolding potential for all. Intend harmony and be guided and flexible in your approach.

Many people believe that one's faith affects Divinity's ability to act in one's life. Another perspective is that whatever we've done or failed to do does not change the always unconditional energy field of the Presence. The field is what heals, and it is always *on*. However, our actions or belief systems may impact our ability to perceive, access, and rely on this healing nature. By closing our eyes and hiding in the shadows while outside at high noon, the sun does not stop shining but is harder to see. Regardless of our issues, divine Love does not fail to constantly pour its healing power through us. The travesty is that fear, lack of integrity, guilt over past mistakes, resentment, or false beliefs may temporarily blind us to this Power and restrict our ability to receive Love's giving. It is like trying to find a treasure while wearing a blindfold and shackles. We can still search for the treasure, but why make it such a difficult struggle? Aligning with spiritual understanding, honesty, and caring motives helps remove such self-imposed blindfolds and chains. Then clarity, strength, and spiritual confidence can emerge naturally.

Many of us have felt undeserving of healing because of what we have done or failed to do in our pasts. We were weak or afraid, we hurt someone out of pride or anger, or we let someone hurt us. If you believe that you are being punished for past mistakes or wrongdoing, you can free yourself through honest regret, making amends, and letting guilt go. You are in a different place now than you were then, so embody the freedom that goes with this new opportunity called now. Divinity gives you a fresh canvas each day. "Because of the Lord's great love we

> "If any of you lacks wisdom, he should ask God, who gives generously to all without finding fault, and it will be given to him" (James 1:5 NIV).

are not consumed, for His compassions never fail. They are new every morning" (Lam. 3:22-23 NIV). The past has no power to stop the continuous omnipotence and presence of Love's care. For this moment be willing to surrender everything else to Love, including all doubts, hurts, regrets, resentments, and mistakes. The Great Healer invites you to seek its merciful field of divine Love for healing, to trust in its care, and to relax into and be comforted, strengthened, and blessed by it.

Spirit's Perfect Structure

Our spirituality is really the degree of clarity and power with which we experience Divinity. By holding in mind feelings of wholeness, freedom, and strength, notice how quickly and easily the body responds. Devotion to such a practice builds momentum. Spirit's dominant formations are perfectly built with the balanced and strong structures of Love and Truth. They have a cohesiveness that cannot be compromised, injured, or torn apart. Claim alignment with Spirit's perfect structure by filling your consciousness with understanding that strengthens you rather than with negativity that undermines you.

All of us have been significantly indoctrinated into societal beliefs and fears about the physiology of bodily conditions. Because of the dominance of media images, this is much more so today than a hundred years ago. At times, we forget that the body must change when consciousness does. Consciousness is primary; body is secondary. Quantum physicists and metaphysicians are both telling us this. The consciousness of the observer affects the outcome (what shows up in form). What we go looking for will tend to be found. Once belief is aligned according with the structure of spiritual laws, our bodies and lives must adjust to honor these same laws. Remember that we each have a body, not vice versa (unless we forfeit our rights from fear or ignorance).

Motivated by forgiveness, compassion, and integrity, we're led to think and act rightly from an empowered place. Love and honesty profoundly influence the health of our relationships. David's psalms put it poetically like this: "Mercy and truth are met together; righteousness and

> "… for you who revere my name, the sun of righteousness will rise with healing in its wings. And you will go out and leap like calves released from the stall" (Mal. 4:2 NIV).

peace have kissed each other" (Ps. 85:10). Workable thinking and honest, loving actions tend to bring healing and peace, because they're in accord with the perfection of Spirit's structure and laws. One definition of the Hebrew term *shalom* refers to a heart that is at peace deep down, having integrous alignment with God. Isn't this the kind of heart worth seeking?

Dominion

We have the power and freedom to rule our own bodies. Healing is founded on claiming and accepting that we are the expression of Divinity, having a birthright of dominion that is only subject to what we hold in mind. There is the only one spiritual Creator, and guess what? It isn't our parents. So what about genes? We have the right to claim our spiritual DNA (Divinely Named Authority)—our heritage of dominion over material DNA. We possess the innate power to consciously choose what we hold in mind to be true and thus what gets projected forth on our bodies.

Cutting-edge scientists are telling us that DNA is actually a blueprint containing thousands of possible instructions instead of just one set. The ones that actually play out in our bodies are not predetermined as once widely believed, but certain genes tend to be switched on by choices that we make and environments with which we surround ourselves. Exercising dominion over limited beliefs about DNA includes bringing consciousness and actions into harmony with what is spiritually true, just, and loving. This creates a healing environment and includes the capacity to act with authority over the creeping things that would try to take our power away—things such as fear, hypnotic programming, and even bacteria. "And God said, Let us make man in our image, after our likeness; and let them have dominion . . . over every creeping thing that creepeth upon the earth" (Gen. 1:26). Have you been establishing your dominion or giving up your rights?

Thoughts, feelings, and actions that are true, loving, and healing vibrate at a more powerful and dominant frequency than ones unlike them. Just one loving motive or spiritually true thought can overrule hours of negativity. Love is that powerful. Ultimately, love is easier and more effective than non-love or negatively.

Not only are we healed by God-consciousness but so is the entire world to some degree. When we feel offtrack, if we will honestly assess where we are, choose to be gentle with ourselves and others, and set an intention to uplift our minds and hearts, we can witness Divinity's power

> If you think your prayer will change God's Mind, you might be reminded that prayer is designed to change you.

and comfort coming through our consciousness. The obstructions to our total healing can be removed step-by-step, as well as instantaneously. Everything is instantaneous anyway; some things just seem to take longer.

Claiming our dominion includes the recognition that, in reality, our spiritual identity is already healed. The Self is at peace and whole now. The Self doesn't need to change; only a false or distorted sense of it does. Dwelling in this understanding can be freeing, because correcting a distorted perception is doable, whereas just trying to physically fix something in the body can seem perplexing. A spiritual shift in our perceptions can dismantle a whole wall of belief systems upon which bodily ailments may have been falsely founded. It is up to us to exercise our divinely authorized dominion and boldly tell our bodies that we have! So, from now on, what will you be subject to?

Heal Relationships

All of the above principles apply to relationships as well. Those you care about can be greatly blessed by your consciousness when it is aligned with spiritual reality—the Allness of Divinity. If a relationship needs healing, it can help to take your focus off of what seems to be missing or wrong and put it on what is already spiritually true and God-animated.

> Simple love is powerful enough to make the weightier things of life disappear.

What you focus on in a relationship tends to become magnified. If you want to experience supportive qualities, focus on those qualities and live them more fully yourself. "Finally, brothers, whatsoever things are true, . . . honest, . . . just, . . . pure, . . . lovely, . . . of a good report; if there be any virtue, and if there be any praise, think on these things" (Phil. 4:8). Dwell on what is valuable, beautiful, unique, and talented about other people and allow those aspects to expand. Be a powerful witness for and magnifier of the best they represent. You have the opportunity to fill your relationships with so much love that higher awareness can displace negative ways of being.

Practice Healing

1) **Expose Feelings that Block Healing:** Bring to mind a physical, mental, or emotional condition that needs to be healed. Take notice of how you feel. Does your body feel weak, tense, or painful? Emotionally do you feel afraid, anxious, angry, or helpless? Recognize where you feel these conditions in your body. What do you believe is blocking you from healing right now? Set an intention to remove the obstruction and then ask and trust Spirit to show you how.

2) **Identify Limiting Beliefs:** Limiting beliefs can seem to interfere with the healing process. Remember, your physical body, business, and bank account respond to what you hold in mind. For example, if you believe that you have a really bad condition, your body will more likely manifest what appears to be a bad condition. Write down the limiting beliefs you are holding about your condition or situation from the first exercise. "I always catch a cold during the winter," "I do not deserve to be healed," "I'm stuck with this, because I've had it so long," or "It runs in my family." Exposing such hidden thoughts makes it easier to shine the light of correcting Truth on them for healing.

3) **Replace "Dis-ease" with Allness:** The great Healer is the infinite field of divine Love, ever present and all-powerful. We can trust in its care, relax into its power, and be comforted, strengthened, and blessed by its activity. Lie down in a comfortable position. Visualize and feel infinite Love filling your whole body with perfect healing light. Remember, you're completely included in this infinite field of Divinity. There is no space where its transforming energy is not operating. Let intelligent healing energy fill all the spaces where there appears to be "dis-ease." Picture and embody the feeling that you are already being healed. Claim your divine birthright of dominion. Where the Allness of God is felt and realized, nothing else apart from this Allness can exist or have activity.

4) **Discover the Lesson:** Every situation in your life serves as an opportunity for you to learn about yourself, others, and life. If a bodily or relational condition hasn't yielded, ask Holy Spirit what the condition is trying to show you. For example, someone who has chest pain might learn that he needs to forgive emotional hurt from the past, release guilt, or be more accepting of the idiosyncrasies of himself or others. From the above situation, ask your body, relationship, or emotions what they are trying to teach you. When you receive the learning, you may no longer need the condition to be there as a teacher.

Chapter 14

Listen

To love someone is to listen to her heart and not just her words.

Listening Is Love

A woman called me to get some help on her marriage. After a couple of sessions her husband agreed to come for couples coaching. On the calls it was evident to me that neither partner practiced listening to the other one. Because of this, neither one felt understood, so conflict seemed to be the way they showed each other that their needs were going unmet. I asked them questions, such as: "Do you know what makes him feel disrespected? Did you ever ask her what she most wants or needs from you? Do you know why it's important for her to talk about her work?" These questions allowed the couple to access their own inner wisdom, and they realized how much better they could listen to and understand one another. Over a period of several weeks they began to hear and feel one another again, and this simple shift was enough to save their marriage.

Deep listening is an amazing gift to give, and it carries with it a powerful benefit—heartfelt connection. The root of communication means to commune, to be at one with another. One of the most satisfying things about being in a conscious relationship is that we can speak and feel that each of us is being understood. Genuine listening gives us the ability to get beyond chitchat and richly bond with people. Imagine how lonely life would feel if no one was there to fully listen to you. When you do feel alone, listening to others can help to change your state by taking the focus off yourself and discovering a whole new world in someone else.

In conversation, do you perceive another's pain, desires, needs, and values? Listening is a primary way to realize soulful relationships and help others feel supported, valued, and loved. Do you regularly hold a space for others to express their thoughts and emotions or help them discover their truth and inner guidance? If you do, you are likely supporting them toward a greater sense of meaning and freedom. People who feel listened to are more willing to be vulnerable, which invites deeper levels of honesty and sharing. Lastly, do you hear what's being said and what isn't? Both are vital.

When we don't listen well, others may feel disrespected and uncared for. Poor listening is one of the primary things that lead to breakdowns in relationships, while conscious attention nurtures and strengthens them. How would you rate the mastery of your listening ability on a scale from one to ten? Have you recently brought tears of love to another just because you made them feel understood? Let's look at several aspects that can support your listening skills and relationships.

Listen with Presence

To be an outstanding listener, give the other person your full attention and interest as if nothing else but him or her matters at that moment. Your loving consideration can make that person feel significant, help him to get clear, allow him to connect to his emotions, and discover what he truly believes, values, desires, and resists. Clarity that results from such focused attention can give that person the power to make positive changes in his life. Distracted listening fosters frustration, disrespect, and confusion. Higher awareness always gives new choices.

Effective listening requires that you be totally present in conversation—not dividing your attention between where you are and where you would rather be. If you would rather be somewhere else or with someone else, the other person will energetically feel it at some level and in that degree disconnect from you. When we love being with someone, it is easy to give her our undivided attention. When we don't, it usually shows up in the ineffective way we hear what she has to say.

Do others feel your love when you are listening? If not, try listening with every cell in your body and not just with your ears. Don't just hear the words but *feel* them with your heart. If you're a visual person, it may also help to visualize what is being said within your mind's eye. If someone is describing a difficult coworker, picture that person talking with the coworker. Maintain eye contact with the speaker to avoid surrounding distractions and to offer acknowledgement. Many people use a combination of auditory, visual, and sensory skills to listen with full presence. Again, your energy and motives will communicate the most.

Listen From Neutral

A nonjudgmental listener allows the other person to feel accepted for being where she is, no matter what her situation or emotional state is. She then has room to expand with the listener. Judgment will tend to box her in; it's like saying that she shouldn't be where she is.

Many people just want to be heard rather than have you fix their lives or solve their problems. Do you give your opinion before fully receiving what the other person has shared or before you are even asked for it? Do you listen without a need to interpret or express an opinion based on your years of experience? Are you attached to how you think the conversation should go, or are you open to its natural course? Are you anxious about what you will say next, how the situation relates to your own life, or how you already know what the speaker is going to say rather than fully seeking to feel his unique experience?

If the other person doesn't feel understood, you probably haven't listened well enough. If you disagree with her or have negative feelings toward her, it will take extra discipline on your part to be neutral about what she is saying. Any time you find yourself pushing your opinion or position in a conversation, there is likely something you need, desire, or fear. With your focus on you, it will be hard to listen to the other person.

> "He who answers before listening—that is his folly and his shame"
> (Prov. 18:13).

Lastly, any information you hear presumes something. Your spiritual perception and neutrality will allow you to hear what the presumption is, without bringing your own presumptions that could distort what is actually being shared with you. If someone says, "I had to put my dog down," find out what that means to that particular person before you presume to know.

Listen for Essence

Although it's important to accurately hear the content of what someone says to us, it is often significantly more important to receive the essence of what's being said. Essence includes, but is not limited to, the silence between the words; tone of voice, inflection, and genuineness; repeated or emphasized ideas; emotions; why something is being said; and what is being left out. Essence is around, underneath, and inside the energy of the words.

The best listening you will do will take place in your heart, not your head. When your heart is open, you'll perceive what is being expressed at the heart of another's words. Compassion and healing are possible when your heart is engaged. The other person can actually feel it and be comforted by it.

Seek to understand the feelings, beliefs, needs, fears, pain, and yearning of the speaker. When you perceive that someone is trying to communicate more than he is saying, if appropriate, be willing to ask questions that help to clarify your knowingness. "What I sense you are getting at is . . ." or "What else do you feel about that?" Then allow the other person the space to discover and reveal deeper levels of his heart and mind. How many times in relationship have you argued with someone about one thing, and when you stopped and truly listened, you realized that it wasn't even the real issue? Instead of making assumptions as if you already know what the other person is thinking and what their motives and needs are, simply ask.

It will also help you to be aware of the context surrounding another's words. Her context includes the location and conditions from where she is speaking (airport, bedroom, car, with company, etc.) as well as what has gone on or is going on in her life (she started a new relationship, is moving or switching jobs, or has an ill mother). Context impacts what's actually being shared and why. If you get people's context and motivation, they will feel moved by the way you pay attention.

> "You can win more friends with your ears than your mouth" (Anonymous).

Listening Questions

Here are some questions to ask in order to more fully understand the heart of your child, partner, friend, relative, or coworker:

1. What is most important to him right now?

2. What does she yearn for or dream about?

3. What inspires or energizes him, and what takes his energy away?

4. What is her greatest fear, pain, or wound?

5. Why is he experiencing the emotions he is?

6. What allows her to feel safe or vulnerable, and what causes her to close down?

7. What is his pattern when he is scared, tired, or overwhelmed?

8. What restores her, makes her feel easier, or brings her peace?

9. What is his communication style (i.e., visual, auditory, digital, and/or kinesthetic)?

10. What makes her feel most loved (words of appreciation, gifts, quality time given to them, touch, understanding)?

By seeking answers to such questions, you may find yourself connecting with others more authentically. Notice if your conversations suddenly become more meaningful and fulfilling.

Listen to Children

Nearly all of us have some kind of connection with children. As parents, relatives, friends, and/or mentors, we have the opportunity to enter the world of children and listen to them in a way that inspires them, crushes and angers them, or bores them to tears. There is a huge difference between really listening to children and giving them advice or telling them what to do. Children tend to respond to adult figures who talk *with* them instead of *at* them or *down to* them. We give children opportunities to express their true feelings by first creating an environment and using language that feel safe to them. Do you feel the need to fix children's problem rather than to openly receive their thoughts and feelings and support them to find their own truths and solutions? Which do you think will help them grow the most into confident, independent adults?

Even though your parents may not have truly listened to you as much as you would have liked, you can still make the most of the opportunity to communicate with children in your life; plus, you can expand on what worked positively for you while growing up. Instead of just talking to your children about *what* they are doing—sports, school, friends, chores, or homework—seek to understand their emotional and spiritual needs. As you may recall from your early years, a child's worldview looks totally different, so you don't have to take their words personally if they respond to you in an immature way. Their words are spoken within their limited understanding—one that is constantly developing, just like yours.

One good way to motivate children to express themselves is to ask open-ended questions and then listen without interruption. If there is dead air space, so to speak, don't rush in to fill it up too quickly. It sometimes takes children time to find what's in their hearts and to feel comfortable enough to express it. Inviting types of questions can encourage dialogue—for example, "Tell me about . . ."; "How do you feel about . . ."; "What do you believe about . . ."; "Why is that important to you right now?" You can then reflect back or summarize in a genuine way what they have shared and then listen further. "That seemed to upset you . . ."; "What I hear you saying is that . . ."; "What I understand you to be feeling is . . ."; "It sounds as if . . . ." Through this caring process, we can teach children how to connect with consciousness and find their own inner guidance. When children feel safe and supported enough to express their budding thoughts and feelings, they will more willingly allow parents or mentors to be active participants in their lives. If this is not already the case, think how much more rewarding it would be for you to give them what they truly need.

Spiritual Listening

When the prophet Elijah received the message that Queen Jezebel intended to kill him, he fled for his life. Later he wanted to give up and die, because his own people had forsaken their covenant with God and because all his fellow prophets had been murdered. At the pit of his discouragement, he listened and heard the voice of Divinity—not in the wind, not in the earthquake, not in the fire, but in a still small voice that motivated him to complete his mission (see 1 Kings 19).

Spirit also communicates through the still small voice in your consciousness. Spiritual intuition is a primary way for you to receive the messages you need. After you reach out for divine guidance, what you receive through your inner knowing is often a sure sign that you have been heard.

How would you rate the quality and consistency of your asking, listening, and responding to the still small voice within you? If you want clear and frequent communication with Spirit, it is available to you throughout your day. It is possible for you to have a David-like experience of feeling listened to: "God has surely listened and heard my voice in prayer" (Ps. 66:19).

> "And this is the confidence with which we approach him: that whenever we ask anything that is in accordance with his will, he listens to us" (1 John 5:14 TCNT).

Responding to inner wisdom, loving inklings, and truthful urges in relationship gives much greater perspective and results. You can perceive what you really need to say or do from a place of grace rather than willfulness. Listening spiritually happens naturally if there are no obstructions to doing so. If there are, awareness can give you the capability and intention to clear them.

Blocks and Costs

As adults we may or may not recognize the tremendous costs to ourselves and others that poor—quality listening has caused. Studies show that immediately after hearing a ten-minute oral presentation, the average listener understands and retains only about half of what was said. Most of us have played the telephone game where the first person in the circle whispers a short statement to the second, such as "Larry built a fishing boat engine out of his own spare parts." By the time the sentence gets around the circle, it has become wildly distorted. "Harry killed his bowl fishing for parts." We laugh at the game, and yet when such distortion happens at work or at home, the miscommunication in our lives and intimate relationships can be quite serious. How many mothers and daughters, husbands and wives, bosses and workers are still feuding over something they *think* they heard, when in fact something else was actually said?

Although there are many others, here are just a few attitudes and actions that block effective listening:

1. Being self-centered or critical.

2. Being dominated by fear or worry.

3. Lacking compassion and patience.

4. Not being present (i.e., scattered, distracted).

5. Reacting with ego instead of listening with heart.

6. Being unwilling to hear another's ideas or viewpoint.

7. Needing to be in control, be right, or make others wrong.

8. Feeling defensive, angry, or positional instead of neutral.

9. Having assumptions or judgments that aren't accurate or true.

10. Missing the essence of what is being said or focusing only on the content.

11. Letting your mind race ahead of the speaker and focusing on what you want to say.

12. Filtering/distorting what you hear based on your own needs, desires, and experience.

Let's look at one of the blocks to listening more closely—number 12, filtering. Your life looks unique to you and logically so, because nobody else has seen it from your eyes or heard it from your ears. You have your own combination of culture, education, career, economic and social status, vocabulary, genes, and family experience. You've had to figure out how to be safe, get love, avoid rejection and pain, and seek happiness in ways that work for you. Because of all these things, you naturally receive information through your own interpretation of how the world works—through your filter.

You can hear another's words, but unless you've had that same experience and background as he has, you may not fully understand him—unless, of course, you decide to bypass your filter! Otherwise, you won't hear from his point of view, just yours. You'll decide what is important and what is nonessential. You'll decide if his words match your belief system. When your filter dominates your listening, only things that resonate with its system will pass inspection. If you were bitten by a dog in your childhood, you may be holding the filter that dogs are mean. When Barbara tells you how much she loves her dog, part of you may not connect with her words. If you do not choose to feel what Barbara is sharing, you haven't truly listened to her.

Fortunately, your filter is not insurmountable. If you stay alert to the fact that you have one, you can transcend it in moments through loving intention and deeper listening. Listening is an act of conscious surrender. It is the willingness to discover and understand the views, desires, fears, and needs of another. It includes the desire to learn and grow—spiritually, emotionally, and intellectually. Imagine what your life would be like if you actively listened with greater humility, neutrality, and heart-connectedness. What changes could and will you make?

Practice Listening

1) **Remove the Blocks:** Identify three behaviors or attitudes that are blocking you from being a better listener. For example, do you get easily bored or distracted? Do you feel irritated or defensive? Recognize the cost that such behaviors and attitudes have on your communication and relationships. What would be possible if you freed yourself from these blocks? What

intentions will you choose in order to use your ears and heart differently in communication?

2) **Be Present:** By being grounded in your body and keeping connected in your heart, you will feel more present in conversations. Notice when you are multitasking while carrying on important conversations. Perhaps your child tries to talk with you while you make dinner and have work issues on your mind. There will be a greater chance for misunderstanding when you don't give her your full attention. This week, pick one relationship and choose to give this person your full and undivided attention whenever he speaks to you. Practice presence. Maintain eye contact, feel the words in the cells of your body, and if helpful, visualize in your mind's eye the situation being described. Give him the feeling that nothing else matters but him.

3) **Listen from Neutral:** With the same person or another, practice listening from neutral. Listen to what she has to say without letting your mind race ahead to figure out what you're going to say next and without judging, interpreting, or comparing her situation to your own life. Let go of your opinion, the need to fix any problems, and the pattern of taking things personally. Create a safe and vulnerable space so that she can genuinely share her perspective.

4) **Listen for Essence:** In your conversations this week, practice listening for the meaning behind the words of others. Remember that sometimes people say one thing, but their tone of voice, inflection, emotions, or body language may communicate something entirely different. If they dispassionately state that everything is fine, you may sense they have real needs below the surface. Consider their context too—what has gone on or is going on in their environments, lives, and hearts? Listen until others really feel understood.

5) **Listen to Spirit:** You have been designed with the ability to hear the still small voice within you. It can guide the direction

of your life with comfort, protection, inspiration, and helpful ideas and resources. Ask Divinity to guide you before you listen to others and to inspire your words before you give a response. Stay open to receive divine communication daily. Since Divinity knows how to get through to you, even amid the winds, earthquakes, and fires of change in your relationships, you just need to hold the intention to hear what you need to. Notice how such spiritual listening supports your relationships.

Chapter 15

Persevere

"Let us not get tired of doing what is right, for after a while we will reap a harvest of blessing if we don't get discouraged and give up" (Gal. 6:9 TLB).

Masters Endure

Beyond mere human efforts, the true depth of our abilities to get through adversity and to move beyond mediocrity and failure comes from the realization of Divinity within. Enduring achievement is not the result of force and grit but of humility in receiving and translating this Presence in practical ways. By accessing divine strength and wisdom in the middle of difficulties, we are transformed and made stronger in character and capacity. If we quit prematurely, we will have to come up against our own fears, limitations, and mistakes again in the future, possibly under more intense circumstances. Spiritual tenacity is developed through experience—those times when we resist temptations to give up, refuse to get distracted by lesser priorities, and resolve to get the learning and victory. Stamina is an innate quality that gets revitalized when we exercise it, slow or fast, through the dark and light, the known and the unknown.

What has it cost you in your lifetime to have given up, quit, or failed to bring to fruition what you were capable of being and accomplishing? What price in quality of life have you paid in your intimate relationships, career, and spiritual pathway? If you emotionally stack up the cost over your entire lifetime, it could feel significantly expensive.

Conversely, think about all the areas where you totally persevered and did what it took to break through roadblocks, move past confusion and doubts, and stay the course through uneventful plateaus. It may have started when you learned how to tie your shoes, read your first words, or ride a bike. Perhaps now you speak a foreign language, negotiate large business deals, or navigate the complex dynamics of a deeply committed relationship. Feel the tremendous benefits you have brought to yourself and others because of your persistence, determination, and willingness to put in extra effort and face your fears when others around you threw in the towel. The way you have endured reveals something about the depth of your love. Hopefully, after reading this chapter, you will build on what has worked so well for you and be willing to reassess where you have been halfhearted.

> Some of the biggest reasons for failure are an unclear vision, interrupted focus, and weak-hearted follow through.

The true masters in any field are those who persist beyond the point most others do. They continue in a direct line regardless of setbacks, painful struggles, and expensive tuition (i.e., mistakes on the way to learning). They don't let resistance from doubters and detractors or hardships stop them. Instead, they seem to gather strength through adversity. Many of the greatest masters have been devoted to knowing Divinity in ways that seem unreasonable to common men and women.

Love for and of the pathway itself demonstrates endurance, whether it is the pathway of salvation, enlightenment, effectively parenting children, or mastering a golf swing. True masters make never-ending improvement, always seeking a new level to master. They show up to that new level with a willingness to overcome and yield what they must for the prize. It is the same with sages and maestros. Goals and clear intentions can be essential along the way, but without endurance, they tend not to happen. Endurance, the way of the Master, is a vital part of a pathway, while goals appear to be merely the by-product of that pathway.

What Lasts

The glitz and glamour of winning, the juice of victory, snatching the award, or resolving the TV commercial problem in twenty seconds can have a deleterious effect on our psyche. Such modern day programming makes us forget that it often takes depth and determination, not quick fixes, to achieve real and lasting success. Love includes dedication to practicing principles, even when it is hard, inconvenient, or unpopular. It means having the passion to go to the edge of our capacities and stretch a little farther and to give beyond what is normal or required. Genuine love may not appear to be very glitzy, and we probably won't see it airbrushed or written about on glossy magazine covers. Yet, enduring love promises much more than temporary satisfaction. It holds the promise of growth in character, capacities, and contribution—things that ultimately can never be taken from us. The difference between failure, mediocrity, and successful breakthrough is often simply the quality of one's persistence.

Mothers who experience long deliveries, caretakers who stand vigilantly during extended patient illnesses, entrepreneurs who do what it takes to make it through start-ups and tough economic cycles, creators who struggle triumphantly to bring their art into beautiful form, students who persist through arduous assignments, and spiritual devotees who search and pray endlessly to feel the divine Presence are just some of the unspoken heroes and heroines of determination. In all these examples, they do so not just for the prize but for the joy of knowing that they're on their chosen paths. What one becomes in her journey of endurance *is* the reward. The other gains may not be lasting or really all that important in the grand scheme of things.

Nolan Ryan, one of the great professional baseball pitchers of all time, used to work out in the weight room for hours after pitching a full game of nine innings. His character and willingness to do more than what was required enabled him to play baseball well beyond the age of most major league starting pitchers today. For some strange reason, endurance is not talked about enough today, even in a world where people painfully give up and forsake essential practice and principles in mass numbers. Some drop out of school, forsake diet habits or music practice, or walk away from relationship growth opportunities and families. Others change jobs instead of giving what they are truly capable of right where they are. Sadly, some even take their own lives.

While wisdom may call an individual to leave a situation in life, if one walks away too soon, the lessons will not have been learned and will have to be repeated later in some other form. Opportunities for expansion tend to be handed to people only when they have truly fulfilled their roles in their current situations.

When I was in second grade, my teacher sent home a report card to my parents that said I couldn't read very well. This belief became tattooed into my mind when my parents showed concern about the assessment. Regardless of this performance handicap, I did my best from grade school through high school, even though assignments would take me four times as long as they did my classmates. While I was in college and still struggling with reading, I learned that metaphysically some things we identify with are just limiting beliefs. When we find a more empowering belief, we do not have to be bound by limitations of the former one, no matter how long we have believed it or invested in it.

A breakthrough for me was the spiritual idea that as an image and likeness of Divinity, each of us reflects the divine Mind. With recognition, we can claim the same abilities as this Mind. I reasoned that if divine Intelligence could read, so could I. Afterward, I felt an empowered certainty that helped me break the chains of the "poor reader" label that my teacher had given me more than a decade earlier.

Following this revelation, instead of fearing or being frustrated with reading, I suddenly loved to read. My capabilities developed steadily as well. Later, the dean of the university awarded me High Honors at graduation. Now, many years later, reading has become one of my favorite pastimes. It would have been easy for me to give up on the possibility of becoming a successful reader, and it's hard to imagine how difficult my life would have been if I had.

> Focused determination unveils inner strength which enables one to persevere successfully.

Divinity Endures

How often have we failed to ask Spirit for guidance or forgotten to be grateful for the grace that has shown up for us? How many times have we made the same mistake over and over, not done what we know we could have or should have, or chosen things that aren't supportive of our life energy? What about the hundreds of times we made something or someone more important than experiencing Divinity? Still, the infinite loving field that is ever present continues to care for us and bless our lives. God's love for us is enduring and unconditional. If we understood and felt this more powerfully, perhaps we would be more willing to be like this Supreme example in the way we treat ourselves and others.

True love comes from a Presence deep within us and does not vary due to outward conditions. It is like the calm depth of the sea that remains undisturbed regardless of the storms raging on the surface hundreds of feet above. The nature of Divinity's love stands with unshakeable stability and is united with us at all times. Often, negative conditions in our lives call forth even greater expressions of care, concern, and compassion from the infinite depths of Love within us. If we answer the call and demonstrate these qualities during challenging times, our spiritual stamina—our capacity to endure—will strengthen and expand.

> "Give thanks to the Lord for he is good; His love endures forever" (Ps. 106:1 NIV).

Men and women who have not developed an enduring character may end a relationship prematurely without ever giving or receiving the real learning, healing, and blessings that were available. In your most important relationships, are you the one who is able to persist? Are you able to give more during the times you don't feel like it? Or is it just easier to end it and find someone else with whom you will also only go so far? By choosing the field of divine Love and stretching your willingness, you can feel both supported and able to support another when he is going through difficult growing edges, pain, fear, or loss. Your own self-worth and spiritual vigor will expand in the process.

If you ever feel strained mentally, emotionally, physically, or spiritually, here are two other ways to sustain yourself: 1) hold in mind those amazing individuals throughout history who have valiantly endured challenges and let their lives help carry you along your journey, and 2) seek to embody qualities that support endurance, such as self-honestly, humility, willingness, resilience, and courage. Life tends to favor those who do not quit but instead are determined to find a way and take action, even when things seem bleak. One of the all-time great examples of this principle is Helen Keller. Her life and that of her teacher, Anne Sullivan, serve as inspiration of what is possible through endurance even in the darkest of times.

The Extra Mile

You may have already endured a lot for what you love, such as pain, suffering, and fear of the unknown or emotional struggle. Yet there may be more to move through. To receive the learning and blessings designed for you, are you willing to transcend rejection, setbacks, failures, mistakes, health and emotional challenges, or looking bad? Many of the greatest people in history have overcome these types of difficulties.

Abraham Lincoln suffered so many setbacks, losses (including the death of two sons), rejections, bouts of depression, and career failures that it could seem incredible for him to be known as one of the eminent US presidents. The Civil War was perhaps one of the greatest difficulties ever faced by a US president, yet one of the reasons Lincoln was a great leader is because he did not quit, regardless of the pressures he faced. His Gettysburg Address reminds us that "all men are created equal." You have the option to quit in the midst of trials and tribulations or move forward through them. Each troublesome life experience you victoriously pass through increases your power to overcome future challenges.

True love enables you to persevere, go the extra mile, and double your efforts, if required, after a major setback occurs. Great business professionals, salespeople, parents, athletes, and spiritual leaders have proven this. Persistence is a huge advantage in every aspect of life from business and finances to health and fitness, and especially in relationship and partnership. If you're not getting the results you desire, you may want to take an honest look at just how persevering you have been when things haven't gone the way you expected.

Enduring love communicates and invites feelings of trust, safety, and assurance. Nurturing growth, lasting connection, and romance all thrive on that which is unshakable.

Inspiring Character

A mother's love is a prime example of love that is unconditionally lasting. Through the decades, my own mother has endured many personal and family challenges, emotional and health issues, and financial stresses. Regardless of whatever her six children have gone through, she has always remained a woman of compassion and love, and she continues to inspire me.

> Along the spiritual path, it is better to move ahead slowly than to quit, retreat, or get lost in harmful, life wasting, byways.

Demonstrating enduring love is what allows us to find new hope and bring our best to each day—no matter what happened the day before. Innately, all of us express some degree of Divinity, which provides the strength for us to move through whatever problem lies before us. But, life is a test; we have to walk our own road to discover if we have what it takes to make it through. Nobody can find this out for us.

The faithful serve to teach and inspire us. We also receive many practical benefits from those who have pressed on. More than a century later, we still use lightbulbs to read and brighten our nighttimes because Thomas Edison loved the ideas of light and invention so much. It took well over a thousand attempts before he discovered the right combination of materials to create a lightbulb that wouldn't burn out quickly. He stayed with it, often working long days and nights, until he successfully tested a carbonized threaded filament.

History is filled with victorious individuals who persevered beyond what seemed humanly possible because their love was so deep and committed. When the signers of the US Declaration of Independence concluded the document with a mutual pledge of their lives, fortunes, and sacred honor, they meant it, proven by the fact that several of them soon lost their homes, fortunes, and lives. But, their commitment for truth handed freedom to millions who would come after them. What they wrote and stood for still serves us today. That which is based on truth and love continues on. That which is not will fail sooner or later. Ultimately, all material conditions and things will pass, and only spiritual essence will live on. With this knowledge, even the most difficult thing can be minimized with a proper perspective, because Divinity's depth, breadth, height, and might within are sure and enduring.

Passion and Perseverance

Inspiration will impel you to pursue a goal, but perseverance will get you through rejection, obstacles, and setbacks. Another president, John Quincy Adams, wrote about how courage and perseverance have the magical charm to make difficulties disappear and obstacles vanish. Perseverance is related to passion, which comes from the Latin root *pati*, meaning "to suffer" (i.e., to endure with patience—to do what it takes to see it through). When you're passionate about something, you will more likely stay in the game and give it your best, no matter what. Your burning desire cannot be put out by mere circumstances. True passion is relentless; it has heart. One way to awaken your passion is to emotionally reconnect with the powerful reasons in your heart that are impelling you to move forward. If you do, then doing the hard thing will become easier. Reasons give us the fuel to overcome obstacles and keep our focus.

Our culture seems to put too much emphasis on feelings and not enough on character. Feelings alone can become confining. Most feelings are just signals that something needs to change in the way we view things or in the action we need to take. If we're afraid, it can mean that we need to get better prepared for what lies ahead. If we're frustrated, we may need to complete some communication or establish better boundaries. Feelings should be our friends not our jailers. Expanding character leads to freedom and is developed by the things we must do and choose to do to serve higher principles rather than just short-term comfort. When we do what is required (i.e., what's in alignment with our highest good) beyond what we may *feel* like doing for comfort alone, we can discover self-fulfilling rewards of enlarged capacities and excellence.

Constancy of the Field

Have you experienced challenges that resulted in incredible struggle or suffering? Marcus Aurelius said that "Nothing befalls a man except what is in his nature to endure." You're designed with the capacity to face your demands. During such times in the future, remember the constancy and presence of the infinite field of Love operating within and around you. Know that there is no separation between Divinity and Its expression (you), so you can endure if wisdom calls you to do so. If you temporarily feel overwhelmed, lost, defeated, or fearful, it may encourage you to know that God never gives up on you. You are spiritually equipped to continue and to feel the spiritual nourishment you need along the way toward victory, freedom, and peace.

There is a profound scene in the movie *I Am David* (Lions Gate Films, 2005). A young boy in a concentration camp was feeling hopeless. He asked his older mentor/friend why he should go on living if life is so bad. With conviction, his wise friend told him that it's only by being alive that he has the opportunity to make his life better. Realizing that your own evolution and that of others is of precious importance, cherish your life and the opportunities you have to make it better. Your commitment to persevere will come from the spiritually and emotionally connected reasons you have kept alive in your heart. With a strong enough why, you can be sustained through just about anything. By persisting in love, you will reveal more of your divine Strength, limitless resources, and infinite possibilities for progress and joy.

Practice Persevering

1) **Sense Divinity's Nature:** Recall how Divinity's love for you has endured at times when you were not at your best. Divine Love is everywhere and always, even when you reject It, blame It for what ego has done, forget to thank It, or make poor choices. Your own strength of heart is an expression of the unchanging, enduring nature of this Love. Practice feeling this Presence in your life and notice how it continually blesses you, no matter what you seem to be going through.

2) **Recognize Your Faithfulness:** Remember a time when you were really committed to something—when you were confronted with an extreme challenge or difficulty—and you didn't give up. Maybe you experienced falls and scrapes when learning a new sport, spent long hours of study to complete a degree, or endured days in the wilderness when navigating a difficult relationship. All the skills that you needed to persist are still within you, ready to be fully activated. Recall and emotionally stack up these victorious feelings the next time you need encouragement in the middle of a trying time.

3) **Endure Relationship Challenges:** Just as those lights of higher consciousness throughout history have persevered, you too can endure through relationship and other struggles. There will be times when people let you down or are difficult to be with. You may face times of poor health, career upset, or dark nights of the soul and yet still have to be around other people! Your character will be tested. Will you stay grounded in the presence of a controlling boss, communicate your needs patiently to your angry partner, or forgive your friend who failed to keep his word? Write down and live three action steps to more truthfully and lovingly persevere with someone or something that is currently challenging you. Then regularly measure what you accomplish.

Chapter 16

Be Present

"Don't be anxious about tomorrow. God will take care of your tomorrow too. Live one day at a time" (Matt. 6:34 TLB).

Are You Here Now?

Presence maximizes the opportunity to realize unity with our Source—the Source of joy, inspiration, wisdom, and power. Presence also makes us feel more at ease, less in pain and suffering, less identified with our ego, and more identified with our highest Self (which has limitless capacities).

Studies in the field of psychology have shown that the average person is consciously present (i.e., undistracted from what is happening at the present time by thoughts of the past or future) only about one-fourth of the time. If that's the case, we could be missing about three-fourths of our lives, because we are not present to consciously participate in them. If our focus and energy is in the future or past, we are absent from the true experience of life happening now. Even if you don't consider yourself an average individual, the above statistics may be a clarion call for you to live more consciously and consistently in the moment to maximize the precious time you have here.

It may be helpful for you to have a trigger or signal that reminds you when you're not present, so you can choose to return there. For many the signal is simply a feeling of unease or disconnection. For others it is when heart-presence seems weak or missing. Decide for yourself what qualities or feelings you embody when you are fully present and when you're not. These distinctions will increase your awareness and empower your choices.

There is a tremendous cost to our relationships and our own well-being for being distracted and not present. Too often, we're busy with past regrets, anger, grief, and pain. We may also spend valuable energy in anxiety, worry, or nervous anticipation of the future. Which category best describes you? The truth is that the future never arrives, and the past cannot be regained. In a sense, neither past nor future is real. The only place we can experience reality is right here and now. We always have just one moment at a time, the only moment when we can receive the ideas and resources needed to resolve our challenges, enjoy life, create our dreams, and live passionately.

> Quit mourning the past. It doesn't belong to you anymore, and it cannot return even with all of your efforts. The present is yours, so own it and improve your life there.

The Now is all we possess, and because it's continuous, it's a truly unlimited resource. The future, which hasn't been designed yet, only exists as a concept. It will be influenced by many things, including our choices and the choices of others. This moment is the only time to share, receive, and experience the wonder and beauty of life. Are you here now?

Open the Gift

This moment is a gift meant especially for you. Perhaps that is why it is called the present. What really matters is the way that you receive it. Will you open this gift graciously or even stay conscious enough to receive it at all? The opportunity of your present will last one moment and then be gone. If you are the type of person who is living in the divorce that happened four years ago or in the possibility of a future promotion next month, you may be missing all the "presents" arriving today. In reality, the always-unfolding now is not based on the last moment or moments from ten years ago. The present is its own special gift—unlike any before—and it should be received spontaneously and preciously. Each now contains unlimited possibility. Your entire career direction, relationship status, and way you identify yourself could shift considerably today if you were truly open to the pristine nature of your new moments. Stop crowding your mind and heart with heavy past and worry-filled future thoughts and feelings, and you'll have more space to experience positive possibility.

One summer I worked at a camp for high school kids in the Rocky Mountains. During a break, I was shooting baskets on an outdoor court when a rain shower started. I was so fully engaged in the joy of what I was doing that I did not want to stop, and I quickly lost track of time (which is typical when we are fully present). Another counselor found it interesting that I continued shooting baskets in the rain, and out of curiosity, she ran over and joined me. We became friends from that experience and deepened our friendship throughout the summer. She did not know it, but I had recently been going through a career change and didn't have a job waiting for me at the end of the summer.

Several months later, she called to tell me about a coaching job at a high school in the Midwest. At first I dismissed the idea, because I was living in California fifty feet from a beach that I loved. Then I remembered the aliveness we both felt while shooting baskets during that rainstorm. This triggered me to become fully present again. As a result, I listened with new and unobstructed ears and became open to her idea. After researching the school and applying for the job, I was accepted and then worked at that high school for ten fulfilling years. Hundreds of wonderful relationships came out of that one experience of being present. Just one moment of opening to the gift of the present can be profoundly life changing.

> In order to maximize your experience, take the fullness of your heart wherever you go.

Moments of Being Present

Let's look at some experiences when we tend to live in present-moment awareness:

- Intimacy

- Emergencies

- Laughter and joy

- Athletic competition

- ravel and vacations

- First-time experiences

- Witness of breathtaking beauty

- Moments of peace and stillness

- Outstanding musical performances and theatre

- Certain careers, such as surgeon, air traffic controller, firefighter, military service, dancer, actor, and public speaker

Choose Now

If you tend to be present during any such experiences, you are likely focusing on something more important than your past or future. You have no resistance to giving your full attention to now-ness. Your day-to-day activities may not seem to require that much presence, but imagine how much more alive your life could be if you gave your full attention to it. Even seemingly trivial things have the potential to become magical moments.

If you find yourself regularly fighting with what is, being worried and fearful, putting off enjoyment until someday, or regretting past losses or mistakes, it is almost a guarantee that you are not present; you are missing much of your life that is unfolding before you. As a practice, notice when you're not giving your full attention to what you're doing. This noticing allows a shift to become present.

In the midst of one of the most difficult circumstances of my life, I turned to a spiritual mentor. He gave me advice that made me angry at the time, but since then, it has helped me again and again. Right after relating my saga of loss, lack, and struggle-filled drama, he said, "You better love where you are, because that's where you are." His words eventually inspired me to face and accept where I was instead of resenting and resisting it. Formerly, I had been in a no-win mentality of fear, worry, and regret. The more I became present and accepting of myself, the more dominion I gained over my life situation. Only then could I see what to do and feel the inspiration to do it.

Do you love where you are, or do you resist it in any way? Perhaps you resist your body, job, debt, or relationship. What you resist will persist! If you are choosing to be here or are feeling joyful, at ease, and peaceful, you are likely living in the now. If you are feeling anxious, tense, frustrated, or angry, you are likely wasting your innate energy in resistance to life. In order to be fully here and now, you must receive this moment with unencumbered acceptance. Besides reducing mental struggle and pain, living life by choosing now is the most fluid, energizing, and abundant way to live. Conversely, resisting anything about the present is a depleting and defeating way to live. This moment has arrived; you can't stop it, no matter how hard you try or how many years you struggle against it. You may as well surrender to it.

What if the present moment is undesirable? You still have needs, desires, and problems, right? Through acceptance of what is, you can still be present to it instead of arguing against it. From this open place, you will more naturally receive what you need to promote your own growth and serve others. Regardless of the situation, you will be more at ease and empowered to see and do what you need to.

It has been said by mystics that there are no problems in the now, because the present comes with everything we need for this moment. Problems exist in thoughts of the future or the past and in our resistance to what is actually occurring. Often what we think we are lacking only exists in a perception of what we think should be or could have been, which is merely speculation. Understanding this can make life easier. Presence is what puts problems in their proper perspective, so they don't dominate us. From a higher perspective, right now is always complete, lacking nothing, and without problems.

There was a period in my life when I was sick and felt like I was dying, I thought I believed I knew what my problem was—the horrible physical state of my body. Ultimately, the condition of my body wasn't the problem; it was my fear of and resistance to it. I began to overcome the fear and resistance by focusing on the love I could express, even with the chronic illness. At first it was difficult even to smile. Later, I felt strengthened and even had glimpses of joy. From that space, it felt easier to create a vision of what I wanted to experience, and to let the past be what it was instead of trying to make it into what it supposedly should have been. As one might expect, my bodily symptoms became less relevant to my new focus. Instead of my body controlling how I could or should feel, I was able to find moments of peace. As life-strengthening moments emerged from choosing now, I received ways to improve my life. Eventually I experienced complete recovery. Yet, the real healing was in a new approach to life: choosing to enjoy and love being right where I am, because that's where I am.

Do you still require things to improve before you will feel better? What if I told you the future will never solve your problems? The future can never actually bring change, because change always happens now! The only way to fix problems is to receive the solution and take action in the present. It is exhausting and impossible to try to fix a problem from the past or in the future.

Much of the pain in life comes from wishing we'd taken a different path. Our memories of the past only exist as an interpretation of the perceptions we had at the time. Two people will remember an identical event in two completely different ways and choose different meanings for the event. Our paths cannot be different than they were. No matter how they look, they were perfect to bring us to where we are today. Let go of the futile craving to be somewhere else or wish that things had been different than they were. Usually, for many reasons beyond our limited scope of understanding, things cannot be different than they are right now. Resting into this awareness, we are able to move forward from a relaxed alignment to reality—a place that enables us to receive what we need to make progressive changes, experience healing, and gain greater understanding.

> If you live in the present moment wisely and deeply, there is no past to bemoan and no future to be anxious about. Let this awareness give rejuvenation to your mind, body, and spirit.

Traffic-Jam Bliss

When you prepare a meal or go to a meeting, how much of the time do you concentrate with loving attention on what you are doing instead of thinking about things such as "My credit card debt is out of control," "Jerry shouldn't have said that to me," or "I wonder if Jane will be home this evening"? When your attention is somewhere else, you cannot fully take part in your life at hand. When you listen to your children, coworkers, or significant other, how much of the time do you fully engage in understanding and feeling what is being shared with you? By being fully engaged with life a lot more than 25 percent of the time, you will become aware of all kinds of opportunities—beauty, pleasure, ideas, people, adventures, and love—that you never noticed before!

Relaxing into the present can eliminate your stress and improve your health. Stress may be viewed as whatever you don't want. The way to transcend stress is to willingly choose what seems to be causing it.

It was ten o'clock on a Tuesday night, five miles from home on a nearly vacant freeway. I was hungry and tired after a long work day that had started at dawn. Suddenly, as I came around a curve, my heart sank. Traffic was completely stopped due to road construction. Before me were miles of red taillights, and not one car was moving. At first I felt numb; then I became angry and stressed. I left the present, jumped to the future, and started to think about how I needed rest, because I had to start work early the next morning. In my mind, it would be a critically important day. Then, in a moment of clarity, I thought to myself, "What if I chose to love being on this freeway right now? How would this affect my experience?" My car had not moved, but my desire to experience the power of the present had.

I turned on some music and began to groove on the bench seat of my Oldsmobile. I opened the sunroof and started to enjoy a jillion stars pulsating above me. I became interested in the driver and passenger on either side of my car, and we shared smiles and head nods. Realizing that I had the gift of a space to pray without interruption, I gratefully did so. Amazingly, for several minutes I truly did not want to be anywhere else in the universe than right where I was—lane three, Interstate 5, five miles from home. It took more than an hour to travel those five miles. Surprisingly, when I arrived home, I felt refreshed, energized, and content—exactly like I would have after a good night of sleep. This feeling carried into the next day, which was productive and fun. Was this experience a trivial incident? Perhaps it was in the grand scheme of things, but the ramifications for larger arenas were truly significant. For me it symbolized that when we let go of fighting the present moment—when we yield to divine Love's potential, timing, and orchestrated activity in us—there is nowhere else to be except here and now. When we fully understand the completeness of this moment, there will be nothing else to want or need.

Let Go

"The kingdom of heaven is at hand" [i.e., here and now], so the Lord taught (see Matt. 4:17), but perhaps living in such a kingdom requires that we bring nothing else to it. Ultimately we have to let everything else go. To fully enter this kingdom at hand, baggage is not allowed—no emotional pain; no feelings of being unloved, misunderstood, or inferior; and no regrets, sorrow, hurt, memories of mistakes, or fears of the future. If we try to take all those heavy bags with us, entering the present will feel like an enormous challenge.

We can frame the past and future with compassion and forgiveness in order to experience something of heaven right where we are. All mortal things must change. When one avenue of delight seems to be shut down, another will open. If we fail to take our view off of the closed road, we may not see what has been made available to us on the new road. There is a Talmudic teaching that instructs us not to cast stones into the well that gives us our water. Divinity is our supply, and life in the present is Divinity's gift to us. When we carry the stones of past thoughts and feelings into the present well of life, the Divine may feel distant or cut off to us. All the power and opportunity of life and all of the healing, creativity, satisfaction, beauty, passion, connectedness, meaning, and love exist in the rock-free well of now.

One way to access the at-handedness of heaven is to come to this moment as if it is the only moment that ever existed. Ted Williams, one of the greatest hitters in baseball history, said that he approached each at bat as if it were his first *and* his last! Perhaps this practice of presence helped him to break so many records. The continuous present is when and where we can experience *our* best and greatest—our unlimited Self. Always-ness is the window through which our unlimited Self shines through. Perhaps the infinite potential for Divinity to express itself through us, in us, and as us, is the kingdom waiting for us at hand.

Creativity

The truly creative person knows that something can happen out of nothing. In fact, "nothing" is the ideal space from which to create anything. Look at the first book of Genesis, the classic spiritual story of Creation. The earth was not made out of something; God made it out of nothing. It was first "without form and void" (Gen. 1:2). When God said, "Let there be light" (Gen. 1:3), there was no obstruction or limitation, no past burden or anxious future blocking the light, so Creation freely appeared. This is a model for us to let the light of our creative ideas emerge in an unrestricted way.

In order to experience the creativity and possibility you desire, enter new moments with the freedom of now—the stillness/lightness that includes the Allness of infinite possibility—as would a painter with a blank canvas and infinite potential. With this approach, Spirit, the ultimate Artist, is invited to be whatever and however it wants to be within us. Our job is to "let there be light"; to find completeness, satisfaction, and eternity in this moment; to allow for something perfectly spontaneous to happen out of nothing, so that we can experience love, contribution, learning, beauty, adventure, and passionate connection each day.

Practice Being Present

1) **Become Conscious:** Make a list of five areas in your life where you most often feel that you live in the continuous now, such as when you bathe your child, make love, or work in your garden. Next, notice if there are moments in your day when you typically go unconscious, such as when you drive to work and wonder how you got there or sit in a meeting and later forget most of what was discussed. During these times, you may be lost in thought, fear, stress, or fantasy. The practice of noticing a lack of presence is an essential step to coming back to the present.

2) **Body Awareness:** Another step to become more available to life is to be more grounded in your body. In order to get centered, first notice how you feel right now. Do you feel overwhelmed, tense, frustrated, anxious, or distracted? Next, sit or lie down in a comfortable position. Feel the weight of your body being supported by what you are resting on. Start at the top of your head and slowly move your awareness down toward the tips of your toes. Notice how being fully in your body helps you to feel more alive to the powerful and peaceful Presence in your heart.

3) **Experience Now:** From your Not Present list in the first exercise, choose two areas of your life where you would like to practice being totally present. Before you start to do these activities, make a conscious choice to practice presence no matter what. Give your complete focus and attention to the activity, including your mind, body, and emotions. Feel the warm water as it flows onto your baby, listen to your spouse's tone of voice behind the words, smell the scent of the orange blossoms in the air as you pull the weeds in your flower bed. Engage all of your senses. Feel the vibrating energy of your heart presence—the peace, joy, love, and gratitude that accompany the experience. Sense that just being alive is enough to make you feel complete satisfaction and joy.

4) **Accept What Is:** Are you resisting certain circumstances in your life? Whenever you think about these situations, notice if you feel nervous, frustrated, angry, or stressed. Now consider the cumulative pain, struggle, and loss of life energy that have arisen from this resistance. When you accept and even love where you are, exactly the way things are, you'll start to feel calmer and more resourceful. What can you declare anew from this accepting place? For example: "I accept the fact that my boss gave Joe the promotion." Acceptance means that you are simply living in true relationship with what is. From this place, you are better able to make positive changes. Practice accepting your difficult situation exactly the way it is. Imagine all feelings of resistance leaving your body. Notice how this helps you feel more certain, capable, and relaxed.

Chapter 17

Feel Protected

"You bless the godly man, O Lord; you protect him with your shield of love" (Ps. 5:12 TLB).

Protect Progress

When my son was born, I felt a powerful, protective energy that I'd never quite experienced before. I wanted him to be able to experience everything wonderful and to protect him from harm, unnecessary pain, and suffering. In the nursery room, my heart wrenched just to see him shiver and cry for a few moments. When people walked in and talked loudly, I asked them if they would please keep their voices down. The way Divinity gives us safety is infinitely greater and wiser than such human efforts.

Spirit is constantly leading you in ways that protect you and others. There is a pathway that best nurtures your soul development and keeps you from unnecessary harm and loss. By its effortless nature, Divinity watches over you and offers protection from pathways, people, and behaviors that do not ultimately support you. Aligning with divine Love's energy can shield you from beliefs and actions that oppose your highest nature and spiritual expansion. Nonetheless, you have free choice. In order for you to best respond to Divinity's protection, it helps to tune into it and understand how its laws operate on your behalf. In this way you can maximize your results, fulfillment, and safety.

Protection basically means to be shielded from injury, loss, or suffering. It is a great concept but doesn't consistency matter? How protected would you feel if there were several periods throughout your days and weeks when you were not shielded at all and were a sitting target? Consistency, like gravity, makes us feel more secure.

Imagine a builder who buys some land and works hard to design the architecture, purchases building materials, and hires workers for the project. Then, just as the structure is nearing completion, the builder allows a demolition ball to destroy what has been built—ruining nearly everything he had previously worked so hard to create. After painfully regretting the setback and loss, he starts to rebuild all over again. Wow, what a difficult way to make progress!

If you look honestly, you may see that you have done the same thing with your life at times. After making progress for a while, perhaps you allowed a thought, person, place, or activity to come in to obstruct or demolish what you had built up. If you are like me, the quality of your life paid dearly for the damages. The good news is that, with awareness, you can build more wisely right from where you are today. You have the opportunity to defend what is good and pure within you—your home, family, business, and places of inspiration or joy—with the vigilance of a wise and diligent builder. All you have to do is ask for, listen to, feel, and follow ever-present divine protection. Doing this consistently would mean less suffering, pain, and loss in your family and personal life. Some of life's pain, suffering, and loss may be unavoidable for reasons that serve your spiritual growth, and yet by staying conscious, you can reduce or eliminate unnecessary upsets, destructive tendencies, and unwise decisions and bolster the citadels of your consciousness and environment.

About seven years ago, I had a childhood baseball card collection that contained mint-condition cards from the 1950s, as well as many other cards from later years. After years of storing them in a closet, I had no idea what the cards were worth. Only when a thief had taken the cards did I do research to assess what had been stolen and discovered that just those cards from the 1950s were valued at tens of thousands of dollars. I'd been foolish in the way I had stored them and didn't realize what I really had until it was gone. Sound familiar? Whatever is unprotected in life is subject to damage or loss. Perhaps for you the loss came in the form of your integrity, peace, investments, connection with loved ones, or happiness. Hopefully, this chapter will give distinctions and strategies for you and those you love to experience a greater sense of protection.

Trust and Protection

Have you ever thought that your life was unfair, difficult, or declining? Perhaps all of us have at one time or another. Joseph, the youngest son of Jacob, was hated by his older brothers because his father favored him. They eventually threw Joseph into a pit and left him to die. Then they decided to make some money by selling Joseph into slavery to some Arabian merchants who were traveling to Egypt. Later, Joseph was falsely accused of sexually assaulting his master's seductive and manipulative wife and was imprisoned for years. No matter what situation Joseph found himself in, he did not wallow in self-pity, resentment, or anger. He knew who he was and that his purpose was to serve the Divinity he respected and loved so much—the God he leaned on for his very life. Joseph's sense of identity and purpose allowed him to feel secure regardless of his circumstances. He eventually used his spiritual gift of interpreting dreams (including the Pharaoh's) to find liberation.

Amazingly, Joseph went from being a lowly accused criminal confined to a dungeon to being second in command over all of Egypt, next to the Pharaoh himself. By taking responsibility for his experience, consistently acting with integrity, and trusting in the Presence of divine protection, Joseph responded to difficulties in a way that empowered him. During a seven-year famine, this enabled him to wisely save multitudes from starvation, including the very brothers who had once rejected him. (See Genesis 37-48). The way you connect with your identity, purpose, and trust in Divinity's protection will have an impact on your life and the lives of others. "As a reward for trusting me, I will preserve your life and keep you safe" (Jer. 39:17-18 TLB).

One night while on a date many years ago, my girlfriend and I got into my car near a restaurant where we had just finished dining. Because there was no parking available on the main street, I had parked on a dimly lit side street. After closing the door, my girlfriend yelled at me, "Lock the door; someone is coming!" After hitting the power button, I turned to see a man in a hooded sweatshirt with a revolver pointed at my head who demanded, "Give me your wallet."

What he didn't know about me was that I had only recently come back from the pit of financial ruin, that I had forty dollars in my wallet, and that I felt strongly that those forty dollars belonged to me, not him. The earnings had come out of the intense heat of a long struggle. To me, the money represented substance of my identity that couldn't be taken away—the perseverance, courage, and discipline that were required of me to come back from the depths. No, he was not going to take what was rightfully mine, and I was certain about that. The truth of my conviction seemed more vital than my human life, and I felt protected by an inner power. Instead of obliging the hoodlum, I promptly yelled at him. "Get out of here!" He appeared startled and probably hadn't heard such a response in prior holdups. Undeterred, he said he was going to "waste me" and cocked the trigger with the gun still pointed at my skull.

Was my stance wise? You can play Monday-morning quarterback for yourself, but at the time, it was just what came out. When you squeeze somebody extremely, you get what's inside of them. The thug squeezed me, and he got the conviction from the experience I'd just come through. If I had given him the wallet, he still could have shot me, stolen my car, and/or raped my girlfriend, right? Instead, I did what my inner voice told me to do, and for some reason the man backed away from the car and ran off. Both my girlfriend and I were totally protected, and her story of the event was later published in a national magazine.

> "God is our refuge and strength, a very present help in trouble"
> (Ps. 46:1).

Ultimately our protection comes from who we are, not just what we do. It may help you to affirm the reality of your protection because of your spiritual nature. You can declare, "I am a spiritual being, so I am always protected." What you powerfully hold in mind to be true will tend to manifest.

Victim and Perpetrator

If we ever intimidate, forcefully control, or abuse another in any way—verbally, emotionally (even with passive-aggressive silence), spiritually, or physically—at some level we will feel inner guilt. This guilt contributes to feeling isolated, vulnerable, and unprotected. By breaking the pattern of being a perpetrator and letting go of guilt, we can feel more fully shielded from the attacks of others.

What about the victim side of the equation? The media, legal, and political machines that seem to control the messages broadcast throughout the world love to dramatize and amplify the victim-perpetrator model. There can't be a victim without a perpetrator, and vice versa. A victim mentality attracts and engages attacks in various forms. A bully needs and seeks out the weakling, the person not prepared to defend himself. At a core level, both victim and perpetrator feel out of control with life situations, choices, and identity. By discovering this pattern and then choosing personal responsibility, the victim-perpetrator model is dissolved to a large degree.

If you feel like a victim in some area of your life, how could you become better about refusing to play the victim, use better strategies, and feel safer? Let's look at several things that can increase your feeling of certainty and spiritual alignment, whether in giving a speech, building a business or family, or walking down a dark street late at night. The first two things that can strongly influence your certainty are what you choose an experience to mean and how you choose to act (based on the meaning you've chosen).

If you heard a loud noise when nobody else was in the building, what would it mean to you? Your actions would be influenced by the meaning you choose. Your results would then come from your actions, based on the meaning you selected. Empowering meanings combined with progressive actions yield positive results. Conversely, disempowering meanings and ineffective actions create undesirable outcomes, especially over the long term. If you look at the results you've experienced in life, you may find that several things affected the meaning you interpreted and the actions you then took. The following five factors likely impacted your degree of effectiveness and happiness and possibly even your feeling of safety and protection. They determined whether you felt phenomenally resourceful and empowered, totally defeated and victim-like, or anywhere in between.

1. Your priorities and focus

2. Your emotional state at the time

3. Your beliefs about yourself, others, and life

4. The quality of questions you asked and the language you used

5. Your spiritual consciousness (and thus capacity to feel and trust in Divinity's Presence)

Awareness of what lies behind your effectiveness and state of being gives you profound opportunities to make progress. Increasing the quality of each of the above factors will tend to lead you toward better results and a more fulfilling experience. This can also impact your sense of certainty and protection. Divine guidance, a supportive environment, and a higher purpose also contribute to feelings of safety and certainty.

Here are ideas to support and protect the quality of your life and relationships:

- **Priorities:** Write down what you are resisting and then what you're attracted to. Assess if these priorities are how you truly want your life to be directed. If not, seek to design the direction of your life the way your heart and soul really want. Then give top priority to your design.

- **Emotional state:** We feel what we focus on. Focusing on fear amplifies fear. Focusing on love drives out fear. What could you more consistently focus on to make you feel better? What are you willing to let go of, quit wasting energy on, or give attention to in order to improve your state of being?

- **Beliefs:** We're more certain about the things we've experienced or have emotionally connected with in faith and/or imagination. Some beliefs serve us, some don't, and some did for a while but no longer do. Knowing this, what do you want to believe and how could you obtain evidence or experience to have more certainty about your new belief?

- **Quality of questions:** Rate the questions you currently ask yourself on a resourcefulness scale of one to ten and seek to ask ones of higher quality (e.g., "What can I learn from this?" and "How can I give more value here?" instead of "Why is life so hard?" and "How come the government/my family/the company doesn't do more for me?").

- **Spiritual consciousness level:** Where you are spiritually has the largest impact on how protected and empowered you feel—to what degree you trust in divine protection. Your motives and clarity of intention strongly influence the expansion or contraction of your consciousness—your expression of divine Power. Each day you can ask yourself: "What is my intention for this day (or this dinner party, trip to New York, conversation with my supervisor, etc.)?" A loving and truthful intention creates guidance, purposeful alignment with divine energy, and increased capacity to feel protected.

You have the ability to impact each of these factors. Therefore, you no longer have to play the victim or continue to attack others subtly or directly. Instead, you can take a very active role in your experience by owning it.

Conscious Choice

Some choices will support what is best for you, and some may not. To make better choices, take inventory of what you have been choosing and the reasons behind your decisions. Your results will give clues about the quality of your choices. Not all of the people you call friends and family may be supporting your desired direction and highest good. Not all the ways you spend your time may serve you. Ask yourself: "Who do I currently associate with, and what activities do I engage in that are detrimental to my spiritual, emotional, physical, relationship, or financial progress?" Maybe it's time to remove the demolition balls in your life.

What if it was possible that you've been getting a hidden payoff for the destructive choices you've made in your life? Examine if you get any satisfaction from temporary pleasure, comfort, attention, material advantage, significance, or revenge, or from feeding another behavioral addiction? Also see if you're avoiding anything, such as perceived pain or unknowns. In order to make choices that support your soul's development, you'll likely have to give up the

> Your conscience will often face what is popular but not necessarily beneficial to you. If you boldly follow your heart, you will not be at war with yourself. If you follow the crowd, don't be surprised if peace eludes you.

satisfaction you have been getting from destructive choices. You may find support by asking Divinity to help you give up your attachment to the payoff you've been getting and/or aversion to the very thing that could help you expand your consciousness and love.

There is a way to get the satisfaction you need in more life-supporting ways. Look at the entertainment you seek, the food and drink you consume, the people you socialize with, and the boss you work for. Review the books you read, the beliefs you hold to be true, and what you declare about yourself. Some of those things are truly beneficial to you, but some actually may be sucking the life energy out of you—bringing a wrecking crew to the good progress you've worked so hard for. With higher awareness, you can make improved choices and thus experience a greater sense of protection of what is most precious to you.

Two-edged Sword

If divine Mind is the source of all intelligence and is all knowing, then it seems reasonable that this Mind must know all the things that are beneficial to you, as well as all the things that are detrimental to you. You might think of this knowingness as a two-edged sword. One side of the sword defends what is valuable to you. The other side of the sword cuts out what would hurt your inner essence. Being all wise, Spirit knows how to show you the impact of the thoughts you think, the emotions you habitually swim in, the people you associate with, and the activities you participate in. Spirit's messages are made unmistakably clear. They may start with an intuitive inkling and then move to louder warning signs long before things become a problem or a crisis. Divinity masterfully knows how to lead you toward those things that truly benefit you and away from those things that detract from your soul-path.

> "God is a circle whose center is everywhere and whose circumference is nowhere" (Empedocles).

What is your job? It is to stay open to and follow the signals given to you. It's likely that you already see them. Signs from your divine Protector have always been present. If you ignore or willfully refuse to heed these signs, progress may feel painfully slow at times. Think for a minute about what you recently knew to be true and yet didn't act on. You knew you shouldn't have started that relationship, entered that business deal, compromised your integrity, or allowed your teen to change your mind. Then you saw more evident warning flags. Your Protector allows you the free will to make choices while actively showing you which way to walk, no matter which pathway you select. If you've made a mess out of one area of your life, Omnipotent Mind is powerful and intelligent enough to disentangle every detail. By definition, nothing is too hard for the all-powerful, ever present, and all wise.

Face the Bogeyman

When I was a young boy, I had a recurring dream of a bogeyman that appeared at my bedroom window at night and terrorized me until I hid shaking under my bed covers. While awake one day, I decided that the next time I had this dream I would jump out of bed, rip open the curtains, and face down the bogeyman. That night I got a chance to courageously work my plan, and when I did, the bogeyman hid his head and ran away, never to return. I felt free! The decision I made to deal with that nightmare has come back to serve me many times over the years. Sometimes protection is the result of directly facing down what most terrorizes us and sucks our energy.

Many years ago I owned a business that brokered real estate mortgage notes (i.e., the pieces of paper that allow one to collect payments from a mortgage loan). After working for months on a particular deal, the seller of the note was ready to close. Just before the closing date, the buyer kept demanding more and more documents from me and wanted to alter the terms of the original deal. At that time, the note buyer was one of the most aggressive and better known individuals in the business. However, I felt he wasn't acting out of integrity, because he didn't deliver what he'd originally promised. The day before the closing, I told him I wouldn't be completing the deal with him. He threatened a major lawsuit, and because his company had millions of dollars and I didn't, I was afraid that he could destroy me legally and financially. My heart pounded in fear.

> "For the Lord God is a sun and shield: the Lord will grace and glory; no good thing will he withhold from them that walk uprightly … blessed is the man that trusteth in thee" (Ps. 84:11-12).

Nonetheless, I made the choice to stand with principle and trust in the Presence of divine protection. The way I saw things, spiritual laws were on the side of integrity, thus would protect me. Soon I was inspired to take some savings and use a line of credit to buy the note myself and was able to close the deal successfully. The weeks that followed were very tense, yet the note buyer had no honest basis to sue me and never did. After facing down this real life bogeyman, I collected monthly principle and interest payments on that note for the next eleven years. This turned out to be a tremendous benefit that had come out of a trying time.

Perhaps you have a bogeyman in your life who needs standing up to—a relative, vendor, bully boss or coworker, an imaginary fear, landlord, or limiting concept. The field of divine protection continuously operates for the benefit of all. Those who align with honesty and courageous love will have an easier time accessing this field.

Protect Childlike and Feminine Energies

Within each of us is a range of masculine, feminine, and childlike energies. It is the nature of the higher masculine energy to protect the feminine and the innocent child, both within ourselves and others.

Feminine energy is creative, nurturing, expressive, connected with the fullness of life, open, receiving, moving, free, spontaneous, and intuitive. The childlike energy is trusting, inquisitive, imaginative, receptive, and innocent. If unprotected, both femininity and childlikeness are subject to harm, physically, emotionally, mentally, and spiritually. For instance, if someone introduces and/or conditions just one false belief, it could mentally inhibit the capacities of one's inner child for a lifetime. One remark can also emotionally scar the feminine sensitivities.

The past cannot be changed, but lessons can be learned from it. Love can heal our perceptions of the past, so the impact of the past can actually change. Calling on the masculine energy brings protection for the feminine and childlike qualities. The higher masculine stands for a humble and honoring sense of service, courage (even in the face of fear), directness, focus, appreciation, clarity of boundaries, resourcefulness, owning one's power and identity, fierce devotion to a higher purpose, and rock-like integrity. The real question is this: what are you willing to do differently today to bring the protecting masculine energy to both yourself and your relationships?

Practice Feeling Protected

1) **Expand Awareness:** Become aware of the protecting Presence of Divinity within and all around you. Omnipotent Spirit is a perfect defender because it is all knowing, all powerful, and ever present. Sit or lie down in a comfortable position. Close your eyes and imagine that you can feel the protecting Light and Presence of God within you and surrounding you. You might want to picture or feel the qualities of Divinity as a warrior-like defender walking beside you or as a protective energy field radiating like a shield all around your body. Feel divine Mind as a resourceful, wise intelligence guiding you through all of your difficult decisions. Receive this safe, encompassing field and let it comfort and strengthen you physically, emotionally, and mentally. As you imagine and feel what God's Presence and protection are like, let it fill every space in your body, mind, and soul.

2) **Align with Divine Protection:** Remember that the key to living a more supported and protected life is to ask for, listen to, and respond to Divinity's safeguarding. Acknowledge and emotionally stack up the times in your life when you have felt protected. You may have been kept safe from an accident, accepting a job from an unethical employer, or getting involved in an abusive relationship. Perhaps you've been protected spiritually or financially. Let this awareness serve to give you greater certainty and feelings of safety.

3) **Establish Support:** Make a list of thoughts, behaviors, people, or activities that currently do not support your spiritual or practical pathway. Notice how these act like a demolition ball to the progress you have made or want to build. Once you have completed your list, ask and listen for protecting guidance about the action you should take to establish better boundaries. Then act on the direction that you receive by taking one step at a time.

Chapter 18

Purify

In order to enjoy the fullness of light, that which would dim light must be removed.

Gold and Dross

The purifying process of spiritual growth can sometimes feel like being in a refiner's fire. A refiner heats gold ore up to more than a thousand degrees in order to evaporate all of the unwanted elements, known as dross. Once the dross has been totally burned off, only the true gold remains. This pure molten gold can then easily be shaped into unique, shining forms of beauty.

Divinity is entirely present everywhere all of the time. Yet, our limited ability to feel and experience Divinity is largely due to our intentions, actions, and spiritual level of consciousness. Spiritual progress results when we remove the impurities and obstructions to this Presence. In the process of removing what is in the way, a higher sense of our God-designed Self, which is always within, is revealed. We do not need to add anything to what Divinity has already created us to be. We simply discover more of our authentic and lasting natures as the distorting nonessentials are eliminated. Our spiritual potentials become realized through purification—the dissolving of that which doesn't match our true essences. If the qualities of Divinity are Life, Truth, and Love, then these must also be our core nature as Divinity's creation. That which does not resonate with these qualities, such as attitudes of false pride, anger, guilt, shame, willfulness, fear, or resentment, needs to be reduced or eliminated in order for us to progress.

When refining pressure takes place in our lives, it can make strong demands on us. We may be required to purge ways of thinking and behaving that do not serve our highest good—things that have been diluting our quality of lives and the lives of those we touch. Once we come through the process, our more purified characters shine through.

> "A person who is pure of heart sees goodness and purity in everything; but a person whose own heart is evil and untrusting finds evil in everything"
> (Titus 1:15 TLB).

Our dross is often the ego-based thoughts, motives, and behaviors that detract from and obscure our priceless spiritual essence. Because dross has no value, why would you want to continue loading your life with it? Imagine how much more beautiful and worthy you'd feel in consciousness and character without that junk clinging to you. Imagine how much the purified gold of your spiritual nature could positively impact those who you know.

Character Purified

To my limited historical knowledge, few have overcome death and ascended into heaven with the widely known exceptions of the prophet Elijah and Jesus the Christ. One could say that the rest of us have some purifying work to do, and while we're still on earth there will be many aspects of our character to refine. As a young adult, I found myself slightly exaggerating my accomplishments in social situations. If I had run a mile race with a time of six minutes and forty seconds, I would tell my friends my time was six and a half minutes. If I had made seventy-five dollars in tips waiting tables, I would tell my coworkers I'd made about eighty bucks.

People think about us a lot less than we think they do, because they are busy mostly thinking about themselves. I suspect that my friends at the time didn't really care that much about my responses and how I rounded up my life. However, I began to suspect that this habit of exaggerating came out of not feeling good enough and was an attempt to make up for that feeling. The other theory was that this was something modeled to me as a child by adults in my life. The bottom line was that exaggerating was dulling the expression of who I was, and at some level, others were picking up on this. My relationships and self-esteem were suffering from this impurity of character.

When I became conscious of what I was doing and the impact it was having, I was driven to make a change. At first, the habit was hard to break, but within several months, it was no longer a habit. A new way of being had been conditioned, which was telling the truth about my achievements no matter how it sounded. As a result, I began to attract relationships that had more integrity, connection, and depth. Earlier superficial relationships seemed to just fade away.

If you took personal inventory right now, what do you believe needs to be purified in your thoughts, speech, or actions? How would it benefit you to do this? Also, what would be the cost to the quality of your family life, workplace, and friendships during the next ten years not to make such changes? What would make it a must for you to do things differently? To want change opens possibility, but true change tends to happen when we must do it—when we find a compelling reason and make a commitment in our hearts to actually do it no matter what it takes. By emotionally connecting with the purpose of change and the costs of not changing, we find additional power to find the resources and overcome obstacles in our paths to progress.

Because no other person can do our inner work for us, it takes a high level of dedication to see lasting change through. At times, others can support our journeys, but we alone bring the desire, willingness, and heartfelt devotion needed. When we start building moments of higher choices with enough consistency, we actually begin conditioning a healthier, more honest, unselfish, and purposeful pattern. I have never heard anyone complain that they have grown or evolved; therefore, the work of eliminating lower patterns and reaching for higher ones must be worth the effort. Remember too that Divinity's grace can enable us to overcome a deeply rooted pattern in an instant. Just asking for Spirit's help brings in powerful resources.

> To expand relationships with other people, look only for the divine in them and leave their imperfections for Divinity to work out with them.

Purify vs. Pollute

What if I suggested that at any moment, our thoughts of others and actions toward them either help reveal their true essence or contribute to polluting their perception of it? We impact our social environment to some degree, and that impact is rarely neutral. When you think about the individuals you interact with on a daily basis, do you serve as a purifying influence to them? If so, is it to the best degree of which you are capable? With the exception of the great beings of history, the rest of us likely still have some cleanup work to do. Pure water can easily clean out a muddy cup if enough water is poured into it. Where does the pure water come from in our own lives? Perhaps from the gift of life itself through all of the feedback and daily lessons we're given to make positive changes.

Divinity as the source of all love designs everything in our lives to bring out the best in us—to purify our hearts, spirits, minds, and bodies. Anything can be a catalyst, from a slow elevator to a sick pet. What we resist in one way will get through in another until our resistance yields to our higher motives and actions. The DUI citation, a mean-spirited coworker, a relative who acts like an enemy, a continual emotional upset in a close relationship, or an excruciating pain can serve to cleanse our hearts if they can get us to change our priorities, perceptions, and ways of being.

There are no accidents in divine Love's perfectly orchestrated Universe, including those things that seem to bring about struggle. Every time you feel like you are beating your head against a wall, you have the opportunity to purify your motives (heart), realign your thoughts (mind), and authentically direct your actions (body and life). During times that you've felt negativity or resistance, did you seek a polluting path or a purifying one? Just by remembering that you are either muddying or clearing yourself in such moments gives you the ability to choose more workable options. The river of life constantly gives opportunities to flush away that which contaminates your divine essence.

> "Blessed are the pure in heart, for they shall see God" (Matt. 5:8).

End of the War

Yielding to a cleansing change in character can often strengthen our bodies as well. In junior high school, I started playing organized basketball. By the time I went to college, the basketball court had become an arena of intense battle for me. Few who play the game would deny that basketball is actually a contact sport, yet unlike in football and hockey, rarely do players wear any protective equipment. Many times during a game, I would find myself in yelling matches, exchanging elbows, or witnessing or experiencing direct-contact injuries. Competition had become war! Even though I liked basketball, it often brought out emotions of aggression, anger, machismo, and defensiveness in me.

For several years I often experienced severe ankle injuries, while many of the other players never seemed to get hurt. This realization forced the question: "Are my injuries trying to teach me something?" I stayed in the question long enough to deeply examine how I had been conducting myself on the court. My ego immediately got defensive, and I justified my actions with the other players and referees based on a victim's view: "The call was unfair," "That guy was a jerk," "The other player threw an elbow first," or "The other team was playing dirty." Until that point, I wanted to be right more than I wanted to play injury-free basketball and actually enjoy the game. Even with the pain, I was getting some weird satisfaction from my viewpoint. This is the same way many people run their lives; they are addicted to the familiar pleasure of being right, even though they suffer from it!

In a moment of humility, the realization came that basketball was not just about me. The game was like an art form of movement from a divine Source, which included all the players, coaches, referees, and even those watching and cheering. My black-and-white view had become a colorful 3-D panorama. The next time I went out to play, I felt part of this grand orchestration and began to witness divine movements of harmony. Amazingly, for the first time I felt just as rewarded when a teammate or opposing player made a basket, outstanding pass, or got a timely rebound as when I did. There was no *I* left in the game. The personal *I* no longer felt like a separate player, fighting, kicking, and scratching to survive and attain recognition. Instead, I felt included in the entire flow of the game, and I loved it! All those years of suffering ankle injuries had led me to what I needed to learn. The battle was over. Since that game, which was more than twenty years ago, I've never had another injury of any kind while playing basketball. Also, no matter what the sport, I've continued to feel camaraderie and joy when playing with others.

Formerly, I had been surviving instead of enjoying an athletic experience. As you know, surviving is not the same as living life to the fullest with freedom and joy. Look at your life and relationships. Is there any experience where you are battling or just surviving rather than really finding joy? Recognize the strange gratification that you get for engaging in the war. Are you willing to receive the purifying lessons you may need to learn and give up the juice of the battle in order to live life more freely and joyfully?

Regardless of what you are going through, the field of divine Love is vibrating in your heart, mind, and body. The process of spiritual purification allows you to progressively feel and resonate with this field, as you remove what would try to oppose honesty and love. When humbly or boldly choosing honesty and love, doors open, emotional scars heal, resources appear, attitudes brighten, talents reveal themselves, conditions of the environment clear, and peace prevails.

> Your lasting wealth and joy will be from what you give and give up, not from what you take or accumulate.

Purifying Interpretations

> "With these promises, dear friends, let us purify ourselves from everything that pollutes either body or spirit, and, in deepest reverence for God, aim at perfect holiness" (2 Cor. 7:1 TCNT).

The most difficult experiences can provide us with the greatest learning. If we don't search for and receive the lessons during such trials or dark nights, we may become bitter and resentful instead of gaining wisdom and grace. Think of some of the most challenging things in your life so far—perhaps the ones that you still have some anxiety or energy about. What is preventing you from moving forward? Your freedom and joy may lie in examining your interpretations, justifications, and resentments about these experiences. Let's look at the facts. Something happened; that is what is true. What may not be true is the meaning or interpretation you gave to it. Ask yourself, "What am I willing to learn from having gone through this? How can I view what happened to me in a way that gives me my power back and blesses others and me?"

How you decide to view your experience is entirely up to you. The great writings tell us that humility always precedes spiritual growth. We may need to realize that we have been spiritually blind before we can see more purely and powerfully. A block is a hindrance or obstruction that impedes progress or achievement. In physiology, it means something that is interrupting normal functions of the body, mind, or heart. What currently feels abnormal in your body and emotions? If there is anything blocking your feeling of what Divinity has created you to be, a willingness to go through the purifying process can help remove the obstacles and free you to be who you were created to be. Today, powerfully prepare your heart and life for good by removing what doesn't belong there. Tomorrow is not guaranteed.

Practice Purifying

1) **Locate the Dross:** You are created in the image and likeness of Divinity. God is pure, and in reality, your true spiritual nature is as well. Yet, in this life there is a need to progressively remove the distorting impurities in character in order to experience and express Divinity. Make a list identifying the thoughts, motives, words, or actions that tend to obstruct your true spiritual Self. Are you impatient when you talk with your spouse? Do you frequently work on personal business when you're at your job? Maybe you harbor resentment because of how your friend or parent treated you. Identify the top three to five things on your list that are hindering your ideal nature. Just by exposing how you're resisting love and integrity can help to melt away the dross that's muddying your gold-like nature.

2) **Purify Character:** From your list in the first exercise, pick one behavior that you'd really like to clean up. Then identify what this behavior has been costing you—how it is obstructing the flow of love and relationships in your life or making you suffer negative emotions such as guilt. Does your restless communication interfere with intimacy between you and your mate? Does your anger rob you of your feelings of peace, joy, or creativity at work? Now take a look at the secret benefit or satisfaction you've been getting for holding onto this behavior. Perhaps you like feeling power over another, getting to be right, or playing victim or heroic struggler. Maybe the behavior gives you a false sense of safety or significance. Are you willing to give up these payoffs and find more workable ways to meet your

needs in order to express your authentic nature? If so, what will you commit to doing differently and by when?

3) **Get the Lesson and Make a Choice:** You cannot control others or the world around you. But you can use awareness to choose empowering meanings and responses you give to events. By viewing everyone and everything in your life as teachers helping you learn and grow, you can receive the lessons behind difficult people and experiences. Recall your most challenging circumstance—a person or situation that you still have an emotional charge about. What is this situation or person showing you? What is a more resourceful way to view your circumstance; a way that brings strength, healing, or progress into your life? With a higher level of understanding, you'll take your power back and ease your suffering. Now, now declare what you intend to change? For example, "I intend to speak clearly and honestly with him," or "I choose to feel compassion for her."

4) **Align with Truth and Love:** In order to align with pure qualities of love and honesty, it helps to focus on what those qualities feel like. Sit or lie down. Bring your awareness into your breathing and body. Focus on the thoughts, feelings, or behaviors that you want to purify. Next, intentionally feel their opposite. For example, if you feel angry toward someone, connect with the feeling of what it would be like to be gentle and easy with that person. Imagine seeing yourself in relationship with the person in this new way, like watching a different movie version of your life. During these moments, you can activate dormant capacities and invite experiences that match your new feelings. Remember, the process of purifying consciousness only requires that you remove the blocks (impure motives, feelings, actions) that are obstructing your innate and highest expression.

Chapter 19

Respect

"Show proper respect to everyone" (1 Peter 2:17 NIV).

Respect and Value

When you think of showing respect to someone, what comes to mind? Perhaps you think of giving that person love, special attention and consideration, honor, reverence, concern, or care. If you respect someone, you probably appreciate and value him, and you don't consciously cause him problems or hinder him from being who he is. How well do you demonstrate respect with those whom you know and care about? Do you consistently show value and concern for them, give them special attention, and keep from intruding on them mentally, physically, spiritually, or emotionally? Don't you deserve this kind of treatment from others too?

Genuine love means to embrace others where they are, honor how the world looks and feels to them, and acknowledge the pathway they have chosen. Without respect, there is no true love. Love means we can magnify the best in others, even during those times when they do not see it in themselves.

Jesus was able to show love and respect for the most challenged people—the alcohol addicted, the unemployed, the sick, the emotionally and physically wounded, and the prostitutes (those who had compromised their souls in an attempt to survive)—because he saw them as precious children of God and, in their own struggling ways, seekers of Truth. He recognized their intrinsic value underneath their issues and lifestyles. He sensed the essence of their lives, and it was recorded that at times he compassionately acknowledged something specific about their past (e.g.,

John 4:17-18). Jesus must have known that spiritually they had the same Father or Source that he did, and that they had the potential to discover their spiritual identities hidden within them. His example can serve to inspire us to spiritually respect that those challenge us.

It seems easy to respect someone for her great accomplishments, intellect, beauty, or financial success. Yet who we really are as spiritual beings is vastly more important than what we have achieved or how we look. Do you find value in yourself and others underneath the surface of appearances, status, and accomplishments? How well do you look for and magnify what is precious in people? Like hidden treasure, true value is waiting to be discovered and cherished.

> "Accustomed to trample on the rights of others, you have lost the genius of your own independence and become the fit subjects of the first cunning tyrant who rises among you" (Abraham Lincoln).

Frequently, people feel devalued by others because of the color of their skin, socioeconomic status, education, body type, or job title. None of these should limit true connection. Spirit leads us to esteem one another because of Divinity's love, which resides in and is uniquely expressed by each person. At the core, our intrinsic spiritual nature is not better or less than that of anyone else. No doubt people seem to express it in varying degrees of transparency. Yet, all are uniquely wonderful and necessary in the conscious evolution of mankind. In the human drama unfolding before us, all are needed on stage. Some make life more interesting and beautiful; others show us love or courage. Some make it full of painfully valuable lessons; others show us passion, diligence, and creativity. Still others show us the downside consequences of lower energies, being slothful, or living in fear. Would we be where we are or know what we do without them, and where would they be without us?

Honor the Real

Do you cherish others' differences, receive their teaching, and honor their individuality? Do others know they are important to you? One year, I felt very frustrated in my relationship with my dad. The way he ran his life and the opinions he expressed seemed contrary to everything I stood for. While I was aware of the fifth commandment given to Moses by the Lord God, which states unequivocally to "honor thy father and thy mother" (Deut.

5:16), I just couldn't shift the way I felt. My feelings seemed justified by claiming that Divinity was my true Father. Nonetheless, this heady perspective failed to solve the strain in my relationship with my dad.

In a moment of prayer and humility, I received the idea to learn more about him. At the next family gathering, I got out a tape recorder and asked my dad if I could interview him about his life. He seemed thrilled with the idea and began the most wonderful storytelling I'd ever heard from him. My dad had to work in a steel mill at age fourteen to help his family pay the bills, nabbed coal from a train boxcar during the Great Depression to heat their home during a freezing winter, and earned money for art school by becoming skilled at playing pool in local halls. My father had boxed semiprofessionally at age seventeen and had written and sketched a book as a gift to the nurses who cared for him while he was in the hospital for an entire year. Listening to him was more intriguing than watching the movie *Titanic*. My dad had had a wonderfully rich and colorful life. He had overcome tremendous physical, emotional, financial, and relationship obstacles and had never given up. The net result of the interview was that I gained understanding, compassion, and newfound respect for him. Since then, I've felt a much better connection with him based on acceptance and genuine esteem.

When we really connect with and understand other people's experiences and views of life, we tend to have more admiration for the challenges they have gone through, the spiritual qualities that have sustained them, and the reasons they are the way they are. In the process of finding compassion and respect for them, we can heal anger, resentment, and separation. Such are the benefits of heartfelt respect.

> Perhaps life is a profound workshop for learning humility as we expand our capacity to love and accept ourselves and others.

Another's Needs and Journey

Respect in relationship is expressed as valuing what's important to the other person and listening until she feels understood. It is seeking to understand others' needs and respond to them with the best we have to give. Do you considerately meet people where they are religiously, politically, economically, physically, emotionally, and socially? A friend once shared how stressful his job can be and how when he first gets home from work, he needs a good thirty minutes of alone time before he can fully engage in conversation with his wife. The stressful drive home rarely offered enough relaxation time for him to let go of the events of his workday. The thirty minutes that his wife thoughtfully allowed him gave him time to restore so that afterward, he could be more fully present with her. If your relationship needs help right now, ask yourself what you can do to more deeply understand and meet the needs of your partner. Be sure to ask him or her too.

Are you considerate of another's time, perspective, ideas, concerns, and emotional challenges? These are all aspects of respect that dramatically influence dynamics in a relationship. Do you allow others, including children, to hold beliefs that you think are wrong or ridiculous? A young man may believe that he's not suited for corporate work. Would you demand that he find a "normal" job, or would you allow him to discover his own creative pathway? A woman may place high value on fashion and beauty. Would you as a partner honor her individuality and support that she likes buying shoes and classy handbags, or would you ridicule her for being impractical?

Each of us is on his own spiritual journey. To our perception, there is something attractive to being where we are and something scary about being in a different place. We need to be where we are in consciousness in order to learn and progress to a higher level. Then we will be attracted by new things and have more expanded perceptions and courage. By looking within, we may find that we no longer hold onto beliefs that we once were certain about when we were less experienced. We learned, grew, and updated our perspectives. We found new things that we were drawn toward and new things we disliked. Just like learning how to ride a bicycle, we likely made mistakes on our journeys and even had to repeat lessons learned, sometimes many times. To have relationships that bring mutual blessing, we must permit others the freedom not to do it right all the time—so they too can discover their inner truths and unique pathways. Isn't this what we want from others? Without this supportive freedom, we might all end up in isolation or with submediocre relationships instead of

> True friendship includes freedom not to get it right all the time; to venture out into unknown waters and learn from one's journey; and to just be, or to be new, without limiting expectations.

benefiting from the tremendous opportunities that wonderfully connected relationships have to offer.

Respect Agreements

We show respect by keeping agreements we've made. Conversely, it is common for people to feel dishonored when we break our promises with them. If we promise to show up at our friend's party and don't, help our spouse with a project and get busy, or commit to taking our children to the park and decide we don't feel like it, guess what happens? Others around us feel disrespected, misunderstood, or devalued; so would we.

When respect breaks down in relationships, it can be extremely difficult to repair. However, there is one way that helps—faithfully keeping our verbal and written promises. This is what builds trust and gives relationships a stable foundation from which to prosper. Even after a rough patch, a relationship that has a focus of love and respect will either be restored or will take on a new form in order to serve a higher purpose.

How a person operates when things aren't going her way reveals a lot about her character. Character means the qualities, attitudes, and values that lead to one's decisions and actions. Are you the kind of person who will do the hard thing just to keep your word? Keeping agreements is one of the most challenging yet rewarding things to do. It will significantly affect your self-esteem, confidence, and spiritual progress. If you demonstrate this kind of respect for yourself, others will more likely trust and respect you. Become aware of the areas where you have been out of integrity with yourself. Decide what you will do to make needed adjustments. Like an accurate golf or tennis swing, respectful action may seem hard at first, but it gets easier with practice.

> "This above all: to thine own self be true, and it must follow, as the night the day, thou canst not then be false to any man" (William Shakespeare).

Diversity and Individuality

It's natural that you notice differences between others and you. Differences reveal significance and variety. Diversity presents the opportunity to appreciate another's individuality, point of view, and contribution. While there is one Earth, there are billions of worlds, because this world looks unique to each person in it. In fact, even within yourself, the world may feel differently on Saturday than it did on Monday; you may have a great relationship one day and feel no passion the next day.

It feels good to be in a relationship with someone who is willing to understand how we feel and see what the world looks like through our ever-changing eyes. Thank goodness there are differences too! Life would be boring without them. Spices make food interesting, and the uniqueness of each person makes life interesting. There is so much to learn from how others approach life. Like walking into a library for the first time as a kid, by appreciating originality and individuality, a whole new world can open up for us. In the infinite scheme of things, we're all just in the sandbox of life anyway, so we have incredible things to learn from and experience with others.

Respect is demonstrated by having no desire to overpower another. It means not forcing our wills on them or telling them what they should or should not think, feel, or do. We respect their rights and their choices. We have no entitlement to rob them of discoveries and lessons they need to learn. We serve them best by example, not by opinions. If our guidance is asked for, we can offer it, but think how *we* feel when someone gives us her unsolicited opinion. Many times we feel encroached upon. A more respectful way of being is to surrender opinions and the ego charge of needing to be right or make others wrong. We can understand others for who they are, how they feel, and the uniqueness of their spiritual journey, one in which they will not always live according to our unique standards, biased rules, or confining expectations.

> "Always put off till tomorrow what you shouldn't do at all" (Anonymous).

Disrespecting Ways

Only conscious awareness empowers us to make higher choices. Here are just a few ways we disrespect ourselves and others:

- Thinking judgmental or critical thoughts. We underrate how destructive these thoughts can be. They bring self-guilt and often precede the decline of a relationship.

- Not communicating when we need to renegotiate agreements.

- Cutting people off in conversation before they finish what they are saying.

- Having an attitude or making comments that are exclusive, elitist, or self-righteous.

- Not asking for a partner's input when making a decision that affects both of you.

- Being prideful or self-centered with priorities.

- Showing a lack of appreciation when kindness, gifts, or love we've received.

- Being inconsiderate or unaware of the perspective and needs of others.

- Being unwilling to seek what works for everyone involved, thus communicating that others are not valuable enough for us to find a win-win.

There are massive costs that come from any one of these unworkable ways of being, including a loss of energy, connection, and enjoyment. Conversely, there are huge benefits to giving heartfelt respect. Discovery, soulful connection, and adventure are but a few. We get to free ourselves of guilt and feel peace for living in integrity and unselfishness. Our own self-esteem is connected with our demonstrable ability to love and respect others.

Other people want your best. Your lover craves the fullness of your heart. Your children seek your playfulness and best example. Your boss requires your creativity and drive. Your parents yearn for you to grow and be happy. Your friend desires your loving attention. The world waits for your contribution. You may be seeking your own acceptance and excellence. Give you best. Your level of self-respect will impact your ability to honor and inspire others.

Your intention to discover another's true essence can progressively help reveal the divine wonder and beauty that exist inside each person you know. With active appreciation and profound reverence for what

Divinity has truly created every person to be, you increase your capacity to experience more of it. In this sense, loving respect has a transforming effect.

Practice Respecting

1) **Express Honor:** Practice honoring your closest relationships in ways that others like to be honored. Identify someone you care about, but with whom you may have difficulty communicating or being with. List five spiritual qualities that you can cherish about this person. Notice how your connection with the person deepens as you begin to focus on, value, and actively appreciate these amazing qualities.

2) **"Be Your Word":** List one area of your life where you're not fully keeping your promises or where you're out of personal integrity. Did you agree to get back to somebody yesterday or tell your spouse that you'd quit interrupting but haven't actually done so? Expose and write down the negative results to you and others for continuing to show up this way. What will you say or do differently from now on? For example, you may want to return a borrowed book, follow through with a family member, or eat more healthy foods like you said you were going to do. Consider the benefits for yourself and others by living in complete integrity with your word.

3) **Respect Others:** Can you respect another person's perspective even if you don't agree with it? Can you respect your partner's yearning for adventure or desire for deeper communication, or your teenager's longing to make some of his own decisions in order to learn to be an adult? List three things you can do this week to create respect and show others that you understand what is meaningful to them. Some ways may not involve words at all.

4) **Plan Positive Action:** Notice any ways that you have been creating subtle disrespect in your relationships. Write them

---

down, and actively seek to eliminate them. Remember, we show disrespect not only by our actions and inactions but also through our thoughts, feelings, and energy toward others. Pick two disrespectful behaviors that you are willing to change. Write an agreement to yourself committing to how you will live anew: "I will find out what my sister needs before making family decisions," "I will voice only supportive comments today" or "I will genuinely acknowledge every kind thing done for me by my spouse and friends."

Chapter 20

Feel Restored

*Instead of fearing or regretting the darkness, use
all that you are to share light.*

Loss Restored

If you're over age thirty, there's a good chance you've experienced an irreplaceable loss in your life. In fact, you may have experienced loss even if you haven't reached the age of thirty yet. The loss may have been a loved one, marriage, home, business, investment, physical capacity, or a dream that you've given up on. What has been lost may have taken years or even decades to create. Those years may now seem wasted or gone forever. You may feel that there's no way to replace what's gone, especially if you've lost a family member or close friend. The biblical Job must have felt that way for multiple reasons. In a short time he lost his entire family, home, business (livestock), wealth, health, and reputation. One can hardly imagine how devastating that would be. Somehow Job was able to survive and keep hope alive. Amazingly, during his trials, he never lost gratitude for God. Perhaps it was Job's way of being that enabled him to trust and stay open to restoration. It is written that eventually Job was given twice as much as he had lost in every area (see Job 42:10). His example proves to us that the sense of loss can be overcome by raising our consciousness above the level of limitation and problems; that grief is a healable emotion, not an eternal condition; and that in a new approach to life we can be made new too.

Restoration is a law of Spirit that we too can understand, access, and experience. Ancient scripture reveals that divine Love constantly maintains the capacity to "restore the years the locust has eaten" (Joel 2:25). Back then, if a locust destroyed a family's crop, they could be devastated economically, which then led to many other disastrous ramifications. The locust that flew into your life may have had a different form, but the law of restoration can apply to you as fully as it did to Job. Let's take a closer look at how this law operates.

What Needs Restoration

After a loss or setback, it seems that people, places, or things need to be brought back. If you find yourself stuck in grief, it may be that your sense of meaning, connection, and spiritual consciousness are what need to be restored beyond material things and people. Restoration may include your sense of hope, joy, possibility, supply, purpose, right activity, resourcefulness, contribution, and love.

Fear often underlies grief and loss, yet there is a way to align one's consciousness in moments with a divine Reality that knows no lack or fear. Job must have found a way to rest in the awareness of the totality of divine Presence in order to feel safe, cared for, guided, and strengthened. How easy it might have been for him to become engrossed and remain stuck in grief, self-pity, or resentment. Instead, he found a way out and focused on what was possible instead of what was tragic or insurmountable. Perhaps his spiritual sense was restored long before his material world was. He must have had an empowering focus. We tend to move in the direction of our focus, and we alone choose that focus, whether it's filled with light or darkness, possibility or negativity, or something in between.

Often restoration comes through unexpected ways, so we need to stay open to new possibilities and forms. Only then are we in a position to receive all that we need in the timely way of ideas, people, and things. Also in order to recognize that which is enduring, we may have to lose our trust in what we've been feebly holding on to. During an emotionally rocky time when my marriage of fourteen years seemed to be collapsing, I made some unwise financial decisions that caused me to lose more than twenty-five years of work, savings, and investments. This, along with the uncertainty of a shaky marriage, was devastating to my psyche as well as my emotions. Concurrently with this, I found myself without a job or savings, in huge credit card debt, and separated from the home, spouse, and friends that I had known for so long. Fear, depression, and feelings of being overwhelmed engulfed me. It seemed there was no way I could dig myself out of this sink hole. Since my teen years, I'd worked up to one hundred-hour weeks, saved with discipline, and invested profitably. Now it appeared to be all for nothing. During restless nights, I wondered how doing so many things well for decades could be undone so quickly and how such sacrifice of time and energy could be regained? More importantly, how could my sense of home and relationship both become restored?

For months I strongly resisted what had unjustly happened to me; I could not seem to stop the downward spiral I was in. My self-identity was in crisis, and I floundered in grief, fear, and loneliness. Then came guilt, because I felt like I'd let myself and others down. Motivation and meaning were disappearing fast, and I didn't know where to turn. Meanwhile, my credit card debt, which was increasing with each passing month, only added more anxious pressure to my mind and emotions.

In this state of consciousness, my health began to fail as well. Many days I struggled just to get out of bed, and soon I was in no condition to work or even look for work. When I reached a dark bottom, I made a decision to quit looking back, to start being grateful to be alive, and to focus on capacities that had not been lost. If Job could get out of his black hole with divine help, so could I. Resourcefulness was one quality that I had always expressed and developed throughout my life. Through up-and-down times, I was able to receive interesting ideas and take action in the face of the unknown with courage.

With this realization, I felt hopeful and strengthened. My health began to improve immediately. Sure, I had moments and days of doubt and fear, but I began to make steady progress mentally, emotionally, and spiritually. One day I felt strong enough to go to an interview for a sales position, one that later helped me to start paying off my credit card debt and meet other bills. Within a year, I was promoted twice, had paid off my debt, and was even able to start a savings account again.

During that same time, my former wife and I went through marriage counseling, and we found a sense of amicable completion with a divorce; afterward, we maintained a friendship. A few years later, I found a stable sense of home at one of my favorite beaches and met wonderful new friends. With a revitalized sense of possibility, several great investment opportunities were realized. Through a change in focus and meaning, and because divine Love's resources are so amazing, abundant, and infinite, my former financial picture was more than restored in just three years.

None of this mental and tangible progress happened until I moved beyond grief and resistance by looking at resources that were still within instead of looking back at the content of what had been lost. Also, I began asking more powerful questions such as "What can I do today to improve my situation?" instead of a question such as "Why did this happen to me?" More energy was then available for me to feel what was possible with Divinity than I'd felt while hypnotized by the dismal circumstances. The turning point was when I'd reached what felt like a critical point of no return. It became clear that I could either attract worse health and relationship troubles and more financial failure or could start realizing some of the abundant resources of infinite Love, knowing and feeling that they were already fully present within me. The Presence of these ideas and resources just needed to be revealed and acted upon with faith, courage, and persistence. Those qualities had never been lost. By recognizing and nurturing them, health and prosperity began to steadily flow again.

> "He restoreth my soul ..."
> (Ps. 23:3).

What We Resist and Why

What have you lost that you are still grieving over or are upset about? Your home, a sense of belonging, a significant other, a job or promotion, health, success, purity, or self-respect? Perhaps you've lost a sense of purpose, direction, or self-confidence. At the time of my losses, I reacted with grief, guilt, and fear. Perhaps the impact of your loss feels more like resentment, anger, or despair.

Emotions usually exist to show us that we need to change either our perceptions or our actions. They are there to serve us and give us clues as to what we truly need to see or do differently. The bottom line is that we're either moving forward and receiving the abundance of possibility or resisting what happened in the dead past and wasting our energy staying stuck in what could (or should) have been. The past is done and cannot be changed. Really, the past only exists as a memory, based on our own unique interpretation of what happened. Moreover, our memory is linked to a chosen slice of time, and by either expanding or contracting that time frame, we can change the context of what happened and thus change the meaning of what happened and how we feel about it. A loss in the short-term could become a gain in long-term growth, depth, and compassion.

Meaning also changes when we unconsciously add or delete information in contrast to what actually happened. We tend to remember only the information that supports our viewpoints. The human mind is an expert at filtering and distorting our experiences. It helps to look for more empowering meanings. Perhaps the loss happened to us so that we can help others through such conditions, become more compassionate, or honor the person who has passed on by making the most of our precious days on earth.

The Love of Divinity is able to restore your sense of health, mental and emotional soundness, family, home, career, connectedness, and self-esteem. With openness and trust in the fullness of this Presence, there is perfection in the way and timing for these things to be healed and restored.

It may serve you not to be attached to the form that restoration must take. There will likely be new forms and priorities. Someone may have lost his home to a flood or fire. That form of home is gone, and yet the same qualities that were represented in that home can be expressed somewhere else. An even higher sense of home can also be experienced. Restoring the essence is more important than recovering the contents, especially because none of us will take any of the contents with us when we leave here anyway. Essence has to do with the inherent and indispensable qualities expressed by something or someone. The essence you loved can show up again, even if a specific individual or treasured belonging does not.

Focus on the essential qualities of Divinity and witness how they are being expressed by others and you. Notice the joy, vitality, intelligence, creativity, variety, and beauty around you. By connecting with these qualities and feeling their aliveness, you'll be expanding your capacity to receive, experience, and share them. Your experience is largely an expression of your quality of consciousness. Where you hang out in consciousness gives you a range of possibilities or potential experiences. Take some time each day to feel what it would be like to already have the restoration you are seeking take place; then receive, speak, and act from this state of being. In those moments, you'll be contributing

> "I have held many things in my hands, and I have lost them all; but whatever I have placed in God's hands, that I still possess"
> (Martin Luther).

to your own restoration by accessing what is actually ever-available to you. Remember, Divinity's resources are infinite, perfect, and ever ready to be received.

Unreasonable Love

Myopia is a defect in vision where the focus of images is solely on the front of the retina, thus distorting the view of distant objects. A person with a myopic view doesn't perceive most of what is going on around them. At times all of us are myopically focused on our own worrisome concerns, thus distorting blocking our view of what exists around us. We may not know everything about how Job was able to move forward into abundance after his catastrophic losses. Scripture does give us one big clue though: "And the Lord restored to Job all that he had lost, when he prayed for his friends" (Job 42:10 LAM). What Job did was totally illogical and unreasonable! At his greatest time of need, when he had every right to focus on himself, his losses, and his unjust conditions, he instead expressed love for his friends and prayed for them.

Is that what you would do at a time of personal crisis? Job likely had greater needs than his friends at that time, yet his captivity was lifted when the eyes of his world expanded beyond his own self-focused troubles and losses. Later, Job wound up with a new family and home, abundant herds, a healthy body, and wealth greater than ever in his life. When Job was ready to receive it, the Lord gave him "twice as much as he had before" (Job 42:10). Job had not failed to love, even unreasonably, which made him able to recognize and accept Love's provision.

In your darkest times, you too can find comfort in expanding your vision, giving love, praying for your family and friends, and living unselfishly. In looking to give to others during unreasonable times, you may be in a better position to see and be lifted above your own problems. Perhaps it is easier to feel the great Comforter when we're comforting another. Expectantly holding to the spiritual law of restoration will better enable you to receive what you really need in order to fill any void you may be feeling. This can happen in a way that you may have never imagined. Remember, the goal is not to physically replace what seems lost but to restore your spiritual sense of what is always available. This inspired, expanded vision then gives you access to abundant supplies in new forms from a limitless and loving Source.

It's important to remember that divine supply shows up continuously and yet only one day at a time. Receive today what you need at this new point in your experience and quit worrying about five years from now, which is just an unreal projection anyway. It has been said that no man or woman crosses the same river twice, because each day both they and the river are different from the day before. Things show up in your life for a reason, a season, or a lifetime. Be grateful for each one.

Resurrecting Deadness

Just about everybody has experienced personal loss in the form of a family member, a loved pet, or something inside them. Possibly a lifelong dream you've earnestly strived for is gone for good, or your once life-filled marriage has hit the metaphorical feeling of when death did you part. Perhaps the thing that has always gotten you by in life—money, charm, or good looks—cannot be relied upon as much as before. Maybe you had a job or circumstance that felt ideal, and it suddenly disappeared. Possibly things were stolen from you, you were another type of victim, or your childlike trust and innocence were violated. Or, you experienced a decline in emotional or physical health. Any of these experiences can leave you feeling like you need a resurrection to bring back the life and energy you once felt. Some have felt dead inside for so long that they've lost nearly all hope and meaning and are living a slow, passive suicide or quiet resignation.

If life has become lifeless to you, there is a way out of apathy, negativity, and darkness. There is a reliable way to feel passion for life again. Give life your passion, and you'll feel life giving it back to you! Connecting with, feeling, and living your own expression of divine Love and Truth to the best of your ability can help resurrect your life. In doing so, the transforming power of divine Grace can help you to feel greater hope, meaning, and strength.

The master example of how to prepare for resurrection was given to us by Jesus on the cross. While suffering from brutal torture, bleeding to death, and slowly suffocating, he still loved in three distinct ways: 1) He cared for his husbandless mother who stood at the foot of the cross by telling John to take care of her (see John 19:26); 2) He gave hope and encouragement to the convicted criminal hanging on the cross next to him (see Luke 23:42-43); 3) He poured out his heart in forgiveness to the ones who had crucified him and misunderstood his life mission and goodness (see Luke 23:34). At the peak of his apparent suffering, Jesus, like Job, lived unreasonable love, and this resurrecting consciousness helped him to experience victory. The Presence of Divinity within him restored him! Although our trial or cross may not be as extreme, we still have the opportunity to love unreasonably and feel the supporting supremacy of restoring Love. In doing so, new life, purpose, and strength are available to us.

By feeling, being, and sharing love, you can regain the will to give, trust, be courageous, receive intimacy, be creative, and live passionately again. Love is the remedy for dark times, and when times get darker, you may be called to love even more. As difficult as your life may seem right now, the resurrecting process does not start with your self—your limitations, circumstances, past hurts, losses, or mistakes. It begins with the infinitely abundant, immensely powerful, bountifully blessing nature of the supreme Self within and all around you. You don't have to grasp all of God's activity and nature. Even a moment of connection is enough to start rejuvenating you.

Take a few moments right now to feel Divinity's Presence, power, comfort, abundance, direction, healing, and wisdom expressing itself as you right now. Feel inspiration and light pouring into and radiating out from your heart. Let nothing stand between you and your God-created capabilities. Inspiration literally means "the breath of Spirit." Its warmth, radiation, wisdom, and intelligent energy may be revealed to you through the voice of a child, a

> "Don't you know by now that the everlasting God, the Creator of the farthest parts of the earth, never grows faint or weary? ... He gives power to the tired and worn out, and strength to the weak" (Is. 40:28-29 TLB).

letter from a friend, a billboard, a radio program, a hug, an idea in the shower, a timely phone call, or the practical words of teachers, saints, and enlightened guides. If you unwittingly try to prevent Spirit from getting through one way, it will easily find another, like sunshine poking through multiple openings in clouds. There is simply no limit to the forms in which inspiration can be communicated to you. Feel directed rather than aimless, confused, or apathetic. The wise part of you knows what to think and do. Your transformed perceptions, attitudes, and willingness to act will lead you to your restoration.

At times of experiencing another's death, I believe there are angelic energies that come to our aid: some reveal divine Strength, and others communicate divine Love. Years ago, my outdoor cat Cookie appeared to have eaten some poison. She came home writhing in agony and foaming at the mouth. Her eyes rolled back, and then she was gone. Cookie lay lifeless before me. With powerful emotions of rebellion against the belief that death could steal her from me in this way, I yelled "No!" at her spirit with all my might, and held to the fact that life cannot be taken. I felt divine Strength surge in my body, and I persisted relentlessly for ten to fifteen minutes even though the evidence before me hadn't changed. Then life returned to Cookie's form, and her eyes sparkled again. She got up and walked normally, and peace and joy filled our home. Months later Cookie went into the guest room where we had an electric blanket plugged in. Without us knowing it, she had chewed through the cord and was electrocuted. When I found her, she again appeared to be at death's door. This time I felt the ministering Presence of Love filling the room, and I just picked up Cookie and loved on her for several minutes until she started moving. Within a few hours, she was fully recovered again.

Share the Light

> "... those who hope in the LORD will renew their strength. They will soar on wings like eagles; they will run and not grow weary, they will walk and not be faint" (Is. 40:31 NIV).

You may have a friend or loved one who currently needs restoration. That person might need to be reminded of her gifts, receive ideas you have to share, have her fears reframed in a more resourceful way, or be given the gift of understanding and time together. She could be greatly benefited by your selfless encouragement, vision, and energy. If she feels your uplifting influence, she might be able to rise above her loss and begin to find life again in new ways. Ask Spirit what you can say or do for this person. Then listen for the answer and follow through from your heart in a timely way. Even a seemingly little word or deed could bring her a sense of new life, hope, and meaning. Your willingness to serve as a vehicle for love can awaken that person's sense of restoration.

Anyone who has a resurrecting experience is transformed. He is blessed with more depth and compassion, which are major assets for inspiring and supporting others. Now Divinity may be calling you to do your part. A spiritual momentum is building that is helping all of us awaken to the fullness of life—a consciousness that spiritually perceives that all good is already present and fully restored.

Practice Feeling Restored

1) **Identify Resistance:** What circumstance in your life have you been resisting or grieving? Perhaps it is the loss of a relationship, a job, or your health. As you think about this situation, notice how your body feels inside. Is it tense, anxious, stressed, angry, sad, or depressed? Where in your body do you hold these feelings? Recognize the cost to the quality of your life and health when you resist situations in this way—a life that still can be filled with joy, love, opportunity, and happiness. What will it take for you to move forward? What do you really need to let go of, and when do you intend to do so?

2) **Accept the Loss:** IIn order to move beyond a misfortune, we have to be willing to accept what happened. Otherwise, the consequences can keep us trapped. When we accept a circumstance for how it is in this moment, life flows through us more easily, and we experience less suffering. Find a comfortable position. Feel the energy inside your body. Now bring to mind what you have lost. Imagine what it would feel like to fully accept this situation for how it is; and for a few moments, act like you do accept it. Next, turn your focus to Divine Presence. Feel the nature and activity of infinite Love restoring all things with power and light, including your health, resources, emotions, opportunities, and the essence of relationship. Remember that there could be new forms. Feel your current situation as if it is already restored. Live today from this conscious feeling of what spiritually already is and see what is revealed to you.

3) **Give Unreasonable Love:** This week, look for ways to practice unreasonable love. Like the examples of Job and Jesus, move your attention and vision off your problems and instead look for ways to cherish Divinity and give comfort to, pray for, and benefit others. Trust that as you express and share your love and gratitude, your uplifted consciousness will help you feel that the Universe is giving back to you through the reliable law of restoration.

Chapter 21

Share

"Blessed be the Lord, who daily loadeth us with benefits"
(Ps. 68:19).

Divine Support

A lot of people would like to change the world, yet relatively few have impelled major change. Not everyone can be a world leader or Nobel Peace Prize winner. Nonetheless, while it may seem impossible to change the whole world, we can always change ourselves. As Mother Teresa once shared, "We cannot all do great things, but we can do small things with great love." All of us have the potential to live where we are with significant love. What if a majority of people in the world showed up to their families, workplaces, and communities with the intention of "What can I do for you?" or "How may I serve you?" If such heartfelt motives were followed up with timely actions, we may come close to experiencing heaven on earth!

Until such a time, we have the opportunity to expand our own sense of heaven, to embody the joy and satisfaction of benevolence in our current relationships. Generosity is a fundamental nurturing quality in all lasting relationships. Without this quality of attitude and action, relationships are prone to wither and lose energy, meaning, and passion.

There's nothing to get! If we live in a universe already filled with infinite Love, then trying to get something for yourself is not going to help you access more of this giving field of Love. It's readily accessed through embodying the nature of the field—through giving. The motive and activity of giving is what multiplies our awareness of what's being given to us. Withholding is what diminishes this awareness.

Life supports that which supports life. Givers are given what they need to be givers. Any time you gave anything from your heart, you likely did so because you were in alignment with the all-giving field of total Love. Giving then flowed naturally through you as an impulsion, and in some degree expanded your demonstrable capacity as a giver. When you look back on those times that you opened your heart and set an intention to help, support, gift, or bless another, you may recognize a pattern that you were given exactly what you needed to be able to do so. When you aligned with that which supported the life of another, you were supported by Divinity to be capable of giving what you did. Because of this, there is no need to waste energy in pride or fear about the outcome of your giving. Thoughts such as "I gave so much, and look at the response I got!" or

"He which soweth sparingly shall reap also sparingly; and he which soweth bountifully shall reap also bountifully ... so let him give; not grudgingly, or of necessity: for God loveth a cheerful giver" (2 Cor. 9:6-7).

"What if my actions won't be accepted or, even worse, are misunderstood?" don't need to obstruct your generosity. Instead, out of a humble and grateful space, feel that you were a vehicle used by Divinity to bring what was needed to serve the highest good at the time. Then your capacities as a giver won't be wounded, limited, or burdened.

Generosity has unique mathematics: it multiplies things through division. When we give to others through service or kindness, we multiply our capacity and expression of love. At any moment in time, we are either giving or taking, and each way of being has consequences. In order to contrast the benefits of being a giver, let us first thoroughly examine what it is like to be a taker.

Profile of Takers

Europeans call those individuals who take energy, joy, and peace away from others emotional vampires. Such self-absorbed individuals literally suck the energy out of the room and out of other people that let them. Takers show up in relationship focusing on what they can get instead of what they can give. They are so engrossed in their own pain, suffering, and past that they clog the present possibility for others and themselves. Takers are needy, and their needs often must be met now! They remain largely unaware of and unresponsive to the desires and needs of others. In conversation, they predominantly talk about themselves, and direct others to talk about them as well. Takers rarely, if ever, ask anything about the other person, and if they do, the questions are usually surface level, showing half interest.

Takers habitually create complicated problems and crises in order to focus attention on them. They are often the drama kings and queens, playing the victim in their own tragedies. The greater the drama, the more significance and connection they feel they can have. Even after gaining a captive audience, takers often resist real help because they would rather continue to rehearse their story and replay the effects of it. At least that way they can hold on to what is familiar. If they lose their drama, what would become of them?

Takers operate from a mindset of scarcity and survival. They don't like to see others achieve freedom and success. They jealously believe there's not enough for everyone, so takers must get theirs first, at any cost to others. Obviously, with this mentality, the means justifies the ends for them, so integrity takes a backseat to results. Instead of being generous, takers are often withholding, inconsiderate, petty, and unkind. They are usually the ones found criticizing and judging others. Permanent healing of the takers' suffering would also mean an end to their drama and bid for attention. It often seems easier for them to maintain the status quo.

Cost of Being a Taker

A taker's actions have consequences. Loneliness, lack, broken relationships, anxiety, depression, limitation, resistance, and exhaustion are some of the effects. Takers feel deficient in a sense of peace, fulfillment, and contentment. They often miss out on opportunities and blessings. They rarely experience the richness, flow, and beauty of life. Their heavy energy makes it difficult for them to feel soulful connection with others, so relationships are a struggle more than a blessing or source of joy. Takers miss out on the present moment, which in itself is a great gift that they never fully receive. And all for what?

> If all you need is within you, then there's nothing to get, nothing to seek outside of the Divinity within you.

To live a self-centered, fear-ridden experience—never having enough but getting to be right about why their lives are the way they are. Fabulous benefits? You decide.

Where can you find one of these takers? Perhaps all of us have been takers at some point. We've had moments when we were tired, sick, emotionally upset, fearful, pressured by time, or grieving a loss. We may not be takers at our center, but in moments all of us have felt out of sync, not quite ourselves, or needy. This realization can give us compassion to understand what other takers may be going through, so we don't have to take their words and actions personally. Instead, we can rise with compassion and pray that others stand by us when we're in a taking mode. Now that the dark side is exposed, let's look at the bright side—life as a giver.

Profile of Givers

A giver is someone who lights up a room like a crystal chandelier. They embody unselfish love and express it through spontaneous generosity and grace. Givers realize that part of what has been given to them in the way of time, talent, or treasure is for sharing with others, and they are glad to do so. They bring joy to themselves by cheering up others. They walk into a space with a desire to know the needs of others and a willingness to respond to those needs to the best of their abilities. With a developed trust that the Universe is designed to bless everyone, givers constantly receive ideas, resources, connections, and opportunities. Their resourcefulness and creativity offer ways to bring beauty, joy, healing, and peace, and not just to those they care about but even to complete strangers. Givers are consistently appreciating and supporting others.

It's not just what givers do that makes them great to be around. It's primarily the energy and attitude behind their speech and actions. They do not give in order to be noticed or receive something back; it is just who they are. It has been said that if you want to get to the heart of what is really going on in politics, follow the money. To get to the heart of someone's character, follow her motives, because they tell the true story. The motives of givers are to benefit and uplift others. They feel better by making others feel better.

In contrast to the scarcity and survival mentality of a taker, the giver operates with a mindset of unlimited abundance. During a vacation, there is a huge difference between struggling to get to a certain place versus enjoying the trip. Only givers get to fully enjoy their moments and life experience. After all, life is a journey, not just a destination. In the end, the only things we can take with us are our experiences, learning, and the eternal nature of the love we've shared with others. All else becomes dust.

Divine Law is clear: we feel and experience more of what God is giving us when we're embodying the nature of the great Giver. In those moments, we're moving in harmony with the unlimited capacities of Spirit. We give to live, as it's been said. When we're giving, we're aligned with the Universal Source of Love, which richly supplies all the things we need, right when we need them. Such are the results of being a giver.

Thoughts and Prayers

Another's prayer can powerfully benefit us in many ways and can even protect us from harm. In 1987, I drove a sports car from Missouri to California in order to sell it there and made the three-day trip alone. In the middle of the night, a few hours from Las Vegas, I was driving exhaustedly on a two-lane highway. Suddenly I received a strong inner message to move over to the emergency lane. As I did, a semitruck flew by on the other side of the highway. As it passed by, a long chain that was loose on its flatbed whipped violently toward my car, just missing my windshield. When I got to a phone, I called my wife who told me that an hour earlier she had been awakened and decided to pray for my safety. Wow, was I thankful she had!

Occasionally we don't think very highly of ourselves; we get discouraged, negative, or into self-sabotage. During these moments, if others think well of us and/or pray for us, we are supported greatly. We tend to underrate the influence that thoughts and prayers have on relationships. Yet, if we're totally honest, we may see that nearly every one of the relationships that have deteriorated in our lives started with less-than-loving or untruthful thoughts. Conversely, the ones that are still growing are being nurtured by positive, honest, caring thoughts and feelings. Prayer can be a powerful way for us to tune into and broadcast such transforming thoughts and feelings.

Other Ways of Sharing

Friendship is not just for enjoyment and learning but also to have frequent opportunities for service. As a giver, you can make a positive difference with your kind words, conversations, notes, cards, and emails. Have you ever saved a card from a friend or relative? Even after moving many times over the years, I've kept many that are very meaningful to me. Perhaps such mementos serve as a way for us to stay better connected to those we care about and to the uplifting experiences we've shared. They serve as a reminder of the innate giving of Divinity that is alive within everyone. Even if some have passed on, qualities and experiences we've shared with them are still very much alive in consciousness.

When timely and appropriate, we can give through our touch. How many men and women in this world are starved for touch or hugs from their significant others or family members? We all need affection; most people need to be held, kissed, and touched. Babies have an increased risk of dying without receiving sufficient touch and nurturing. Physical affection is one of the ways all of us feel alive and cared for. Appropriate touch can help heal the core fear of rejection.

Within you is the ability to give to people both mentally and emotionally. When you allow others to express themselves fully, they will feel more accepted and understood. In fact, to feel understood is to feel another's compassion, which alone can be very comforting and healing. In 1958, the psychologist Harry Harlow studied primates to see if infant monkeys preferred food (lactation) over affection. His experiments found that it was the latter! They actually chose the emotional component of love over food in order to survive. When people give, a natural hormone called oxytocin is released. This actually calms and soothes the person doing the giving. It may also cause the brain to create an attachment with the person she cares for.

Giving emotionally includes maintaining healthy boundaries, such as caring for oneself enough to avoid enabling another's undesirable actions. Spirit's guidance and the wisdom of your own heart will lead you in what is yours to give and receive.

Gifts can also make another feel very loved. Choosing the right gift takes thoughtfulness, time, planning, and often money, which normally requires precious life energy to earn in the first place. So when you receive a gift, feel the depth of caring that someone is giving to you. The love behind the gift is even more important than, yet not separate from, the gift itself. Charity with others can free one from downward spirals of doubt, worry, self-criticism, and fear. Saints have taught that charity is the bond of perfectness that allows one to walk confidently with God (e.g., Col. 3:14-15).

> What you give is what endures, and if you receive like a true giver, you will feel the limitless circle of Love.

Receiving is actually an act of giving too! It graciously completes the circle of love. You might create feelings of hurt in a relationship when you do not freely receive what someone is offering you with good motives. Not being a good receiver is like saying no to the yes flow of the Universe.

The Great Giver

"Every good gift and every perfect gift is from above, and cometh down from the Father of lights, with whom is no variableness, neither shadow of turning" (James 1:17). This verse reveals the nature of God's giving to us: *how* Divinity gives to us (with light and joy), *what* Divinity gives to us (unlimited good and perfect gifts), and the consistency and permanency of Its giving (neither variableness nor shadow of turning). What an incredible standard to follow. What is the effect of God's giving? Divine giving satisfies our spiritual needs and wholesome desires.

Jesus taught his disciples (students) to ask for their *daily* bread. We tend to want our needs met not just for today but also for the months or years ahead. Nonetheless, Divinity's giving meets our needs one day at a time. So, that's when we need to receive what we need.

Another of Jesus's disciples, John, said, "If we love one another, God dwells in us, and his love is perfected in us" (1 John 4:12). People are running everywhere trying everything to find love "out there." Many have given up in frustration or exhaustion. What Jesus and John taught is so simple: love Divinity and express Its giving nature in relationship. If we'll put our focus on giving love instead of searching for love outside of us, we may find satisfying love living within us more powerfully.

Benefits and Blessings

The infinite field of divine Love is benefiting and blessing us all the time. This Presence is perfectly delivering to us what we need—those things that are best for us at this point in our experiences. This is often the case when we don't even know we need them. Love has timing that is perfect too, and timing makes all the difference. Divine timing may seem slow or fast, but it is never late. We are usually given more than we are able to receive. It is only our fears and limiting mind-sets that prevent us from receiving the fullness of benefits.

Do you feel that the Universe is constantly seeking to benefit and bless you? For a few moments really connect with this feeling. As a reminder of this activity, you might consider setting your wristwatch or cell phone to give a tone at the top of the hour. This type of reminder has several benefits. First is the recognition that life is more about Divinity's activity and purposes than just your concerns. Second, you can recall the inspirations and blessings you've witnessed that show Divinity's care for you and others. The third effect may be to open your heart and mind to witness and receive even more blessings for the remainder of the day.

Normally, we can only receive what we're open to receiving in our minds and hearts. You may be unaware of helpful things going on all the time, such as opportunities, protection, connections, or synergy that are too perfect to be less than divine. If you're open to them, you'll be able to perceive them and benefit from them. What if today you chose to feel the hand of Divinity participating in your life, giving to you, and enabling and impelling you to give to others?

Practice Sharing

1) **Get Honest:** Are you more of a giver or a taker in your relationships? Without self-judgment, write down several ways that you see yourself each way. Next, notice where you feel stuck in drama, drained in energy, or resistant to getting the real help you need. Recognize the cost to your relationships and the quality of your life when you are taking or staying stuck in your story.

2) **Ways to Give:** Write down three ways that you currently enjoy giving to others. Perhaps you like to give presents, cook special meals, write notes of appreciation, share photographs, or spend time in uplifting phone conversation. You give to others by your positive thoughts of them and by choosing to see the best in them. Praying for someone is also a special and wonderful gift. Build on your strong points by expanding ways you already like to give and stretch yourself with other forms of giving.

3) **Deal with Takers:** Remember that we have all been needy during times of pressure, sickness, fatigue, or fear. Recognize when others are being takers in relationship with you. Then seek compassion and understanding for what they may be going through. Choose to operate from the standard of not expecting things from takers and maintaining your intention to be a giver to them when it's wise to do so. See if this way of being brings ease to your relationships and/or leads you to new ones.

4) **Receive the Gifts:** Divinity is the great Giver, and if you look around, you may discover that you're being given to all the time. Divinity gives you beauty, life, inspiration, provisions, and opportunities to enjoy, grow, and contribute. Recognize Divinity's giving nature and activity and feel more safe, comforted, and cared for. Imagine feeling this Presence perfectly meeting all of your needs right now. When you embrace this nature of Love, notice how you feel inside. Next, declare your willingness to receive the gifts that divine Love has for you each day. To increase your awareness, start a journal of the many ways God is giving to you or set an hourly reminder to reconnect with the feeling that you're being abundantly provided for.

Chapter 22

Surrender

*Anything that does not contribute positively to you or another
may be unnecessary in your life.*

Real Progress

Every step forward, whether in business, spirituality, or relationship, requires letting go. You literally leave the place where you are in order to move toward the next place. The form of that place may be a perception or behavior. It may be physical, emotional, mental, and/or spiritual. The place could be related to a value, rule, focus, habit, or meaning you have attached to an experience. In fact, if you're feeling stuck in some part of your life, ask yourself, "What do I truly need to let go of?" The answer you receive could be the key to improving the quality of your relationships, home, spiritual practice, and career.

We have to be willing to be new and take new actions to have better things and experiences. A receptive heart and mind must first be present in order to receive new ideas, to gain perspectives, and have new relationships. Something that is familiar to you may need to be released. As the Master's parable indicated, "New wine must be poured into new wine skins" (Matt. 9:17 LAM). New wine, or inspiration, doesn't sit well in an old and brittle, tightened-down mindset. It's not easy to embrace an original idea or new experience when grieving the loss of a job, relationship, or former stage in our lives. Yet, real and lasting progress only comes from forgoing whatever is holding us back, in order to feel free to move forward.

This applies to relationships as well. Ideally, one or both partners will do what's best in order to nurture and strengthen the bond, and seek to give up whatever would damage it. I've noticed that when I feel anger coming up in a conversation with my spouse that it's probably not the best time to explain my point of view or to be heard. By giving up the momentary tendency to be right and make my partner wrong, taking a few minutes to calm down, and then finding a better time to discuss the matter, has yielded much better results in our communication and relationship.

You probably have a good idea of the feelings, words, and behaviors that have damaged or could damage your relationship. The real questions are how badly do you want to hold onto them, and do you want to be right or happy? You need not give up your true identity, individuality, or divine qualities, such as kindness. Rather, you are called only to surrender attitudes and actions that block your best qualities from shining forth. As you do, your relationship can prosper. As you resist true surrender, the relationship will feel limited and limiting. At any moment, your relationship is either growing or dying. There is no neutral position. You are responsible only for your own choices. Your partner will make their own choices, and if they don't eventually ramp up with your growth, this may present a challenge. Nonetheless, trust the process, take care of your business, and let your partner take care of his or her concerns.

After six years of marriage, Dan woke up one day and realized how fractured his marriage with Helen had become. When humbly searching his heart for answers, he realized how critical he had become of her. He saw the damage that his attitude and behavior had caused to their relationship in terms of declining affection, communication, and peace. After an inner struggle, Dan willingly gave up his critical way and replaced it with appreciation in order to nurture Helen and restore their relationship. In this way, he did not yield what was most valuable; he protected and nurtured it.

Clear Distinctions

We surrender when we feel safe or when we're out of options. When we don't feel safe, our survival mechanisms kick in to resist surrender and hang on to what's familiar. Yet, survival instinct can be overridden with conscious choice to access divine Grace. This Grace is a Power that meets our every need when we trust in It. Grace reminds us that our survival and identity are based on the Presence of infinite life-giving Love, not on our egos' sense of self or limited efforts. In degrees, we surrender a contracted sense of self to an ever-expanding one—what we believe we're not capable of to divine possibility. We're on a journey of realizing no separate existence from Divinity, and much has to be let go of to arrive—to discover we've never left home.

We'll consciously leave where we are only when the place we would rather be becomes more important or engaging to us. Ask yourself what you need in order to feel safe, to let go of negativity or resistance.

All of us are non-stop decision makers. In a sense, we surrender something with each decision we make. For an example, we may give up a night at the gym for our favorite TV programs, some extra sleep to get a jump on the weekend yard work, comfort-filled chocolate for our diet program, or our composure for the temporary pleasure of uncorking some anger. Some decisions are more workable than others; some yield more desirable results than others. Some support our desired destination; others detract. In the remainder of this chapter, we'll focus on surrender that contributes to our ultimate spiritual progress and helps us earn the right to express higher understanding by giving up ways that dim understanding.

The concept of sacrifice may conjure up a belief that you have to give up, compromise, and/or forsake what is most important to you. As you may have experienced, this type of behavior often results in pain and resentment. Real sacrifice does not require any of this, and, in fact, it is just the opposite. The word *sacrifice* basically means the destruction or surrender of something for the sake of something else, presumably something more vital. True sacrifice is about fully standing for what's more valuable to you. Spiritually, it's about throwing in the towel regarding what seemed important to your ego in order to yield to what is crucial to your spirit.

> What you're willing to give up will create space for your next experience.

Surrendering has the benefit of taking you farther down the pathway of your ultimate freedom and joy. In choosing to lay down a false sense of life, you progressively discover your true Life, which can never be taken away. Letting go of the nonessential helps reveal what is truly essential to your heart.

Spiritual Priorities

Right now you may be feeling led to let go of something that seemed precious to you for the sake of that which is most precious to your soul path. Your deep yearning may be calling you to detach from lesser priorities in order for you to advance spiritually. It's been said that God is more concerned with your growth than your comfort. Forward progress doesn't always look or feel comfortable. In fact, being too comfortable for too long may be a sign that you're not growing. Life doesn't always have to be uncomfortable to grow; we can grow through grace too. But, think back to the times you evolved the most. You may find that challenges helped you do so.

As we progressively disidentify with a fearful, self-centered, and ego-dominated self, our hidden magnificence within will be expressed more freely and beautifully. This spiritual identity is already complete, at peace, and lovable. It lacks nothing, so there is nothing to fear. It lives in original, timeless moments of completeness and perfection, so it doesn't have to regurgitate the past or be anxious about the future. It *is* life, so it doesn't have to worry *about* life. It's free, so there's nothing that needs to be done or achieved to become free. Tune into this vibrating magnificence in the middle of your chest and abdomen.

Surrender is not about giving yourselves away, at least not your true Self. Surrender that blesses a relationship is about giving up fear-based ego patterns in order to satisfy what your highest Self and the highest in another are calling forth. This kind of sacrifice does not lead to resentment. Rather, it aligns us with the infinite field of divine Presence and allows the highest good for all concerned to be brought forth. Think about it. Have you ever felt resentful about achieving spiritual progress, or any other type of progress for that matter? True and lasting progress is always worth the journey.

Resentment could result when you give up what's true and most valuable to you in order to satisfy the desires of your ego or the ego-demands of another. For example, a friend calls with an invitation for a wild weekend. You know in your heart that the timing is not right for you,

> "Spiritual work is thus an endless surrendering, letting go, turning away from, withdrawing from, and ignoring that which is irrelevant and essentially unrewarding" (David R. Hawkins, M.D., Ph.D., *The Eye of the I*).

because you have a meaningful project to finish. But, you compromise what's true for you and go anyway, because you don't want to let your friend down. You justify in your mind that this is what a good friend should do. Abandoning what's in your heart for some social concept will likely lead to inner guilt, resistance, or resentment. Dishonoring your heart always has negative consequences. If you think about past results for doing this, you may realize that it indeed led to regret, inner conflict, or suffering. With awareness of such consequences, you can choose more wisely in the future.

What about those who come to you in need? Shouldn't you sacrifice your needs for theirs? With the priority of being guided by Divinity, you can respond to a call to help someone, and it doesn't have to feel like a sacrifice in the traditional sense. Even though it may interrupt what you're doing, you'd still be honoring what's most valuable to you. Yet, if you use an everyday call as a pointless distraction from what Spirit is impelling you to focus on, then you may pay for the compromising decision with regret or loss of self-esteem.

True surrender does not require that we give up Truth but rather that we boldly stand for it, so we develop the character needed for more demanding times, just as many spiritual warriors have done before us. A true warrior conquers his own inner weaknesses in preparation for larger battles. Until we become enlightened, there is still much to do in the way of overcoming falsehood, ego-based desires and fears, and nonessential distractions.

Nothing to Add

It is said that a boy walked past Michelangelo while he was chiseling a beautiful marble sculpture, and said, "Mister, how did you know he was in there?" We're all potential Michelangelos working on ourselves, chiseling away what no longer serves the best in us rather than adding something that wasn't there in the first place. Our divine Creator has already completed His work. Our true, beautiful, perfect, and complete nature lies within us, waiting to be more fully revealed. Spiritual devotion, divine Grace, and purposeful action have the effect of chipping away the nonessential in order to reveal the statuesque in us.

We cannot know the fullness of our spiritual nature until we have removed the pieces of our thoughts, feelings, motives, and actions that distort and cover up who we really are. Every time we surrender those blocks to knowing and expressing Divinity through truth and love, more of our godlike identity unfolds. We will be tested many times, and our priorities and choices will determine whether the heart of us gets honored or dishonored. Our intention and actions will lead us closer to or farther away from experiencing our core identity. "I am the Lord your God; consecrate yourselves and be holy, because I am holy" (Lev. 11:44 NIV). Which statement is truer for you: I use God, or God uses me? Which one would give you better results going forward?

St. Paul described surrender that leads to spiritual progress as dying daily (i.e., to the willful or ego-based sense of who he was) in order to be like Christ Jesus, a master of yielding to the divine Will. Paul also had clear intention about expressing Divinity's nature and getting rid of all that corrupts it. To the Ephesians he wrote: "put off your old self, which is being corrupted by its deceitful desire, to be made new in the attitude of your minds; and to put on the new self, created to be like God in true righteousness and holiness" (Eph. 4:22-24 NIV). That process of putting off is none other than releasing the perceptions, desires, and ways of being that hide or distort the genuine us, the best of who we're capable of being.

> Of course you're capable of showing forth the power and love of Divinity; in reality everything and everyone is.

Motives and the Way

Motives are based on desire. Why you do things comes from what you want and what you want to avoid. Like everyone else, you are wired to go for what you believe is pleasurable and avoid what you believe is painful. If you feel resistance to the stretching going on within you right now, ask yourself, "What is it that I truly want (or want to avoid)?" Clarity about your true desires may help you navigate growing edges.

Motives matter in every area of life, including that of surrender. If love is the dominant motive, you'll be able to focus not on what you are giving up or on how difficult things are but on what you truly want. Your desires and intention will impel you, whether they include freedom, devotion to knowing Divinity, the commitment to living your values, or striving for excellence in sharing your talents.

Higher motives may reveal the futility of former payoffs we'd been getting from trying to be right, making others wrong, feeling better than others, and getting even with or controlling others. We probably won't change until we recognize the secret satisfaction we've been getting for such motives and until we find a desire for higher rewards such as joy, true connection, and awareness of Divinity. Our shift in perceptions or action doesn't have to feel like traditional sacrifice. It may feel like we're standing for a higher principle or purpose in order to achieve a goal, meet a necessity, or live for the good of something beyond ourselves.

When we have a powerful enough reason, we can do just about anything. Time, space, and monetary limitations are transcendable with a committed heart of love. When the Presence within inspires us, we may find ourselves giving up temporary pleasure and comfort for more lasting benefits of healing, inner growth, and contribution.

At the end of our lives, we'll have paid the price for discipline and have been rewarded self-mastery. If not, we'll have paid the painful price of regret for letting ourselves and others down. Either way, there is a price to pay, yet only the former has lasting rewards. We've all witnessed examples of those who have lived disciplined love, such as mothers and fathers, entrepreneurs, teachers, coaches, spiritual mentors, innovators, and public servants. The average Olympic athlete trains more than seven thousand hours before the training culminates in their TV performances. Their excellence, borne out of willing commitment, brings us joy. True dedication has a way of inspiring others and moving them to action.

Self-concern is typically an anxiety-based state of being that can feel like a cage at times, limiting and small. As a young boy, I wrote something in a booklet that has served as a reminder many times since: "When you're feeling down, do something nice for someone." When we reach out in concern for another, suddenly our whole world can open up. Surrendering the downward pull of self-centeredness for the expansive outreach that lifts us up is a reward in itself. Caring also blesses others and can be life changing for them. Our capacity to love is enlarged as we share it, because it is being drawn from an Infinite Source, like a flowing river that expands its shores.

> Greatness isn't inherited from the great; it is born out of the dedicated and courageous lives of men and women.

Early Christians were identified not by their knowledge of scripture or big churches but by how they loved one another. Their standard was to "serve one another in love" (Gal. 5:13). They gladly gave their homes, money, encouragement, teaching, and healing to each other. The powerful energy and realness they demonstrated attracted many others to live that way also. It is interesting that before they were called Christians, they were called The Way. The way we live and the motives that drive our actions are always more important than the labels we attach to ourselves.

Blessings for Surrender

One of my favorite movies of all time is *Life is Beautiful* (Miramax Films and Mario and Vittorio Cecchi Gori, 1998). In it, Italian star Roberto Benigni, as Guido, lives a life of devotion to his wife and son. He risks his own life (which ultimately he totally gives up) and gives hope, encouragement, and unconditional love to his family. Guido courageously shields his young son from the horrific realities of being in a Nazi prison camp by creating make-believe games to redefine his son's lack of food and warmth, living conditions, and separation from his mother. He keeps romance alive with his wife by finding a nearly impossible way to play classical music, especially recognizable to her, over the prison camp's sound system. The film, which won three Academy Awards, seemed to serve as a vehicle to awaken man's potential to love, even in terrible conditions.

Many people never experienced from their parents the degree of unconditional love portrayed in the movie. But the question for today is this: what are we willing to give (and give up) in order to experience and share such unconditional love? What judgments, restricting feelings, words, or actions are we willing to let go of? One of the great acts of love we can give to the world is to progressively give up the selfish desires of the fear-ridden lower self in order to discover the security of genuine love and honesty.

In the process of unconditional giving, we may find rewards and blessings that we were not looking for. A person may volunteer to help the needy in his community and meet someone who later offers him a job or even a hand in marriage. An inspirational speaker may give free speaking engagements and later be invited to speak on television to promote her new book. A young person who selflessly

> Only a man or woman who does more than is required can enlarge his or her abilities and truly feel free.

gives up a social weekend to help build a house for the homeless may develop leadership, resourcefulness, and compassion. The universal law of Love shows again and again that there is no loss to our soul when we sacrifice lovingly and sincerely for the good of another, while honoring what is most valuable in our own hearts.

The Greatest Surrender

> At the end of your life, regardless of the results, you'll have lived for something, and you'll have given up many things in order to have whatever you do. Instead of living by default, consciously decide now what's worth living for and what you'll surrender to have it.

Many believe that the ultimate surrender came from the purely good man Jesus of Nazareth, because he gave up everything—except devotion to God—for the benefit of every man, woman, and child. He had a clear mission, which he boldly stood for, and readily gave up anything that was in the way of it. Regardless of what he went through, he never compromised love and truth. Whatever difficulties we're going through, there's a proven way out. The Christ in us is fully capable of leading us through them in the way of honesty and love. When we yield up that which does not honor the Divine within us in little ways, we develop the desire, humility, and strength to make larger demonstrations.

Do you know your mission for your time on Earth? What is it that you ultimately desire to bring forth and leave as a legacy? What is your motive for being here and doing what you do? You may not be called to give your human life for another as Jesus did, but you will be given opportunities to remove what is in the way of your life's purpose, perhaps through giving a helping hand for an afternoon, through a word of encouragement during a busy day, or by the work you choose. You may find yourself giving up anger or willfulness or doing more than your fair share when you see your partner tired after a long day.

Through such motives and acts, you can find a higher degree of joy, peace, and purpose. Those you help will be blessed as well, and the ripple effects carry forward to the entire consciousness of humanity. Ultimately when you surrender to the Highest within you, you are living a profound prayer; an increasing realization of unity or "at-one-ment" with divine guidance and capacities.

Practice Surrender

1) **Notice the Distinction:** Think of a time when you dishonored what was true in your heart and did something out of a false concept of sacrifice. You may have thought, "A good person should . . . ," "To save face, I better . . . ," or "My friend will not like it if I don't . . . ." These motives are not the same as when divine Love moves you. Take a look at the results of the choices you made based on a false sense of sacrifice. Did they lead to pain, suffering, or resentment in your experience or that of another? How would you do it differently knowing what you honestly know now?

2) **Prepare to Surrender:** List three attitudes or behaviors that your higher Self is calling you to surrender. It may be the way you interrupt people, the way you pose to get attention from your friends, or the fear that prevents you from acting courageously and honestly. Ask Holy Spirit to help you give up that which is hiding the real you and know that you will receive the help you ask for.

3) **What's Worth Surrendering For?** Through chiseling away each unnecessary piece of marble, Michelangelo got closer to his beautiful finished sculpture. In the same way, when we remove what's corrupting or distorting us, more of the best and the beautiful within us stand forth. Get clear about what is most meaningful to you in life. What is really worth living your life for? Is it honor, family, healing, freedom, or knowing and serving Divinity? With your top priority in mind, what is one change you will make to more fully align with what's truly important to you? Why must you do this, and when will you do it?

Chapter 23

Trust

"If our consciences are clear, we can come to the Lord with
perfect assurance and trust, and get whatever we ask for
because we are obeying Him and doing the things that please
Him" (1 John 3:21-22 TLB).

Success of Trust

An officer of the NASDAQ Stock Exchange spoke at a conference I attended many years ago. Although I do not recall his name, I will always remember the essence of what he said. He told the audience that companies prosper or fail because of trust. He showed that when people trust a company, they invest their money in it, become its vendors and clients, and buy its products and services. If a company does not maintain trust, it won't be successful and prosperous in the long term, or it will quickly loose whatever success it seemed to have in the short term. If a successful public company stopped producing quality products, its customers would look for a competitor to meet their needs, and the price of the company's stock would likely plummet. Top companies know that they must work daily to build and maintain trust in order to survive and succeed. True and lasting success is built on trust, not only in companies but in all of life, including relationships. Without trust, what's really left?

You can look at the quality of trust in your life from four different perspectives: How well you trust in your divine Source, how well you trust yourself, how well others trust you, and how well you trust others. Are you able to surrender control of your life to Divinity, at least in moments? Do you trust that a loving Power is caring for you and guiding you in every detail of your life? Do you really trust yourself to follow through and stick to your values and inner promises? Can others count on you to do what you say when you say you are going to do it? Do you possess the qualities, motives, and actions that others can rely on? Are you considerate, honorable, and honest? Finally, can others easily take advantage of you, or do you even know what makes them trustworthy or not? These are vital questions. The results of your answers may radically affect your power, the quality of your relationships, and your level of success in life. Let's look more closely at each area of trust.

> Who and what you trust will have a great impact on the results of your life.

Trust in the Supreme

It doesn't matter if you relate to Divinity as a Higher Power, Source Energy, The Universe, The Self, Divine Consciousness, God, Infinite Mind, Spirit, or Christ. If you are like the vast majority of the population, you probably agree that there is something beyond your mortal self and what you can see and touch—a divine Power that created everything and presently gives life to all things. You are included in the totality of this animating field of energy. The immensity of this Power and Presence ultimately governs the existence and movement of all things, including you. Saint Paul discerned that Divinity "giveth to all life, and breath, and all things" (Acts 17:25). "All things to all" means that everything and everyone are included, and nobody is excluded no matter what they did or didn't do in life. With this awareness, you have several choices each day. You can refuse to accept divine Love's presence in your life, ignore or forget about it, or choose to progressively relax into it and be blessed by it.

For a fresh approach, instead of focusing on God as an entity, it may be helpful for you to think in terms of trusting in principles and qualities of Divinity, such as constancy, omnipotence, reliable Truth, comforting Love, all-knowing Mind, and eternal Life. Trust in these attributes of Divinity is developed by seeking to understand, witness, and align with them. There are principles that you already trust in, such as gravity. You don't have to psych yourself up to get enough faith in the principle of gravity, because you have years of experience with it. With awareness and follow-through, faith in spiritual principles grows more powerfully as well.

You can increasingly align with the heavenly purpose of letting yourself be loved and provided for.

After graduation from college, I made a trip to the rustic island of Molokai in Hawaii to visit some of my Hawaiian friends from university. One morning we were out surfing about a quarter mile from shore. Suddenly the waters became very turbulent, so much so that I became fearful for my safety. We did not know that a potential hurricane was gathering power about one hundred miles away. The riptides and storm surf became so strong that all of us were being carried out to sea. I had heard stories of small boats being carried hundreds of miles off course during such conditions because of interisland oceanic currents. Fear gripped me when I realized that we could be getting close to those currents. After becoming exhausted from paddling, my only choice was to place complete trust in the divine Presence. I really didn't see another way out. It felt like my body just relaxed as I turned everything over to the mighty hand of God. My consciousness became filled with the nature and care of divine Power, and I felt that we would be protected. A few minutes later the currents completely shifted toward the land, and we were eventually carried to the shore. Other than some minor scrapes from rocks, all of us got out of the water safely and gratefully.

You may have had such an experience that seemed beyond coincidence. You know in your heart that it was only Divinity's care for you that brought you safely through. Being able to actually trust the Presence is an amazing and wonderful feeling that stays with us always. Like most things in life, such trust is developed step-by-step until it becomes more natural. No doubt it is easier for us to feel trust at a time of crisis when we've come through a lot of less threatening experiences that supported our growing certainty. Every time we shift from anxiety back into trust, our faith-capacity increases.

Divine ideas come with their own safety and supply. It's up to us to use them. This applies to relationships, finances, health, and every other area. Our capability to realize safety comes from Divinity's Allness, which includes knowing what we need and how to deliver it to us in understandable ways that serve our growth and other's.

Staying conscious of this may help you progressively give up the need to control your external world or your future. No matter what your life situation looks like, you have the opportunity to know that you're part of a much greater plan. Look for the bigger picture and seek to be part of the orchestration that is moving everyone involved, including you. In this way, you won't have to make your problems and responsibilities bigger than Life itself, because they actually aren't. Choose to feel at ease by understanding divine Intelligence, Power, and Presence to be greater than anything you're facing. Much like the mighty ocean currents, there is a flow that we can adjust to. One guarantee in life is that there will be changes and new demands made upon us. Nonetheless, the qualities and principles of Divinity will remain constant for our access and ultimate benefit.

What we focus on, especially with emotional intensity, will tend to expand in our lives. By focusing on God's infinitely powerful, tender nature and activity and living in alignment with principles of humility, truth, and love, we'll tend to have less fear and doubt parading in front of us. We strengthen our trust in the Presence by making *It* our focus and priority. It is our spiritual design to trust Spirit, and it is the most natural thing to do when the ego—or fear-dominated obstructions to this trust are reduced or removed. With negative thoughts, fears, and selfish tendencies minimized, it will seem easier for us to feel and rely on Divinity's field of Love.

Divinity's nature includes gentle kindness, tender compassion, powerful strength, constant discipline, perfect timing, abundant care, infinite goodness, spontaneous creativity, and so much more. Appreciate, understand, and progressively embody these qualities and thereby overcome fear and darkness and expand the certainty of your trust in the Supreme. Through clear intention, conscious awareness, and experience, a deeper trust in the Divine is revealed like the rising sun.

> "God goes before you and will be with you; he will never leave you nor forsake you" (Deut. 31:8 TLB).

Trust Yourself

Do you trust yourself? Do you keep promises with yourself? Do you believe in your own empowered word to declare something and have it occur? Along with inner reliability, the Presence within you gives you spiritual intuition about what you should say or do and when you should say or do it. When you rode your first bicycle or drove your first car, you progressively knew how to ride or drive from experience. Hearing and following your inner voice is developed the same way. Do you remember your summer days as a kid when you wanted to learn something new? You started where you were, dedicated yourself to progress, absorbed the learning, and practiced persistently until doing the hard thing got easier. Most areas of life are difficult until they become easy. Be easy with *yourself* and know that a refining process along the way leads to more clearly trusting your inner voice. In life, you really only have one main task: to let self-imposed limitations and fears go and allow Divinity to become dominant within you to unleash your capabilities. Then you are letting God be God in you, replacing limitation with God-possibility.

What else can help self-trust? Keeping your agreements and acting with integrity is vital in building your self-esteem, self-confidence, and self-trust. Say what you mean, do what you say, and then watch self-doubt subside and self-confidence rise. Motives are also important in developing confidence, because pure motives will give you an untainted heart—the kind of heart that feels easy to trust.

Your inner voice will become clearer when it is not obstructed with motives, words, and actions that try to deceive others. We can fool some of the people some of the time, but we can never really fool ourselves in the long run. We know at a core level whether we're practicing integrity. If there is any doubt, ask such questions as, "Was there a more honest way to say that?," "Was my motive unselfish?," or "Will I be glad I did this a year from now or at the end of my life?" Spiritual wisdom will show us how we can be even more honest in certain areas. Life is like an onion skin—there are a lot more layers than we think before we get to the pearl.

By everything you think, feel, say, or do, you're contributing to either an atmosphere of trust or mistrust. When you know what to do and then do something else, you'll likely feel weaker mentally, emotionally, physically, and/or spiritually. The fact that you're feeling weak in a certain area may be a clue that you need to realign with stronger personal integrity. Take a few moments to feel what it would be like to have confident trust and trustworthiness in your life. You may feel a sense of freedom, positive energy, power, or peace. Now that you have anchored that feeling, what could you say or do differently today or this week?

> Trust your pure insights; they can lead and protect you much more than you may realize.

Principles of integrity and self-trust apply equally to every area of life—spiritual practices, eating habits, exercise, education, workplace, and relationships. Ask yourself if your desired quality of life is worth enough for you to strengthen your self-trust. If yes, then go for it!

Do Others Trust You?

President Abraham Lincoln once rejected a man named as a potential cabinet member. When an aide asked why, Lincoln simply replied that he did not like the way the man looked. Being shocked, the aide stated that a man is not responsible for his appearance. Lincoln corrected him by saying that every man over the age of forty *is* responsible for the way he looks. Perhaps Lincoln sensed that a man's face reflects his trustworthiness after years of motives, choices, and actions. What are you doing and how are you being that allows people to trust you? Are you reliable and loyal? Are you believable? Do you have the kind of character that people look up to? Does your communication build bridges with others or tear them down? Do your thoughts and feelings of others build connection or separation? Does the way your face looks and the energy you broadcast create confidence in others? Do they move people toward love or fear?

Trust enables growth, intimacy, success, and fun. When trust is not a dominating quality in a relationship, unease causes weaknesses in the bond and difficulties in communication. Imagine being on vacation and wanting to go parasailing. You watch the first tourist lifted up by the boat operator have a major accident. Then you see the same thing happen to the second tourist. If you're next in line, what would you do? Anything else but parasailing, right? It's difficult to have fun and fully engage in an experience without feeling safe. Likewise, true joy in your relationships only happens when others feel safe with you—when you are trustworthy.

The fact is that in the minds of others, you're either trustworthy or not. There is no "kind of trustworthy." If you're up for the challenge, ask three people you know best how trustworthy they think you are on a scale of one to ten. Then, if you really feel bold, ask a couple of people who don't like you very much or who aren't close to you. Also ask why they feel the way they do and what you'd need to do differently to make your score a ten. The answers these people give you could be radically revealing. Others watch how you walk your talk and how you live your core values. They see if you do the hard or unselfish thing when you could take an easy way out. They (including children) even see you when you think they are not watching. Is your life an example or a warning? No matter what you've done up until now, what will you do with the time you have left?

Life is full of surprises and sometimes crises. How much do others trust you during crunch times—those times when your character is exposed and tested? My sister once risked her own life to save two children who had broken through an icy lake and were in danger of drowning. Others frantically stood by and watched them struggle in the freezing water. She later received a heroine award for being a woman of character and courage.

Your character is broadcasting a particular frequency level of trust. Those you spend the most time with may have a similar frequency. Notice that we can meet someone and immediately feel the quality of his or her character (e.g., "She's a great woman," or "He seems shady to me."). Credibility or lack thereof is discernible to many others as well. Ultimately, you are the one who creates the experience of trust that others give you by the quality of character you have, the motives you entertain, the feelings you display, and the choices you make. Who you have become is what others trust or mistrust. Hopefully this is encouraging to you. George Washington, the first one to be entrusted with the highest office in America, considered the most enviable of titles to be that of an "honest man." What do you consider to be most worth going for in your life?

> What seems advantageous to you depends on the perspective you choose. If it brings you pleasure now but causes you to lose the level of respect you once had for yourself, it can hardly be counted as a win, unless you learn from it.

Trusting Others

We don't always see things as they are; we tend to see things as *we* are. Everyone sees life from her own perspective. The drug dealer thinks most people are into drugs or are criminals. The college professor believes that most people are or should be motivated by learning. The soccer mom believes that parents should actively support their kids' interests. Who we have become, even more than just what we do, affects our ability to trust others. People who are trustworthy tend to believe that most others are too. People who are not trustworthy tend to believe that most others aren't. Each perspective comes with benefits and costs, because not everyone we think is trustworthy actually is. But, to assume that nobody can be trusted would make for a very limited experience.

Spiritual discernment can save a lot of unnecessary trouble. Inner wisdom will let you know whom you should not trust, if you give heed to the warning signs rather than ignore them. Think about painful relationship experiences in your past. Didn't you receive caution flags before the emotionally climatic events? Right now you probably have new signals about with whom you should be in a relationship and from whom you need to separate. The important question is this: are you willing to separate from those you should, regardless of how invested you are with them? If a man tells you about some real estate business deals where he has stretched the line to make extra money, why should you trust his interactions with you? Given similar circumstances where he thinks he can secretly gain something at your expense, he might try the same type of thing with you. What benefit is there for you to ignore such warning signs? Is the connection with such a person really that satisfying? Whatever satisfaction you're getting from the status quo, you might have to give it up to put your life on a safer foundation.

You know people by their energy, motives, actions, communication, relationships with others, priorities, contributions, and experiences with you. Do they help build up and heal others, or do they impact them negatively? Do they find value and meaning in the same things you do? Do they support the best within you, or do they tear you down passively or aggressively? If you are a sovereign adult, you are the one who gets to decide who to have relationships with, including your own relatives.

What about expanding your ability to trust others? Sometimes a limiting belief or untrue concept may keep you from trusting others, and this may have a hidden cost. Thoughts of past relationships may hold you back from exploring new opportunities. If you believe that all men cheat or that all women are needy, then you will operate your life on something that is simply not true. There are millions of men who don't cheat and millions of women who are beautifully selfless givers. With your limiting beliefs, you will get to have your own private world where the beliefs are true for you. The question is: do such beliefs truly serve you and others? Do they allow you to live an abundant life filled with unlimited possibilities and amazing experiences?

There are times when we're called by Spirit to trust others more. The English people had to learn to trust Winston Churchill (who had been formerly known as the "warmonger" but who had been right all along about Adolph Hitler's intentions). The early Christians had to learn to trust Saint Paul (a former persecutor of Christians), and you may have someone in your life who, seen in the correct light, now deserves your trust. If you are looking for closer relationships, you'll need to develop a deeper sense of trust and allow others to step into their greatness around you. This may include your willingness to open up and not be so afraid of getting hurt. Because we each operate based on our own values and rules, occasionally we let people down, and they let us down. That's life. Perhaps we need to get over it, revise our rules, and give others another opportunity to shine. Ask for their confidence, and give them yours one wise step at a time. Then check in honestly with the new results.

Isn't it time to break out of the prison of limiting concepts and false beliefs in order to experience more of the fullness of relationships? Each day presents you with growth opportunities to trust Divinity, trust yourself, wisely trust others, and expand trustworthiness in your progressive pathway to personal freedom and infinite Love.

Practice Trusting

1) **Trust Divinity:** How often are you aware of Divinity's influence in the details of your life? List three reasons why you don't ask for and feel divine guidance more consistently. Maybe you're too busy or believe that God only helps other people. Maybe you believe that even if Spirit did communicate with you, you wouldn't be able to hear it. Recognize how such limiting beliefs are obstructing you from trusting divine Love more fully. How could you update them and what could you focus on to feel more empowered and loved?

2) **Trust Yourself:** Write down the areas of your life where you live with integrity and honesty. Notice how it feels to be able to trust yourself in this way. You strengthen trust in yourself when you keep your word, have good motives, and live honestly. Now list three things that you've committed to but have not followed through on. The list may include a promise you made, a project

that needs to be finished, or a friend who needs help. What's it going to take for you to feel in complete integrity with yourself on these things? Take one positive step today and another this week and notice how these actions make you feel.

3) **Build Trustworthiness:** List the names of three people whom you trust and include the reasons why you trust them and the qualities they broadcast. Notice how they listen, speak, and act. What is it that makes their character strong, and how could you model them in your life? People trust you based on what you have become and how they see you live your life. What are two things you can do this week to build trustworthiness in your relationships? It may be doing what you say you're going to do, keeping people's confidences, or showing up with an unselfish heart. To build the trust of others in you, treat them the way they would like to be treated as well.

4) **Trust Others:** Acknowledge the signs and caution flags all around you. Trust what you spiritually discern about people and activities and make your relationship decisions from this Spirit-led heart-knowing. You may feel impelled to expand your trust in others or to completely disassociate from some. Act boldly to build and maintain relationships with others who have trustworthy qualities and character and, if wisdom calls, be willing to gracefully let the other ones go.

Chapter 24

Understand

"Wisdom is the principal thing; therefore get wisdom: and with all thy getting get understanding" (Prov. 4:7).

Universal Need

One of our greatest needs in life is to feel understood. A friend or partner who understands what is important to us and why it is connects with our hearts and souls. When our feelings, needs, and beliefs are understood, we feel assured, comforted, and loved. When part of us is misunderstood, we can feel hurt, pain, or alienation. Misunderstanding almost always leads to confusion, conflict, or a loss of energy—the very elements that tend to tear a relationship apart. In the process, we may even question our own self-worth; some part of us may feel insignificant. Many people have a core ego fear that they will end up alone and unloved. Being understood helps heal that fear, and it gives a foundation for relationships to grow.

The deeper someone discerns who we are, the more we feel engaged and energized. We also feel safe and nurtured. That safety allows us to trust another and to let him or her know us physically, spiritually, and/ or emotionally. When our hearts are open we are more honest about who we are, how we feel, and what we desire, need, and fear. For most of us, passion and adventure in a relationship begin with understanding and end without it. If you're feeling disconnected from someone you were once close to, this chapter can give you distinctions and choices toward mutual understanding that can positively transform your sense of relationship.

Intimacy and Peace

Are you missing closeness? Closeness is the result of knowing what's in another's heart and vice versa. Connectedness comes directly from giving understanding and being understood. Disconnection is the default setting when there is no understanding or when the unspoken crowds space to create a feeling of emotional distance.

Think for a moment about misunderstanding that exists between two people you know. At some level, you too may feel impacted. Every relationship affects more than just the two people involved, often like a chain reaction. A worker who misunderstands the words of a boss verbally reacts to them. The deflated employee goes home and doesn't listen to her child. The forlorn child goes to school and acts angry with her friend, and so on. Each one of these individuals longs to be understood. Giving understanding has a similar domino effect, only in a positive way. Imagine how your relationships could be if you had a willingness to understand others more deeply, especially when in the past you would not have done so.

You may not always agree with someone else's viewpoint, but you can open your heart to find out how she got there. Her pathway and perspective is valuable to her, and when you acknowledge them authentically, she will feel your love and respect. Do you know why someone you're distanced from has come to feel and believe what he has? Perhaps if you did, you might expand your perspective and have compassion for him. Each person has had millions of factors, interpretations, and choices affecting what they have become. We might think we have a man all figured out, but really we may not have a clue how his world looks to him or why it does. No matter how others show up, they need our love; and they may need it the most when it appears that they don't deserve it.

Although I did not have a nasty divorce with my first wife, no divorce is easy or pretty. Untying our closely intertwined lives after fourteen years of living together was very difficult for me emotionally, even though I felt we were traveling different spiritual directions. Fortunately, my former wife and I have both been willing to continue to understand one another even after we separated. We've explored how the other felt while married, what was great, what we learned, and what we each could have done differently. This mutual understanding has helped to bring healing and peace. It has also freed us to still care for one another and yet experience new relationships unburdened by the past.

Understand the Other Person First

Feel what is currently at war within you about one or more relationships. Do you feel angry, wounded, or deflated? Do you wonder if your friend or partner feels hurt or misunderstood too? For a few moments, ask your higher Self if there is something that you can do today to know the other person's perspective and heart more completely. With a change of heart, you might be led to give a prayer, a thoughtful phone call, an email, a visit, or simply ask her to share how she's feeling and what brought her to that place.

It is amazing how quickly healing takes place between two people when one reaches out to listen fully to the other. St. Francis of Assisi left us a prayer that unselfishly inspired that we can seek to console rather than be consoled and to understand and love rather than to be understood and loved. By taking the saintly first step to understand, you can positively change the dynamic of your relationship. Your unselfish intention and heart-directed actions will create an opening for connection to be reestablished or for the form of the relationship to change in a way that serves the current highest purposes for each of you. Understand the other person first and then witness what happens. For a reasonable time, decide that the important thing that matters is how the other person feels and sees things. Watch how the dynamics between you change.

Often when we do not feel understood, we get defensive, bring out attack weapons, and claim our territory. We want to regain control over something that feels out of control. If we feel hurt, we close down communication and disconnect. After all, we're right, so we shouldn't have to yield; the other person should! But look at the results of this attitude. Where has it gotten us? It's natural to look at a situation from our own eyes. Rarely do we remember to step over the line and look at things from someone else's perspective. We get secret satisfaction from holding on to our interpretation rather than seeking

> To understand our "enemy's" pain, needs, desires, fears, wounds, and view of us and to compassionately answer their concerns, is a way to gain wisdom and allow for possible resolution.

to feel another's. For the relationship to improve, someone has to be humble and courageous enough to cross the line in the sand and give understanding by saying something such as, "Help me to understand exactly how it looks and feels to you." If sincere, we're willing to genuinely listen to the response, without the need to present ours, until the other person feels complete.

Then Be Understood

If you truly take ownership for your own experience, then you'll realize that being understood is 100 percent your responsibility. With this perspective, you'll possess more power to take wise action. Is there something that you could say or do to have someone more clearly know what is meaningful to you? It may take courage, but the bigger risk to the longevity and harmony of the relationship may be in taking no action.

If you're feeling misunderstood, look at what you're doing to create or condone that experience. What are your motives: to be the hurt one, to sit in righteousness or resentment, or to let fear run you? Just what are you saying or leaving unsaid, committed to or apathetic about, forcing or allowing? Sometimes what is unspoken is crowding the most space. If you feel the disconnection growing but say nothing, you won't have to wonder why you feel stuck or unloved. Honest awareness allows you to do things differently, whether that means to have a better attitude, clean up communication, state your truth more boldly and completely, or get in better touch with your or another's emotions.

For another to understand you, you have to understand yourself first and foremost. Personal transformation includes doing the inner work to clarify your own desires, motivations, passions, dislikes, judgments, values, rules, emotional patterns, fears, needs, and beliefs. It also includes examining how you tend to language things internally and with others and to see if each of the above tendencies actually supports both you and your partner. The clearer you get about who you are, the better you'll show up to allow others to understand you. You can't expect your partner to figure out who you are for you—that's your job!

To create more understanding, focus on what you can control: *your* motives, speech, and actions, not on what your significant other should do. Honesty, wisdom-led vulnerability, and completeness are all highly important to build bridges of understanding. Saint Paul wrote with clarity and excellence, courageously creating understanding in lands both foreign and at home. This kind of communication helped to prosper relationships in the early Christian church. Perhaps part of the reason for the tremendous growth that took place then was because of how he advised others to live "speaking the truth in love" (Eph. 4:15), which is a great standard for creating understanding.

> "Keep yourselves in the love of God ... and of some have compassion, making a difference" (Jude 1:21-22).

Acceptance and Realness

Even when someone else is not willing to understand you, you can still find some peace by accepting the relationship for what it is and not trying to make it into what it isn't. Only by being in honest relationship with what is can you end internal resistance and take appropriate action to create the experience you truly want. If your cantankerous aunt has caused problems in your home on every holiday for the past ten years and your needs continually go unacknowledged after numerous communications, why do you keep inviting her over? Call the relationship for what it is—an unnecessary pain in the butt! Then you'll be free to create the holiday environment you want in your home. Accept what is and what has been and then seek to create the experience you would rather choose by responding with positive action.

Another aspect of getting real with your relationships is admitting that many times you react from misinformed or incomplete information or from an emotional trigger instead of from the actual reality of the situation. Frequently, *your* truth is not *the* Truth, and you can damage relationships by assuming it is. In the grand scheme of things, your truth is an infinitesimal factor in life, even if it is correct. There is always more to find out and learn, always another perspective to consider. Also, your opinions, which often change or diminish as you evolve spiritually, can interfere with your ability to see the experience or heart of another clearly. Judgments are decisions that cut off other options. Life is way bigger than that, so if your relationship feels boxed in, open the judgment flaps, look around you with new eyes, and feel how expansive things become.

Sometimes we feel rejected or misunderstood because, unknowingly, we're not being authentic; we're posing. Our acts are the masks we probably put in place earlier in life (and have refined since then) in order to be accepted or to get love in an insecure environment. In some ways, we may not accept ourselves, so we continue to use our acts to make up for it. We didn't think we were good enough the way we were to get enough love or acceptance. Instead, to gain attention or certainty, we used humor, flirtatiousness, intellect, athletic prowess, or an ability to make money.

After years of unconscious habit, we may think our masks are us, but some part of us longs to take them off. To relinquish an act and reveal our heart-centers can feel scary, so we default to the familiar in any situation that feels uncertain. A simple solution to being more accepted by others is to accept ourselves as we are, which includes the good, bad, and ugly; the weak, fearful, and frustrated; the mistakes; the parts of ourselves that would rather be shooting a nature photograph than running a board meeting; the erotic parts of us that we don't talk about; and the parts that aren't as smart as we feign to be when we tiptoe outside of our well-rehearsed area of expertise. Until we become enlightened, all of us have some pretenses to transcend. The real part of us is yelping like a caged Labrador to come out and play.

A normal reaction when we get into the energy of something that seems phony is to become angry or resistant or to even walk away from it. Think of a comedian who tells a joke that totally fits his personality and life experience versus someone who tells a joke that seems borrowed or contrived. We laugh and connect with the former; we energetically boo the latter. Rejection is our natural response, because our souls want the real deal.

Other people want the authentic from us too. We shouldn't have to try to be something we aren't in order for people to like us. If they only connect with the fake us, they're not really helping us in the long run anyway. Most young children don't wear masks, because they feel no need to hide who they truly are. Their divine innocence still easily shines forth unobstructed, and they naturally get attention because of their power and love radiating forth. Remembering that the heavenly kingdom (i.e., an authentic experience of peace, dominion, closeness to God; being accepted and understood) is within us, these words about a childlike heart may take on special meaning: "I tell you the truth, anyone who will not receive the kingdom of God like a little child will never enter it" (Luke 18:16 NIV).

Energy of Words

Dr. Masaru Emoto's internationally acclaimed research on water crystals viewed with high-speed photography reveals conclusive evidence that words can have either a constructive or destructive effect on the physical formation of the crystals, depending on the energy of the words. Phrases such as "you are beautiful" and "thank you" create beautiful designs resembling geometric snowflakes. The energy of words such as "hate" and "you idiot" form distorted, broken-down structures in the crystals (see Dr. Emoto's amazing works: *The Hidden Messages in Water, The True Power of Water,* and *The Secret of Water*). Perhaps you have experienced the effect of negative words on the structure of a relationship. What we say to and about another can have a lasting impact. All of us should treat our words more preciously. Words can transcend time and space and be used to bring the power of love to where it is most needed. Kindness uses a language that anyone can understand.

Does any tension or conflict exist in your family or extended family today? Are there members of the family who are not talking to each other? Chances are that it started with words that led to a misunderstanding. Perhaps it did not even seem like that big of a deal at the time. Then it festered, fed on personal interpretations and defensive emotions, and escalated. Now the story has taken on a life of its own; the rift has become well grooved.

Even a seemingly small verbal assault can do huge damage over time. Remember the slight that Ishmael delivered to Sarah, Abraham's wife, several thousand years ago? She saw him mocking her (see Genesis 21). What was the outcome? Ishmael and his mother Hagar were cast out of the family and consequently lost their inheritance. Perhaps the tension and misunderstanding that was started then has multiplied through centuries of hurt, anger, conflict, death, and destruction. In some ways, it has lasted up to the present day, as seen and felt in the conflict between the Israelis (Sarah's offspring) and the Arabs (Hagar's offspring). Yes, words definitely have energy.

If we want a world with more harmony in it, then we must take the lead by reducing or eliminating the launch of verbal and internal assaults. War tends to exist where governments and their people live without a standard of truth and love. History shows what is positively possible, because there was an era in ancient China where peace reigned for several hundred consecutive years.

What is the standard you live by in your home and workplace? Do you control your words, or do they control you? Before the reptilian part of your brain prompts you to speak to your offender, ask yourself, "Will saying this or participating in this conversation bless everyone involved? Will I be glad I said this a year or five years from now?" The intention of your words will give them nurturing power or destructive potential. The choice is yours.

> "Knowing God results in every other kind of understanding" (Prov. 9:10 TLB).

Tension is resolved one unselfish step at a time. It takes love and courage to move in a healing direction. One humble act of understanding has the power to change a life. What if Ishmael had begged forgiveness for his remarks? What if Sarah had been more understanding of his youthfulness and jesting? How would the next four thousand years have looked? How much emotional pain and slaughter could have been avoided? If progress is what you want, then what are you willing to do to step out of your shoes and sincerely understand the person who is challenging you? Are you willing to find out what another believes, feels, fears, and yearns for? If so, you'll be in a better position to allow divine Grace to bring movement and healing to the relationship and to be more fully understood yourself.

Practice Understanding

1) **Understand Others:** When seeking to understand someone else, you may discover that the person acted out of hurt, fear, or defensiveness from feeling misunderstood about his or her values, rules, beliefs, needs, pain, or desires. Recall your most difficult relationship and imagine yourself watching the experience through the other person's eyes. Include the ability to understand how the other person was feeling and why. Then journal about how it feels to experience the situation through the other person's eyes, ears, and heart. Write down any revelations or action steps that Spirit communicates to you as a result of your journaling from the other person's perspective.

2) **Feel Understood:** Identify any situation in your life where you don't feel understood. What impact is this having on you? Take an honest look at your own motives in the situation. Were they completely honest and unselfish? Is there any way you could speak the unspoken or communicate more honestly and lovingly in order to achieve the outcome you want? Sit or lie down in a comfortable position. Quiet your mind by bringing your awareness into your body. Feel the hurt, pain, tension, or stress that has stacked up from this situation. From this place of discomfort, ask yourself, "What would it take for me to feel understood? What action am I willing to do this week to feel more complete?"

3) **Bring Peace:** Choose, declare, and write the feelings that you want to experience within yourself and your relationships. "I will be peaceful," "I choose to love her," "I will understand him," or "I intend to express compassion today." Next, describe the benefits you'd gain from creating such a quality state of being. Clarity and intention precede action, so witness what you are led to do over the coming days and weeks.

4) **Take Action:** A key step to resolving conflict with someone is to experience a change of heart within, before attempting to take action. Taking action before your heart has changed often creates more pain and problems! Any steps you take with an understanding heart will have a better chance of bridging the relationship. If you need guidance, you can humbly pray for understanding and compassion. From the space of a softened heart, list and schedule one or two things you're willing to do in order to bring connection or healing in one of your relationships.

Chapter 25
Unify

Unity comes from elevating one's motives, actions, and consciousness. Disunity is the result of deceit, inauthenticity, and self-centeredness.

Unifying Fundamentals

In order to bring maximum unity to a relationship, you must first find accord within yourself by moving in the same direction as your soul's desire. If you don't move with your soul, you'll bring inner conflict to your relationships. Your destiny unfolds from your intention and decisions, which set the course of your actions. If you want to be a high-level tennis player, you'll take entirely different actions than a person who intends on designing fantasy video games. Unity between you and a partner will be strongly influenced by whether you are moving on the same pathway with the same motives.

Intentions are important, but in order to have substantial results, devotion is required. Devotion is the willingness and determination to access resources and do whatever it takes to overcome fears, obstacles, and distractions in order to realize what you desire to be, do, or have. This is how you have accomplished many things in your life up until now. Clear intention, motives, and devotion are the common elements that bring success individually, in families, in business, and in other relationships.

Conflict tends to start and escalate when falsehood, fear, or selfishness prevail; when we are not moving in the same direction as our souls; when clarity of intention is not chosen, communicated, or agreed upon; or when we have motives that conflict with the highest good of all concerned. "If a kingdom is divided against itself, that kingdom cannot stand. And if a household is divided against itself, that household cannot stand" (Mark 3:24-25 LAM). Without unity, life is a bigger struggle. Disunity usually includes anxious and constricted energy that tries to control another in dishonest ways. Controlling another person invites resistance and inner

> The direction we're moving in is at least as important as where we are and how we got here.

guilt. Conversely, where honesty prevails and where there are concordant hearts and actions, we feel part of each other, and the most amazing things can take place in our homes and relationships.

Synergy Math

Unlike arithmetic, the math of unity shows that one plus one does not equal just two; it is much greater than two. The synergy between two people can yield much better satisfaction and results than if they were working independently. In terms of quality of life, true partners can create five, ten, or twenty times the results than an individual can alone.

Inner harmony makes us feel strengthened, supported, and supplied. Conversely, when we're not aligned within ourselves, we're usually struggling against someone or something. Instead of using our energy to create, we spend it to resist, and often what we resist is another person. This can result in losing focus and motivation, becoming lost in negativity, or feeling worn down. Much less energy is available for what we originally wanted. The good news is that we can make a shift at any time.

During my early twenties, I worked as an assistant superintendent for a home builder in California. One morning while making my rounds, I found the masonry and concrete flatwork contractors in a heated argument at the model homes. I stepped in to stop the impending fight and to discover the underlying issue. The masonry contractor was supposed to lay a complicated brick design for one part of the driveway, and the other part was to be concrete surrounding the masonry. The two contractors disagreed about the way the architectural plans read. Upon reviewing the plans, I realized that the plans were actually not clear enough, and there appeared to be no immediate solution. Both contractors had costly crews and equipment standing by, and both were ready to storm off the job site in anger.

Part of my job was to keep the project on schedule, so I held in mind that both of them were capable of expressing divine intelligence, and both of them wanted to do excellent work. I told them that together we would find a solution that worked for all. The three of us took a deep breath and became quiet for about ten seconds. Then the masonry contractor got a design idea, which all of us agreed was a great solution. Both contractors completed their work with outstanding craftsmanship. To this day, the driveway of that home in Laguna Niguel has a special meaning to me, because it reminds me that no matter what the divisive outlook is, positive results can come from taking the high road of working together.

Compared to business interactions, the impact of motives, intentions, and devotion in personal relationships can be more energetically subtle, and the results of disunity or unity can be respectively very disturbing or exceptionally rewarding. One couple I know sits down together each New Year's Day and identifies common goals, desires, and plans for them and their family. The outcome of this has been a wonderful support to their marriage. They know where they are going and that they are heading there together for the same powerful reasons.

At my parents' fiftieth wedding anniversary, I asked my mom if she had any regrets in her life. "Yes," she told me, "I wish that we'd never moved to California." My parents had left Ohio and moved to California forty-five years earlier. My mom was sitting before me revealing that she had forfeited what she had truly wanted. It appeared that she and my dad had not made a decision that worked for both of them. I wondered if this undercurrent of discontent had affected her happiness and the unity of her marriage in any way. I wondered what else could have been possible for them had they found a unifying solution.

When you don't communicate your needs and what's true for you, compromising may lead to hidden resentment and disconnection from inner power. If compromise for you means being forced to do something you don't want to do, you may have an association of pain with finding a solution and thus may choose to avoid the conversation. Remember, though, the unspoken can have negative consequences too. If you have to unwillingly give up something for someone else or for some less-than-worthy reason, you may feel a growing crack in your bond. A better solution is one where neither you nor your partner compromises anything in the conventional sense. Instead, you work diligently to find a solution that works for both of you as a relationship, so each one feels satisfied for having nurtured the relationship without forsaking their most vital individual needs. The process of getting to such a place may take some work and deep communication. Pure motives and willingness will make the process easier. Wherever you commingle with others, life will be easier if you keep the motive to help them and, at the very least, not hurt them.

Consciousness Impacted

Unity has to do with wholeness, oneness, being in agreement, experiencing harmony, integrity, and continuity. When we feel another's desires, pain, needs, and fears, a compassionate bridge is formed that helps to heal the belief of separation. Many great spiritual writings have pointed to the fact that all of us come from the same Source or Creator. "Don't we all have the same father? Didn't the same God create us all?" (Mal. 2:10). At some level, everything we do affects both us and the whole of humanity. Even a hurricane starts in another part of the world as a tiny puff of wind. A war originates in somebody's mind before it erupts into battle. We live in a universe of interconnected consciousness. Therefore, when we help another, we're helping ourselves, and when we hurt another—mentally, emotionally, physically, or, worse still, spiritually—we're also hurting ourselves in some way. We may feel the impact through self-guilt or in our own inability to feel and express our best for a period of time. If we could grasp the rippling impact of our thoughts, feelings, words, and actions, we would probably choose them more responsibly. As we progress spiritually, the entire world benefits to some degree, and if we retreat spiritually or cause an impediment to another, the whole world is impacted negatively.

Nature shows us that things that work together grow and prosper. Rain, nutrients, and soil minerals feed forest plants and trees. The sunlight then invites their upward growth. Things that are opposed, divided, or energy-consuming bring temporary or long-term destruction in some way. Where there is disunity in a business, marriage, or group, relationships are weakened, energy is consumed, and creative power is reduced. True love brings energy that isn't consumed; rather, it flows freely and continuously multiplies from an unlimited source.

Hold in mind someone with whom you're having a conflict or weak connection. Now recognize that in consciousness you're one with that person because you have the same life Source; then feel linked in with the Infinite energy that is divine within you and the other person simultaneously. After this experiential connection, especially if you felt it with emotional intensity, witness if you have a positive shift in your relationship. By aligning with the infinite field of Love, you make yourself available to the benefits that it generously offers—supply, peace of mind, guided connection, unmistakable timing, soulful experiences, and profound joy.

Unifying motives, speech, and action come from going to higher common ground to find common ground. By living in a higher state of consciousness, there is less to fight about. The Self, your godlike nature, reveals itself when you disidentify with the divisive nature of the ego. The ego, which likes to be separate from others, gets de-energized in moments and in degrees whenever you choose love and truth. The desire to experience unity based on truth and love will expose ways of being in you that need to be released, such as pride, jealousy, or fear. In your moments of decision, you'll move closer to or farther away from unity, so unity is a process more than an event.

Even after all the marvelous things they had witnessed for three years, the Apostles disputed among themselves who was to be the greatest. Upon hearing this, the spiritual CEO Jesus told them to let "he who is a leader be like one who serves" (Luke 22:26 LAM). What if we adopted this way of being in our workplaces, homes, and intimate relationships—that of serving and giving value as the measure of how much of a leader we are? Each one of us has a unique and important part to play in the entire symphony of Life if we're willing to serve our Spirit-animated role and appreciate the roles of others.

No Other Power

The foundation of divine Love is oneness and wholeness, not division. One who is moved by Love has the intent to bring together and build on what is like-minded, often even when there seems to be differences. These types of people have a way of transcending circumstances and appearances and finding the divine spark within themselves and others. Divine Love knows no lasting opposition, so there are not two sides to Love. There is only one side—the Allness of God—which includes the entirety of Creation, including you. "Therefore, he who is not against you is for you" (Mark 9:40 LAM).

Based on a dualistic and limited perception of things, opposition is ultimately an illusion, because there can be no opposite of Allness; there is only the belief of its absence, as if Divinity didn't exist in a certain person or place. If we hold to the false belief that there is another side having real power to oppose Divinity's expression, this belief will tend to project onto the screen of our lives and form an experience filled with conflict, disharmony, and fear. We'll get to be right about what we hold in mind to be true. Collectively, we're projecting the experience of the world we see today.

Ignorance is not the opposite of understanding, just its absence. Darkness is not an actual substance; it is lack of light. There appears to be a spiritual dark side that can lie and destroy, but this is not power. It only operates by hypnotic and false suggestions. It appears to have life only when we give it life and a home when we give it one. A choice in falsity, heartlessness, or fear seems to give dark energies temporary authority and activity. Ultimately, spiritual darkness can have no influence over us unless we believe and follow its suggestions or hypnotic spells. When we contribute to disunity through falsity and nonlove, we're adding to our own hypnotic trance! Where truth and love dominate, there is harmony. Where false beliefs, critical judgments, or negativity are fostered, disunity will deepen. Like a light dimmer switch, falsity and lack of love dim our experience of peace. When we think, feel, and live by standards of honesty and true caring, we thereby diminish the spell and reconnect with the Presence, the true Power within us. The enlightened beings are the ones who have awakened to non-duality and are no longer ruled by the belief in a power other than that of Divinity. Where there is no opposition, there is unity. "Let every soul be subject unto the higher powers. For there is no power but of God" (Rom. 13:1).

When I was a teenager living with my parents, I was getting ready for a date with a gal I'd recently met. My dad came barging into my room and started yelling at me about going out with this girl. I yelled back, "You haven't even met her!" I believed he had no right to tell me whom I should and should not date. The tension escalated quickly. With my dad shouting at me nose-to-nose, I glimpsed the futility of

"May God who gives patience, steadiness, and encouragement help you to live in complete harmony with each other—each with the attitude of Christ toward the other" (Rom. 15:5 TLB).

the conflict between us. Then I prayed silently, "Dear God, I don't know how to love this man right now, but I know you do, so please show me." Instantly a surprising wave of compassion flooded over me, and I felt nothing but tenderness toward my dad. Perhaps his anger was a sign that he was hurting inside, frustrated with his life, or feeling out of control. I may never know. I just stood there not saying a word, looking deep into his eyes with compassion. Instantly he became silent, gave me a look of wonder, and walked away. When there is nothing left inside of us to oppose another, the other person will find it hard to push against us.

Twelve Behaviors That Unify:

- Honor Divinity

- Keep agreements

- Show cooperation and kindness

- Share common values and vision

- Act with loving motives and integrity

- Surrender ego reactions and practice humility

- Be more accepting and supportive to yourself and others

- Awaken your own consciousness (and remove the blocks to it)

- Give value and seek to serve the highest good for all concerned

- Have the willingness to learn, grow, and put forth needed effort

- Communicate honestly; make your needs known and understand another's

> "Only humility will lead us to unity, and unity to peace" (Mother Teresa).

Behaviors that Divide

One of the quickest ways to break up unity in any partnership, organization, or nation is by adding something that does not belong (i.e., an impure substance, concept, or action), something that does not support life, truth, and love. For example, it's been said that during the fourth century, the Emperor Constantine, who had witnessed a sign whereby he was converted, declared that Christianity was to be the official religion of the Roman Empire. In doing so, thousands of people were added to the church, many of whom were not interested in Christlike motives or lifestyle. This resulted in the potency and harmony of the early Christian church being contaminated by all sorts of beliefs and practices, some of which may have been in opposition to pure Christianity. Soon there was a dramatic decline in the miraculous healing power and concordance that formerly had been so evident among the original followers of Jesus.

This same type of thing happens in businesses where someone or some concept that is not in alignment with the company's philosophy gets added to a department. The productivity and unity within the enterprise soon declines. Marriage is another obvious target for disunity, when one or both partners participate in extramarital affairs, pornography, or other self-interested or addictive behaviors. Impurity is often insidiously disastrous to a bond. If you are experiencing virus-like disunity right now, ask yourself: what elements are undermining the purity of the relationship? It could be selfishness, gossip, deception, compulsive habits, low-energy TV programs, or simply a lack of nurturing. Once you uncover what is creating a rift, you can do something about it.

Having an "I'm right and you're wrong" attitude also divides. Self-righteousness and criticism foster separation. Humility and appreciation are the antidotes. When we consider only what's best for ourselves instead of everyone involved, we're inviting discord, which may eventually seem like inviting a pack of wolves to fresh meat. A more loving standard is to seek to give the greatest good for the greatest number of people involved, including ourselves.

Miscommunication also divides. This includes communication that leaves information out and/or adds information that is not quite accurate or is meant to distract or confuse another. Like gasoline on a campfire, untruth enflames conflict. Making assumptions without verifying the validity of them can also cause dissention. Checking facts and correcting false presumptions and statements will build more certainty and unity. Great communication includes sharing and understanding each other's desires, pain, fear, needs, and dreams. A lot can be healed through any one of these.

Fear can be incredibly divisive and is at the root of most conflicts. When we're afraid (as we have all been at times), we intensely focus on our fears and needs and may be unaware of the division it is creating. A man I know had suffered a neck injury more than thirty years ago and had only recently told his wife that he had lived with an ongoing fear of becoming paralyzed by moving his neck the wrong way. It's likely that the fear impacted their relationship on numerous occasions.

At one time or another, we may have been afraid of our state of health, job, income situation, social standing, or an unpredictable relative. We may hold limiting fears that nobody finds us desirable or that we don't know how to say the right thing socially. Fear can seem to obstruct our authentic expressions and abilities to best respond to a situation or person. Most often fear is at the core of anger, resentment, and hurt. It needs to be exposed and healed. If left unchecked, fear may distort our vision, weaken our devotion, and zap our energy. It won't enable us to feel unity, because we'll feel temporarily disconnected from our hearts.

John, one of the Apostles who seemed to have understood the love of Jesus, wrote that "The one who fears is not made perfect in love" (1 John 4:18 LAM). Fortunately he did not stop there but gave us the way to remove fear in the same verse: "There is no fear in love; but perfect love casts out fear." Connecting with the love in our hearts and allowing divine Love's activity to flow through us toward others is the antidote that will displace fear. Knowing this, we're never stuck with fear, because there are always opportunities to express love.

Deep Connection

Perhaps one of the most enjoyable, wonderful, spiritually challenging, and growth-motivating things to experience on Earth are deeply connected relationships. With an increased awareness of what is blocking unity in your relationships, you can seek concord by letting go of the limiting beliefs, fears, motives, and actions that divide. In their place, feel the strengthening Presence of divine Love, a field of energy that is always within you and others, motivating you to cast out all that opposes honesty and love. Alignment with the field of infinite Love naturally impels you to embody thoughts, motives, and actions that bring you closer to the authentic Self of others. When your true heart meets the unencumbered heart of another, harmony is much more likely to happen.

Practice Unifying

1) **Recognize the Costs:** Identify a relationship or situation in your life where there is disunity. Recognize the pain, suffering, and loss this division is giving you mentally, physically, emotionally, and/or spiritually and what it may cost you and others over the next one, five, and ten years if a resolution is not found.

2) **Clarify Motives and Intention:** With the above situation or relationship in mind, write down your motive and intention for reconciliation or healing. Your intention is what you decisively want to become, do, or experience, and your motive is the reason why. Writing uses your physiology to place a feeling or thought into physical form. When you have a clear intention and emotionally inspired motives, you can more easily carry them through with others. Together with devotion, such powerful clarity promotes healing and unity.

3) **Recognize Behaviors that Divide:** Make a list of the behaviors that you believe are creating division in your most difficult relationships. Do you listen carefully, stay open minded, and think kindly of the other person? When you feel hurt, do you criticize, emotionally explode, or withdraw from the relationship? Actions have consequences, and you're responsible for how you choose to respond to difficult people in your life. In this way, you create your own heaven or hell. When you consistently choose behaviors that divide, there is no easy way to create a solution that works for everyone.

4) **Practice Behaviors that Unite:** Pick two of your behaviors that divide and commit to doing the opposite. For example, you

might decide to stop thinking negative thoughts about a friend who has hurt you. Instead, you decide to focus your thoughts and actions on what is valuable about them, and appreciate how they contribute to you and/or others. Or, instead of leaving conversations half-finished or inaccurate, commit to completing them honestly and thoroughly. Notice the results your new behaviors invite. Remember that common ground is best found by going to higher ground.

Chapter 26

Be Willing

Possibility, power, and resourcefulness abide in a willing heart.
Unwillingness houses feelings of limitation, fear,
and separateness.

Power of Willingness

In order to be applied and integrated, every concept in this book starts with willingness. It is the one thing that no book or other person can give us; it's a choice that must come from within. Along with honesty and love, it is a pivotal quality that determines the outcome of relationships. Willingness is the springboard for learning, growth, connection, and excellence. It is the element needed for us to find jobs and expand the quality of our lives. It helps us to move from limiting patterns to divine patterns, from ego to Spirit, from the animal toward the angelic. It is the quality of character that enables us to give up short-term gains for long-term growth.

Humility is inherent in a willing heart, and it's the very thing that eliminates the belief of separateness and unites us with wholeness. When we choose to transcend our confining lower patterns during an act of kindness, we find more of our true Self, which knows no limits.

Unwillingness is resistance, and resistance generally makes life more difficult. Without willingness, we reinforce the belief in a separate ego, stay stuck, and are unable to receive the inspiration, resources, and people we need to move forward, solve problems, and expand our consciousness—our awareness of ever-present Divinity.

Willingness lubricates the sticky parts that can occur in marriages, businesses, and other close relationships. It begins in one's heart and precedes all actions of love. A willing heart allows one to overcome pride, laziness, and the habitual need to control others in order to be of service and enjoy lasting satisfaction. It takes a willing attitude to face core emotional issues and fears, to explore new interpretations of life, and to realize new possibilities. An infinite world exists, yet a new one can open up to us only with willingness. Ways to enjoy a more expansive life are found by looking at ourselves, our situations, and others in original ways and by readily raising our standards and giving more than we're used to giving. How expansive is your life feeling right now? Chances are that your depth of willingness is directly related to the emotional quality of this feeling.

A love-motivated person cares about others and says yes when there is a need that he's capable of filling. Love impels us to step up to the plate, go the extra mile, and do what's needed. Willing people are ready to help, learn, partner, and figure out a way. They contribute to life, and life powerfully and caringly contributes back to them. Ultimately, willingness isn't about doing what we should do but about an eagerness to put short-term self-interest aside in order to serve a higher and enduring good (our own and another's).

Willing Partners

One of the benefits of spiritual growth—doing our own inner work—is that we then have something alive to share in our relationships. Just as a firefly lights up a summer evening because it's moving, you too will be able to bring light to your relationships when you are moving, becoming more of who you are capable of becoming. Remember that at any moment you are either growing or dying, progressing or regressing. There is no middle ground. The idle status quo of your relationship is actually a slow breakdown in disguise. With a significant other, your willingness facilitates heart-connection, learning, deep listening, and feelings of support. What kind of partner have you been lately? How willing have you been? How much movement and life have you given to the relationship, and if you're not in one, to past relationships?

Spiritually evolving people don't always walk around in a state of nirvana. They seem to regularly face obstacles, setbacks, tests of devotion, pains, and losses, in both wilderness and desert-like territories along their journeys. Perhaps you can relate. What a tremendous benefit to be in a relationship with a supportive partner throughout such a pathway—someone who comforts you when you feel war-torn, reminds you of what's great when you can't see it, and prays for you when you don't see a way out of a difficulty. Do you have somebody in your life who sticks by you and cherishes the essential you as you work through your ego patterns, physical trials, emotional wounds, and spiritual blind spots? Do you show up like this for your partner and friends?

Relationships have lives of their own, so when one partner is out of sorts, the other feels it. A helpful partner can make all the difference in bringing restoration. Before things get heated, are you typically motivated to find a win for the other person as well as for yourself? Do you stand on the principle that there is a way for both of you to have your needs met so the relationship wins too? Supportive partners understand that this win/win principle is more important than one person being right and making the other person wrong (which is the classic win/lose—an unwillingness to understand and meet the needs of another's heart). Lose/lose is where neither partner is willing to meet the other's needs, so obviously the relationship loses as well.

Roommates may have a conflict about how warm to keep their home during the winter. One person has a high metabolism and is too warm, while the other often feels chilled to the bone and wants to turn up the heat. Unwilling attitudes would make the situation difficult to solve, yet there are ways to do so. Perhaps the cool roommate offers to wear layers to feel warmer. Hearing this, the warm person offers to wear less clothing and/or raise the temperature slightly. Because of willingness, the relationship is strengthened. Seems simple enough, right? That's what willingness does—it makes seemingly complex and frustrating things simpler.

Conversely, think back about everyone you've ever lived with and recall the two or three worst conflicts you have ever experienced. Now play the same movies again, only this time edit them with absolute willingness, starting with you and including the other actors in the scene. Do you get a different screenplay and outcome? Now come to the present, the relationship you're in right now that's presenting some challenge or flatness. Fast-forward this life movie two to five years out. Do you like the results you foresee? If not, what would it be like if you showed up, starting today, with a profound sense of willingness? How much pain and angst would this save? How much clarity, understanding, and perhaps even passion would this help bring to your situation? Also, what effect might this have on the way the other person shows up for you?

Relationship: Not Fifty-Fifty

Willing people are givers by nature. They don't worry about doing more than their fair share or fear losing a horse-trading, tit-for-tat game. Instead, they gladly do their parts, and often more, without keeping score. You see, the ideal relationship is not fifty-fifty; it is more like one hundred-one hundred. When both people individually accept that they're fully responsible for the relationship and commit to giving their best, the needs of the relationship are abundantly met under any condition.

Your 100 percent will vary in appearance during demanding times. There may be occasions when you or your partner feels tired, under pressure, or just not feeling well, so your best will look less than normal. Still, if you're consistently giving your best, your partner will feel this and will be more likely to give his or her 100 percent to make up the needed slack. Over time your emotional, physical, and spiritual investment in each other can accumulate vast resources for you to make it safely through the valleys, plateaus, and dark places where you may eventually find yourself.

If your bank account was unexpectedly found cleaned out, you would react and probably look for another bank. Many people bail on their relationships because they don't have many secure assets built up in their relationship bank account; they believe there aren't enough reasons to stay around. Approaching your relationship with a 100-percent attitude will create more certain reasons to stay around and invite your partner to do the same. Fifty-fifty is a sure way to suck the life out of a relationship during the trying times and make the valleys seem like bottomless pits.

Willing Words that Wow

There are six words that can do wonders for any relationship: "What can I do for you?" If sincere, this serving attitude can enable the other person to feel understood and supported, bring back romance, and open up new and wonderful possibilities. By individually answering this question, each partner can receive clear direction to be there for the other partner in more fulfilling ways. With such feedback, you can understand your partner's needs without having to guess and be the hero or heroine for meeting those needs.

There are seven other words that can shift a relationship positively: "What do you need most right now?" Most people feel more valued and cared for just by having such words spoken to them. Wouldn't you at times? Our needs change dynamically with many cycles of life, including the different stages of life we are in—various seasons, careers, emotional state, financial status, health, family ups and downs, and evolution in consciousness. Some needs are more prevalent on Mondays; others are predominant throughout one's life.

Usually men have a central need to feel like they have what it takes to please their women. That's why a smiling woman is so attractive; she reinforces the possibility that a man can make her happy. Many women have a core need to feel valued by and delightful to their men—to feel they have what it takes to captivate and hold their interest. All of us have the need for certainty, variety, connection, and feeling special, yet not always in the same order or intensity. Nonetheless, willingness goes a long way to help meet these fundamental needs in relationship. If they're not met, dispassion, conflict, or even breakup can result as the partner attempts to get his or her needs met in another way. Just a few sincere, timely, and willing words can make a huge difference.

Synergy and Energy

Willingness builds bridges between people and allows for positive energy to flow across them. We cannot have a true sense of teamwork and synergy without eager participants. Have you ever been in a meeting with a room full of reluctant coworkers? Those meetings can feel like agony, and they can be a huge energy drain and waste a lot of time. Conversely, a group of entirely eager people tends to be fun, productive, and efficient. Your life can feel more like this too if you show up to your home, workplace, and friendships with the light-bearing nature of openness and readiness instead of heavy resistance and defensiveness.

The opposite of resistance is freedom, and partnering in a cooperative relationship feels more like freedom than the proverbial *ball and chain* experience. The energetic experience is one of expansiveness, connectedness,

> "Do what you can, with what you have, where you are" (Theodore Roosevelt).

and spaciousness. When difficult situations present themselves, the mental shift of willingness opens up room for new possibilities and movement. Focus is shifted from what feels restrictive to what feels motivating and creative, because willing individuals will most readily learn the needed lessons and thus be wiser and stronger to meet future demands. Setbacks become launching pads for upward wings of progress. "Bring it on" is an enthusiastic mantra of those who are willing, because they look forward to who they will become in the process. Presidents Theodore Roosevelt and John F. Kennedy seemed to embody this attitude, and as true statesmen, they infused it in many other Americans as well.

It's Up to You

Do you accept and completely own your own experience? How you choose to respond to everything in your life is totally up to you. Only from this perspective can you fully participate in your own learning and growth. Otherwise, you are giving your power to something or someone external to you. Do you come from the place where you can honestly say to your partner, "I'm ready to understand how things look and feel to you. I'm willing to take total responsibility for my part in this relationship and heal what needs to be healed in me"? Stand from an empowered place of knowing that the experience of your bond is your responsibility, so if it must change, first you must change. If you want more romance from your partner, then be more romantic. If you desire better communication, then ask better questions, listen more deeply, and speak more honestly. If you feel like your partner is not much fun, create the experience of spontaneous pleasure. Your results will show you how you are being. With an open heart, anything is possible. "If it must be, it's up to me" is a great attitude that can bless any relationship.

When you make positive changes, the relationship must shift. Sometimes the result will be renewed romance and connection, or it may result in ending a relationship or adjusting to a new form of it so that you can move on to one that is more in line with who you have become.

Several years ago I was involved in a community service project with seven others. After a few weeks of working together, I became angry and frustrated, because I felt four of the participants were dead weight. Something had to change if we were going to meet our project time line. My perception changed when I realized that each person's 100 percent was totally different. Each of us had a different personality and skill set. Our group had an essential mix of visionaries, networkers, leaders, and analysts, and I began valuing each person's assets and unique capacities. What had appeared to my limited senses as laziness in some people was possibly the best they had to give at that time. I also recognized that I'd been so wrapped up in a critical, energy-sucking attitude toward their nonperformance that I was not giving anywhere close to my best.

With this shift in understanding, I became willing to do whatever it took to get the project done on time. Amazingly, several of the others also stepped up and contributed significantly more than expected. By the end, our project was a success, especially in terms of the learning that took place and the ultimate harmony of the group. Once you have sincere eagerness, you could pray something like this: Dear God, according to your will, please give me the wisdom to know what to do, the clarity of how and when to do it, and the courage and strength to see it through.

Allowing Perspectives

Do you allow people to be who they are without trying to change them? Do you let them grow in a way and time line they believe is best for them? Isn't that what Divinity does with us our entire life? We've all had periods of going nowhere or seemingly backward, and we've had times when we've traveled down less-than-perfect roads. Didn't those byways help us become who we are today? Growth often comes from an experience of trying something new, even if it doesn't work out as expected. When evaluating our own or another's lifetime, time frame changes perspective a lot. If we look at a decision over a two-day period versus a two-decade period, our sense of what was best or successful can appear radically different. If we consider the impact of a decision for just us or another, we have one perspective. If we think about the impact on everyone concerned (such as extended family), we may have a completely new definition of progress or success.

All of us do what we think is best for us (even if we're mistaken) until we learn there is something even better. Is there someone in your life wanting you to value his feelings and pathway as important? What if you let that person choose his own road and gave him the opportunity to learn from his choices? Sometimes what we think is a mistake for someone else is actually the best choice for that person in the long run for reasons we cannot comprehend now. We may learn the value of letting him be by watching how perfectly things play out.

A wise mentor of mine often stated, "You don't get into heaven in pairs." No matter how close we are to a significant other, we're still unique individuals on individual spiritual journeys. Nobody can do our work for us. Nobody can give us willingness. Are you willing to let someone have her own journey and experiences even if you're married to her? Do you even let her discover what her ultimate pathway is, or do you use every opportunity to keep her chained to and dependent on you? In marriage, we are both individuals and partners. The relationship will suffer if either person feels boxed in or sedated. Both parties need to be respected and allowed to expand their interests. We all need to stretch and test ourselves in order to be transformed and to feel alive. At times we have to do this completely on our own. The world will change; so must we.

Some people get so used to doing things as a couple that it seems foreign to do something individually. A person must first find independence in order to contribute healthy interdependence. Interdependence is when two or more independent people work together for a greater good. This is entirely opposite of codependence, which tends to smother the energy, joy, and higher passion out of a relationship (due to attachment to the other person instead of mutual spiritual alignment to a higher purpose). A man or woman who has not matured into his or her independence will find it difficult to have an interdependent relationship built on trust, devotion, and freedom.

> Why should you cling to another for your identity and joy instead of accessing Divinity within you as the Source of all that you need?

Blocks to Willingness

What has typically blocked you from having an open and willing spirit? You may find that it was fear of some type that prevented you from taking on fresh opportunities or responsibilities or exploring new relationships and experiences. Perhaps you didn't want to fail, be embarrassed, or lose something. You didn't want to expose the belief that you don't feel good enough. If you find yourself reluctant, you may have the subtle fear that you aren't going to get your own needs met by moving in the new direction. The fear of the unknown can feel uncomfortable. Also, you may be holding on to an outdated concept keeping you from expanding. Perhaps you have unrealistic limits about how long something should or will take. You may doubt your abilities, resources, or emotional or intellectual capacity to handle potential changes. Many beliefs are imaginary, and exposing such beliefs can make it easier for you to let them go. Falsity exposed is easily overcome by the light of truth.

Unless we stay conscious, we tend to base the potential of the future on what has happened in the past, but it's an illusion that this moment is based on the past. Instead, this moment has infinite potential and possibility of its own accord. It is showing up new. Are you? Claim that you're at one with divine Love's field of unlimited potentiality, which gives you the full capacity right now for the demands being made upon you.

Willingness removes blocks and allows us to bust through social concepts of what we *should* do because of our social class, education, race, economic standing, age, gender, or religious background. Instead of being bound by these labels, we can be freed by Spirit to experience expanding potential and fearless expression of who we divinely are. With an open mind and heart, we get to experience the wonder of life that previously had been blocked by confining programs and attitudes.

Weigh the Costs

There are tremendous costs for being reluctant—costs that most of us have paid at one time or another. When we're feeling closed down and stuck, our relationships feel stale, unsatisfying, or disconnected. At some level, we'll actually push others away, because an unwilling attitude sends the message that "I don't want to be with you right now," or "I don't want to give you my best." What do we expect our partner's response will be to such messages? Is it any wonder why he or she pulls away?

With unwillingness, our problems will tend to feel bigger than us. The fact that time is ticking may add pressure to the sense that our life situation is not getting any better. We cannot expect it to get better while we remain resistant. Possibilities, solutions, and resources that are right in front of us will go unrecognized. The quality of our lives and of those around us may suffer as well. These costs apply to health, fitness, finances, home, career, relationships, and spiritual growth.

We feel disempowered in proportion to our unwillingness to accept responsibility for where we are, how we see things, and the way we're being. The bottom line is that nobody is acting out your life for you. You have the lead role in your own life drama. If you don't like the movie, you can change the screenplay (by designing a compelling future and acting on it) and the actors (by how you're showing up and who you're surrounding yourself with). Without willingness, you'll feel less able to alter how your life movie plays out.

Unwilling people tend to be dominated by fear and the need for survival, instead of living lives of love, generosity, and grace. If the former describes you at times, the major cost for holding on to such a mental state is that you may never fully know true and secure intimacy, including the feeling of being understood, respected, and valued. As importantly, you may not experience a deeper sense of loving another beyond what you think you're currently capable of. Finally, you will not learn as much as you potentially could in a world so filled with wonderful things to discover, experience, and share. By emotionally stacking these costs, you may feel more conviction to give up such resistant ways of being. You'll only get to live today, this week, this year, or this life one time. When the time passes, you'll have demonstrated either neglect or willingness to show up for yourself and others, give your best, and expand your consciousness. Neglect or willingness: which will it be?

> "I expect to pass through life but once. If, therefore, there be any kindness I can show, or any good thing I can do to any fellow being, let me do it now, and not defer or neglect it, as I shall not pass this way again" (William Penn).

Benefits for Being Willing

The price we pay for eagerness gives much better returns. Sure, we may be have to dig deeper, give again, try a new way, find the courage, get help, learn a new skill, communicate differently, seek healing, or ask Spirit. Nonetheless, the benefit of saying to the Universe that we're ready, willing, and able is that the Universe will readily respond in similar ways with amazing people, resources, and inspiration.

What if we absolutely knew that willingness would help us find answers and wisdom; courage to act in the face of fear; support from friends, family, and mentors; soulful experiences; and new ways to listen and be heard? Our commitment to excellence is what brings enduring results. Commitment begins and continues with willingness. Today is another precious opportunity to be willing. The quality of your life and those around you depend on it.

Practice Being Willing

1) **Count the Costs:** Journal about ways you have been resistant throughout your life. Maybe you've resisted forgiving yourself or others, facing the truth about your financial debt, making necessary health changes in the form of diet and exercise, or taking the passion in your committed relationship or job to the next level. Now, without self-judgment, write down and feel what it has been costing you to be so unwilling. Then list what you would rather be, do, and experience. Once you acknowledge where you've been and are now, and get clear about where you'd rather be, you can plan and take steps to improve your experience with more empowered choices. Remember that you get to write the new screenplay and be the lead actor in the movie of your life each and every day!

2) **Use Willing Words:** Holy Spirit is guiding your life all the time. You may be so caught up with your to-do lists that you forget your role in the bigger scheme of things. Imagine if you woke up every morning with a willing heart, asking Divinity, "How may I serve you today?" Pick one person in your life and ask him or her, "What can I do for you?" or "What do you need most right now?" Notice how your enthusiasm and follow-through changes the depth of your connection with this person and how it opens up new possibilities for your own growth and contribution.

3) **Be Eager:** On a weekly basis, what percentages of time do you approach life with a willing attitude? Are you ready to support and care for others, stay open to new ways of doing things at work, and seek help in overcoming your own fears or emotional wounds? List two or three areas where you feel yourself holding back and not giving your best. Now list five ways you can be more willing. This week apply some of your top picks and notice the results.

Epilogue

While the author's hope is that the preceding ideas, questions, and exercises are of life-changing value to you, words about and experiences of love are vastly different phenomena. To really know something is to be it, and to know something about a subject as infinite as Love still leaves one in the sandbox of Life with much to learn, embody, and share. Nonetheless, just one experience of love is enough to uplift one's life and the lives of many others.

In light of this, the author may be led to develop a sequel, companion workbook, blog, or other ways to share with fellow travelers on the path of unconditional love. May you be strengthened and blessed on your journey as you give the greatest gift you can to others: the expansion of your own consciousness toward infinite Love.

Acknowledgments

I offer deep gratitude to Divinity as the Source of all life, truth, and love and for being the inspiration for whatever in these pages speaks to these things. To my wife Charlene and son Nicholas, thank you for all that you share and teach in the way of love, for standing by me through all that life brought my way over the past seven years, and for bringing me deep joy daily.

I am grateful for the many spiritual teachers, authors, and friends who have had the courage and devotion to stay on their own paths to kindly share their growth and wisdom with me. I'm also thankful for those who generously shared honest feedback during the writing, editing, and integrating of these pages, including Jen Tucker, Lorraine McLachlan, Malcolm P. Galvin III, Christine Blank, Joseph Ho, PhD, Marlene Adams, Michelle Nason, Valerie Vette Vincent, Laura Lynne Dyer (who was the women who inspired me to travel to Austin for the writer's workshop), Jared McLachlan, Linda and Dennis Blank, Jill Kasick, Kathleen Coppe, John K. Power III, and Yvonne Reed. May all of your lives be blessed! I greatly value the graphics knowledge and cover design help I received from Gary Dufner and Gerald Blank. Lastly, I give profound appreciation to the line editors, Sonia Martin and Joy Martin, for their expertise, care, and stamina.

Permissions

Scripture quotations marked (TLB) are taken from *The Living Bible* copyright © 1971. Used by permission of Tyndale House Publishers, Inc., Carol Stream, Illinois 60188. All rights reserved.

Quotations by David R. Hawkins, M.D., Ph.D. are taken from: *Discovery of the Presence of God*, by David R. Hawkins, M.D., Ph.D., © 2006, page 64, and *The Eye of the I*, by David R. Hawkins, M.D., Ph.D., © 2001, page 123, respectively, and are used by permission of Veritas Publishing and www.veritaspub.com. All rights reserved.

Quotations by Mother Teresa are used by permission of the Mother Teresa Center. All rights reserved.

About the Author

Mark is a Certified Coach, Consultant, and Facilitator of Change passionate about shifting perceptions and actions of clients worldwide toward success, fulfillment, and evolution in consciousness. His clients and workshop participants have found breakthroughs in relationships, emotions, health, finances, spirituality, creativity, and careers. Readers have found that Mark's writings bring a fresh blend of strong masculinity and compassionate wisdom. Mark can be found at: www.BeingLove.net and www.LifeCoachMark.com.

Additional Copies of *Being Love*

Additional copies of *Being Love* can be ordered at major retail book sellers and online at Amazon.com, BarnesandNoble.com, and BeingLove.net. To inquire about volume discounts on orders of ten copies or greater, please send an email to BeingLoveBook@gmail.com or call (407) 429-5288. Thank you for your interest.

Contributions

If you would like to support the distribution of this book, your contributions of time, talent, or resources are welcome. Please send an email to BeingLoveBook@gmail.com or call (407) 429-5288 to find out how to submit your contribution. Thank you for your consideration.